To Malcolm
in celebr
birth!
January 1746

Peter

L's

# FOREIGN DIRECT INVESTMENT AND MULTINATIONAL ENTERPRISES

*Also by Peter J. Buckley*

CANADA–UK BILATERAL TRADE AND INVESTMENT RELATIONS (*with Christopher L. Pass and Kate Prescott*)
DIRECT INVESTMENT IN THE UNITED KINGDOM BY SMALLER EUROPEAN FIRMS (*with Zdenka Berkova and Gerald D. Newbould*)
EUROPEAN DIRECT INVESTMENT IN THE USA BEFORE WORLD WAR I (*with Brian R. Roberts*)
FOREIGN DIRECT INVESTMENT BY SMALLER UK FIRMS (*with Gerald D. Newbould and Jane C. Thurwell*)
HANDBOOK OF INTERNATIONAL TRADE (*editor with Michael Z. Brooke*)
INTERNATIONAL ASPECTS OF UK ECONOMIC ACTIVITIES (*with Robert D. Pearce*)
INTERNATIONAL BUSINESS STUDIES: An Overview (*with Michael Z. Brooke*)
MULTINATIONALS AND EMPLOYMENT (*with Patrick F. R. Artisien*)
NORTH–SOUTH DIRECT INVESTMENT IN THE EUROPEAN COMMUNITIES (*with Patrick F. R. Artisien*)
SERVICING INTERNATIONAL MARKETS (*with Christopher L. Pass and Kate Prescott*)
STUDIES IN INTERNATIONAL BUSINESS
THE ECONOMIC THEORY OF THE MULTINATIONAL ENTERPRISE (*with Mark Casson*)
THE FUTURE OF THE MULTINATIONAL ENTERPRISE (*with Mark Casson*)
THE INDUSTRIAL RELATIONS PRACTICES OF FOREIGN-OWNED FIRMS IN BRITAIN (*with Peter Enderwick*)
THE MULTINATIONAL ENTERPRISE: THEORY AND APPLICATIONS

# Foreign Direct Investment and Multinational Enterprises

Peter J. Buckley
*Professor of International Business*
*Centre of International Business*
*University of Leeds*

Foreword by Edith Penrose

First published 1995 by
MACMILLAN PRESS LTD
Houndmills, Basingstoke, Hampshire RG21 6XS
and London
Companies and representatives
throughout the world

ISBN 0–333–61370–8

A catalogue record for this book is available
from the British Library.

10   9   8   7   6   5   4   3   2   1
04  03  02  01  00  99  98  97  96  95

Printed in Great Britain by
Ipswich Book Co Ltd
Ipswich, Suffolk

To Alice Louise

# Contents

# PART III  ASIA-PACIFIC ISSUES

# List of Figures

ix

# List of Tables

# Foreword

The University of Bradford has the oldest business school in the United Kingdom and one of the best known. Its publications are as diverse as its teaching programme. This latest collection of articles by Peter Buckley, some by himself alone and some written with others, including members of the staff of the Bradford Management Centre, surveys various aspects of the operations, growth and spread of international firms.

The twentieth century will perhaps be looked at in retrospect as the century of the 'global' firm. Although commercial international entities existed long before the dawn of the century in trade and some major industries, such as the international petroleum industry, and grew in importance after the First World War, they became of major significance after the Second World War and began to dominate the international economy. This was of course due to revolutionary innovations, particularly in transportation and information technology, and its spread required innovation in management practices.

Since the middle of the century there has been a veritable explosion of academic interest in this subject with the phenomenal rise of Japan since the Second World War and the more recent economic explosion of development in Southeast Asia, The foreign firm is a special case of the growth of firms, as Buckley points out, but a firm in growing abroad encounters a number of special circumstances not faced by other firms expanding only within their national boundaries. At the same time, once a firm has entered a foreign market, its growth continues, again requiring special types of managerial strategies. Very many firms, after having ventured into a foreign country, quickly expand their operations into still others and become in a literal sense international, sometimes 'global', firms.

Much of the literature on international firms has centred primarily on 'case-studies' relating to particular enterprises or industries, but in Part I of this volume Buckley presents a useful comprehensive discussion of the wider generalizations he believes can now be safely arrived at. There are also included here a number of special studies of international activities related largely to the United Kingdom and Part III has three essays on Asia-Pacific relations.

One of the strengths of these essays is the analysis of management strategies and processes in servicing foreign markets, entering into them operating internationally within them. There is much emphasis on the central role of management, often neglected in studies of multinational enterprise generally, and the processes of internalization. It is noted that firms grow by replacing imperfect or non-existent markets by internal ones, but they also grow by taking over other firms, and more ambiguously by making joint ventures.

Joint ventures in the form of non-equity alliances are becoming central to competition among international firm. The discussion of joint ventures in this book and the largely statistical analysis of international joint ventures of the United Kingdom over the 1980s is a valuable contribution to the growing literature. Firms find it profitable to make contractual associations with several other firms often in order to make use of the research and innovations of others while sharing their own. This gives rise to 'networks' in which a number of firms, without losing their identity, join in forming alliances within which each firm has a specific role to play. There is usually a leading firm with some degree of control but the boundaries of the individual firm are often difficult to discern. Competition between alliances is now becoming so prominent that the usefulness of the firm/ market dichotomy so central to traditional economics analysis is increasingly called into question.

EDITH PENROSE

# Preface and Acknowledgements

This book contains eleven articles written or co-authored by me during 1989–94. As is usual in my work, I have been helped enormously by my co-authors who all have strong Bradford Management Centre connections. I would also like to thank Edith Penrose for contributing the Foreword and for the help she has given to me and my staff during her term as Visiting Senior Fellow in Managerial Economics at the Centre.

I am grateful for the permission of the copyright holders to reprint the articles included. Chapter 1 first appeared in *Journal of Marketing*, Volume 7, No 1, 1991; Chapter 2 in L. Zan, S. Zambon and A. Pettigrew (eds) *Perspectives on Strategic Change*, Kluwer, Norwell, Mass, 1993; Chapter 3 in *Hitotsubashi Journal of Economics*, Volume 32, No 2, December 1991; Chapter 4 in *Management International Review*, Volume 33, No 3, 1993; Chapter 5 in *The Journal of the Economics of Business*, Volume 1, No 1, 1994; Chapter 6 in *Managerial and Decision Economics*, Volume 10, No 3, September 1989; Chapter 7 in *Journal of General Management*, Volume 17, No 2, Winter 1991; Chapter 8 in *British Journal of Management*, Volume 5, No 1, March 1994; Chapter 9 in *Pacific Review*, Volume 4, No 4, 1991; Chapter 10 in Nigel Campbell and John S. Henley (eds), *Advances in Chinese Industrial Studies 11*, Part B, JAI Press, Greenwich, Conn, 1990; and Chapter 11 in *International Business Review*, Volume 2, No 1, 1993. I would like to record my thanks to the editors of the volumes concerned.

Once again my thanks go to my former colleagues at the Management Centre and to the other institutions which I visit – the Department of Economics at the University of Reading and the University of Paris I Panthéon-Sorbonne. My main debt for word processing goes to Mrs Chris Barkby and for secretarial assistance to Mrs Sylvia Ashdown.

*Bradford*                                         PETER J. BUCKLEY

# Notes on the Other Contributors

**Keith Glaister** is Senior Lecturer in Strategic Management, School of Business and Economic Studies, University of Leeds.

**Eugen Jehle** is Managing Director, SIFO, Netherlands, and Honorary Visiting Research Fellow, University of Bradford Management Centre.

**Hafiz Mirza** is Senior Lecturer in International Business, University of Bradford Management Centre.

**Christopher L. Pass** is Senior Lecturer in Managerial Economics, University of Bradford Management Centre.

**Kate Prescott** is Lecturer in International Business Management, University of Bradford Management Centre.

**John R. Sparkes** is Professor of Business Economics, University of Bradford Management Centre.

# Introduction and Overview

This volume represents a selection of my published papers between 1989 and 1994. It covers three themes which have been basic to my research in the past ten years: the development of theory, the theory and practice of foreign market servicing strategies by firms and the Asia-Pacific Region.

## I  DEVELOPMENTS IN THEORY

The first section of the book covers five pieces on developments in the theory of multinational firms and foreign direct investment. The first piece attempts to map out the likely developments in theory in the 1990s. This is a hazardous exercise in any field of endeavour, but particularly so in the field which is expanding quickly and multi-dimensionally. It attempts to chart a way between excessive eclecticism and inertia and it looks to the construction of a robust theory based on few axioms with wide relevance. It alludes once again (Buckley, 1991) to the difficulties of true indisciplinarity. It is not sufficient to 'bolt on' new concepts – a considerable effort has to be made to go back to basic issues and build anew.

The second paper in this section takes a simple hypothesis – that the international expansion of the firm is a special case of theory of the growth of the firm – and elaborates upon this theme. This is the tradition of my work dating back to empirical studies of the internationalization of smaller firms done in the late 1970s and 1980s (Buckley, Newbould and Thurwell, 1988; Buckley, Berkova and Newbould, 1983; Buckley and Mathew, 1979, 1980). Alternative perspectives on the theory of foreign direct investment are useful tools for the development of strands of theory. A protracted debate has occurred between myself and Professor Kiyoshi Kojima on the relative merits of the internalization approach versus a macroeconomic approach (Buckley,1983,1985; Kojima, 1978, 1989, 1990; Kojima and

Ozawa, 1984a, 1984b). My contention here is that Kojima's macroeconomic approach is a special case and that he misrepresents the internalisation approach. Developments of the approach by Kojima turn it into a special case of a special case and have been outdated by events. It should be possible to develop Kojima's approach into a variant of the strategic trade theorising but Kojima makes no effort to make the link. The debate between 'Reading' and 'Japan' has helped to clarify issues and to induce some cross fertilization between 'micro' and 'macro' approaches.

A further contrast in theory is between international business, based largely on an economics tradition and international management, based much more on strategic management. Chapters 4 and 5 attempt to elucidate this contrast, to find areas of commonality and to draw on the best of the international management tradition to the benefit of international business research.

Chapter 4 attempts to 'put management back in' to the theory. There is a certain irony about this because the whole thrust of internalization is the replacement of the market by management fiat. This chapter thus is a vehicle for a discussion of the infra firm implications of internalization decisions. The simple view of internalization as the 'buy or build' decision can be opened up to encompass different types of strategic behaviour and extensions allow consideration of dynamic elements and alternative growth strategies.

As with Chapter 4, Chapter 5 has a section which discusses the management of research and development. This issue has achieved salience not only as the most prominent special case of the general case of growth by internalization presented in Buckley and Casson (1976) but also as a key object of study in its own right (Casson, 1992).


## II  THE FOREIGN MARKET SERVICING STRATEGIES OF MULTINATIONAL ENTERPRISES

Chapter 6 is an empirical study of the structure of British industry's sales in foreign markets. It examines the exports from

British parent companies together with their licensed sales abroad and the sales arising from British foreign direct investments. The total foreign sales of British companies are thus (TFS) = X + L + I. This formulation raises a number of interesting issues. One of these issues is the divergence between the interests of British owned companies and those of Britain (as represented, perhaps, by the British government). It may be in the company's interest to service a particular foreign market via a direct investment but is this in Britain's interest, given that the investment transfers activity, jobs, technology away from Britain and may substitute for British exports? It may be that the alternative to direct investment is no sales from UK interests at all. Government policy generally is to stimulate exports at the expense of the other forms of market servicing but in an increasingly global economy this stance may be in need of revision.

The next two chapters revert to the level of the firm. From the macro picture presented in Chapter 6, Chapter 7 examines individual changes in market servicing stance by a small sample of firms in three tightly defined sectors. The impact of these changes on competitiveness is traced. Competitiveness is defined as a dynamic process made up of the interaction of performance, competitive potential and management processes (Buckley, Pass and Prescott, 1992). This chapter shows that even minor changes in foreign market servicing stance (from, for instance, exporting through a foreign agent to a foreign sales subsidiary) can have a major impact on competitiveness. Moreover, 'within mode' shifts (e.g. a change in the *type* of exporting) can also improve competitiveness to a surprising degree.

Joint ventures and alliances (Buckley, 1992) are increasingly important means of doing business abroad. Chapter 8 examines the patterns of UK activity and the distribution of UK international joint ventures based on an original investigation. Joint ventures are increasing in numbers and occur largely between the UK and its European Union partners and the USA. There is a distinct sectoral bias in the reported numbers of joint ventures, with four industries (financial services, telecommunications, aerospace and 'other manufacturing') accounting for over half the activity.

## III   ASIA-PACIFIC ISSUES

Chapter 9 examines the impact of the Single European Market Act (SEM) on the Asia Pacific region. It speculates on the medium term reaction of firms from the Asia Pacific region to the SEM and outlines the potential opportunities and threats which face them. The ability of Asia Pacific firms to see Europe as a single integrated market should balance increased protectionist tendencies.

The great interest shown in penetrating the Chinese market by foreign firms has been one of the key elements in international business activity in the early 1990s. Chapter 10 examines the taxation implications of joint ventures and other forms of entrepreneurial cooperation between foreign and domestic Chinese firms. Fiscal progress in China is seen as a major determinant of the future success of 'open door policies'.

The final chapter examines the contrast between UK and Japan in terms of business–government relations. Close contacts between industry and government are often suggested as key determinants of the relative success of Japan in international competition. This piece examines the institutions of both countries in the particular context of two industries: pharmaceuticals and petrochemicals. The empirical work included in the chapter consisted of interviews of industrialists and government functionaries in both countries.

## References

Buckley, Peter J. (1983) 'Macroeconomic versus the International Business Approach to Direct Foreign Investment: A Comment on Professor Kojima's Approach', *Hitotsubashi Journal of Economics*, Volume 24, No 1, June, pp. 95–100.

Buckley, Peter J. (1985) 'The Economic Analysis of the Multinational Enterprise: Reading Versus Japan?' *Hitotsubashi Journal of Economics*, Volume 26, No 2, December, pp. 117–124.

Buckley, Peter J. (1991) 'The Frontiers of International Business Research', *Management International Review*, Volume 31, Special Issue, February, pp. 7–22.

Buckley, Peter J. (1992) 'Alliances, Technology and Markets: A Cautionary Tale' in Peter J. Buckley, *Studies in International Business*, London: Macmillan.

Buckley, Peter J., Zdenka Berkova and Gerald D. Newbould (1983) *Direct Investment in the UK by Smaller UK Firms*, London: Macmillan.

Buckley, Peter J. and Mark Casson (1976) *The Future of the Multinational Enterprise*, London: Macmillan.

Buckley, Peter J. and A. M. Mathew (1979) 'The Motivation for Recent First-Time Investments in Australia by UK Firms', *Management International Review*, Volume 19, No 1, pp. 57–69.

Buckley, Peter J. and A. M. Mathew (1980) 'Dimensions of the Market Entry Behaviour of Recent UK First Time Direct Investors in Australia', *Management International Review*, Volume 20, No 2, pp. 35–51.

Buckley, Peter J., Gerald D. Newbould and Jane Thurwell (1988) *Foreign Direct Investment by Smaller UK Firms*, London: Macmillan.

Buckley, Peter J., C. L. Pass and Kate Prescott (1992) *Servicing International Markets: Competitive Strategies of Firms*, Oxford: Blackwell.

Casson, Mark (1992) *Global Research Strategy and International Competitiveness*, Oxford: Blackwell.

Kojima, K. (1978) *Direct Foreign Investment: A Japanese Model of Multinational Business*, London: Croom Helm.

Kojima, K. (1989) 'Theory of Internalisation of Multinational Corporations', *Hitotsubashi Journal of Economics*, Volume 30, No 2, December.

Kojima, K. (1990) *Japanese Direct Investment Abroad*, Tokyo: International Christian University Social Science Research Institute Monography Series, No 1.

Kojima, K. and T. Ozawa (1984a) 'Micro- and Macro-Economic Models of Direct Foreign Investment: Towards a Synthesis', *Hitotsubashi Journal of Economics*, Volume 25, No 1, June, pp. 1–20.

Kojima, K. and T. Ozawa (1984b) *Japan's General Trading Companies: Merchants of Economic Development*, Paris: OECD.

# Part I

# Theory

# 1 Developments in International Business Theory in the 1990s*

## 1 INTRODUCTION

It is rather presumptuous to attempt to predict developments in a wide field such as international business theory during such a turbulent period. However, recent developments in international business suggest that the subject area is sufficiently mature and core concepts are so well embedded, that predictions are not entirely foolhardy. Part 2 of this paper examines the key empirical issues in the world economy which international business theory should explain. Part 3 examines the tools of international business theory and Part 4 questions whether they are adequate to the task.

This paper takes a personal view of the development of theory. It draws in particular on the internalization approach whose two key axioms on internalization decisions and location costs were developed by Buckley (1988). It thus represents a version of the 'Reading School' approach to the theory of the multinational firm. It is recognized that this is not the only theory of international business, but it is not appropriate here to review potential and actual rival theoretical approaches. It is possible to envisage convergence of theories – a greater incorporation of strategic management concepts perhaps – but for reasons of exposition, this issue is not treated here.

*Journal of Marketing Management*, Vol. 7, No. 1, 1991, pp. 15–24 (reprinted by permission). An earlier version of this paper was given at the International Symposium 'MNEs and 21st Century Scenarios' organized by the Workshop for the Studies of Multinational Enterprises, Tokyo, July 4–6, 1990. I am grateful to the participants for their comments.

## 2    EMPIRICAL ISSUES IN THE WORLD ECONOMY OF THE 1990s

Several important trends seem likely to influence the world economy throughout the 1990s:

1. An increase in both competition and collaboration between firms (Jorde and Teece, 1989). (a) A search for improvements in competitiveness at national, industrial, firm and product level and increasing attention to the source of competitiveness. (b) Increasing use of joint ventures, alliances and other collaborative devices between firms.
2. Political changes including deregulation, political, economic and financial integration and change in trade policies. (a) The increased pace of the deregulation of industry particularly in former command economies. This will direct attention to the management of newly privatized industries. (b) The process of integration in Europe (EC), North America and possibly Asia is likely to continue. Developments to 1992 and after will lead to increasing economic, political and financial harmonization in the EC of the twelve and it is likely that more members will join. (c) The development of trade policies is difficult to predict. The general trend of deregulation does not always extend to the international market and integration moves are frequently accompanied by rising external trade barriers.
3. Technological imperatives will continue to be important in international business. The increasing resources put into research and development play a major role in international competition. The impact of radical learning in inducing spin-offs and the management of radical innovation as well as developmental changes in product and process innovations will play a major role in international competition and the institutions of the world economy.
4. Social changes, too, will influence international business. Demands for improvements in social conditions are determinants of future patterns. Clear indications of the growth of 'green' issues are already with us. Demand for greater equality and equality of opportunity influence fiscal regimes as issues of 'life-style' determine consumption patterns and regimes of work.

5. All of the above changes are likely to lead to considerable re-structuring of the world economy and of its constituent parts at national, regional, local, firm and intra-firm levels.

6. Most of the above issues will primarily concern the developed, industrialized world. The relationship between advanced countries and the less developed countries, as mediated through international business operations, will remain a crucial issue.

## 3 THE CONTRIBUTION OF INTERNATIONAL BUSINESS THEORY

The above empirical issues set the agenda for a purposive theory of international business. Any theory must attempt to explain and predict these emerging phenomena. Because of the diverse nature of these factors, a successful theory must be wide-ranging and interdisciplinary while not so general as to be vacuous. The theory proposed here based on internalization theory, location cost and transaction cost minimizing behaviour is sufficiently rigorous to meet the challenge.

### Some Criticisms

The core theory of international business has been subject to close scrutiny and has had to weather the storms of criticism, not least from its proponents, including myself (Buckley, 1983, 1988, 1990). This is because it has been unthinkingly applied in its most general form without the necessary restrictions and qual-ifying assumptions. Its empirical impact lies in its special appli-cations to particular configurations of the world economy, not in its general axiomatic basis. Figure 1.1 from Buckley (1988) is an earlier attempt to elucidate this point.

A recent set of criticisms is contained in a perceptive article by Charles Kindleberger (1988). Kindleberger makes three sets of points which may be construed as criticisms of internalization theory. These are: (1) many foreign investment decisions are 'close cases' and similar firms may make different decisions

*Figure 1.1*   Structure of the theory and testing: an example

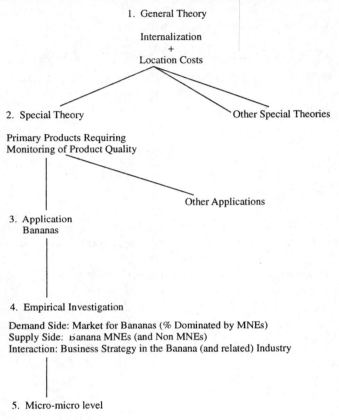

1. General Theory

Internalization
+
Location Costs

2. Special Theory

Other Special Theories

Primary Products Requiring
Monitoring of Product Quality

Other Applications

3. Application
   Bananas

4. Empirical Investigation

Demand Side: Market for Bananas (% Dominated by MNEs)
Supply Side: Banana MNEs (and Non MNEs)
Interaction: Business Strategy in the Banana (and related) Industry

5. Micro-micro level

Incidence of costs – measurement of transactions cost

when facing similar decision sets; (2) multinational firms are not unified firms but rather are loose agglomerations of profit centres; and (3) joint ventures are difficult to fit into the theory because they are inherently unstable and do not work in the long run.

The 'close case' argument is an interesting one. Kindleberger alludes to the vacillations of the European car makers Volvo and Volkswagen on their potential entry into manufacture in the United States of America. It is implied that the fact that the decision in both cases was so close and that the two firms did not make the same decision refutes any general theory of foreign direct investment. This would be so if the theory were attempting broad generalizations at a macro level (as perhaps Aliber's approach (1970, 1971) does). However the firm level elements are crucially important as in the firm's reaction to uncertainty. Moreover, the assessment of competition and of the firms' own competitive advantages at a given time are crucial. It is also important that transaction cost factors and location costs change over time and may cause the exporting versus foreign investment decision to switch. The fact that in these cases the measurable costs of each mode seem to be so finely balanced meant that intangibles – uncertainties about the ability of the firm to achieve a given level of market penetration, costs of distribution, reaction of competitors – could swing the balance of the decision. The role of management decision making also plays a part. It is perfectly conceivable that even were the external circumstances facing a firm identical (which they never are) that two firms would choose alternative paths based on their evaluation of probabilities of outcome. Management discretion in imperfectly competitive markets has long been a precept of business theory.

The organization of the firm is an issue tackled by Kindleberger. He takes the view that (many) modern multinationals are loose agglomerations of profit centres rather than unified decision takers. This is not incompatible with internalization theory. Indeed, it is one potential outcome of growth by internalization that the firm is explicitly organized as a complete internal market with shadow price signals being used as an internal co-ordinating mechanism between quasi-independent profit centres. Head office thus operates as a central brain, allowing resources to be allocated by an agreed pricing system. Once such a shadow pricing system is implemented, managers can make 'independent' decisions, and resources are allocated automatically within the firm. The more rigorously such a system is implemented, the larger are the organization consequences. Thus break-ups, spin-offs, diversment and divisionalization are direct consequences of the application of internal pricing rules. The internal flexibility and responsiveness of such a system to change means that the organization becomes highly fluid. The boundary of the firm is defined by the span of the internal pricing regime and its resource allocating mechanism.

Kindleberger's view of joint ventures is of great interest given their increasing importance in such contexts as foreign investment in Japan, Eastern Europe and less developed countries. His view is that joint ventures are inherently unstable and are essentially a short-term expedient measure for the purpose of acculturation and are likely to lose their joint status (either becoming absorbed by one partner, disappearing in a take-over of one partner by another or becoming independent) in the long run. In view of the importance of joint ventures to current theorizing (Buckley and Casson, 1988), this is an issue to which we return.

**The Current State of Theory**

It is folly to believe that the current theory of the multinational firm has solved all the problems. At the moment, it represents a framework for problem solving. Its key components – a theory of how firms grow and a theory of the location of economic activity – combine effectively to explain the ownership structure of the world economy and the directions of growth of multinational firms. It is important to develop this to include a theory of management direction. It has not yet fully encompassed the role of management decision making, as the criticisms by Kindleberger make clear. At one extreme, management simply is the embodiment of decisions programmed by changes in external markets (a pure economic approach). At the other, management appears to have complete discretion (as in globalization models).

Several attempts are being made to introduce a positive but prescribed view of management into the theory. These are based on a more careful delineation of the functions of the firm (Buckley, Pass and Prescott, 1990; Casson, 1990), the role of culture as it impacts on management decisions (Buckley and Casson 1988, 1990) and entrepreneurship (Casson, 1982).

It is however, fair to say that internalization theory has already gone a long way to encompassing dynamics into its purview. (Buckley, 1983, 1988; Casson, 1990). The analysis of internalization decisions based on external costs (Casson, 1981; Buckley, 1983) and of switches in modes of market servicing as a reaction to cost and demand changes (Buckley and Casson, 1981) are examples of this development. The new generation of work goes further in systematizing the role of management and, in so doing, widening of the conceptual base of the theory is necessary.

## The Functional Make-up of the Firm

Modern firms are multifunctional. It is important to distinguish production, marketing and research and development as key areas which have to be co-ordinated (Buckley and Casson, 1976; Casson, 1990). However, going beyond this, it is important to sub-divide marketing into distribution, the agency function (attracting new customers) stockholding and promotion (Buckley and Casson, 1976; Buckley, Pass and Prescott, 1990). The role of channel management is extremely important in accurately predicting the growth of firms, and the total distribution system must be managed (Brown, 1984; Buckley, Pass and Prescott, 1990).

Making such distinctions may complicate the theory, but make it much richer. Casson (1990) shows that the configuration of firms is explicable by the externalization of certain functions, while Buckley, Pass and Prescott (1990) show the key role of internal flows of information between functions.

## Culture and Management

The role of culture in influencing management decisions has long been a subject for debate (Weinshall, 1977). However, it is only recently that its importance for the theory of the multinational enterprise has been made explicit. This integration of fundamentally economic concepts with those of organizational behaviour and anthropology is one of the most exciting developments in international business theory. The management of co-operative relations is an important focal point for discussion of the impact of culture on management, as is the culture clash which occurs in multinational investment in less developed countries.

A careful examination of the often superficial concept of 'competitive advantage' can lead back to the notion of cultural influences on management. Buckley and Casson (1990) suggest that the development of an entrepreneurial culture and geographical factors which confer entrepôt potential as an initial locational endowment may go some way to explaining the pattern of differential growth and ownership in the world economy.


**The Role of Entrepreneurship**

It is a feature of the up-to-date nature of international business theory that internal entrepreneurship (intrapreneurship) within the firm is a subject of great research interest in its own right. The exercise of discretionary decision making within the firm and the harnessing of such behaviour to meet the goals of the firm is a major problem for large corporations.


4   CAN THE THEORY MEET THE CHALLENGE?

Section 2 of this paper listed a formidable set of challenges for a theory of the multinational firm. Six key points were made:

1. The changing balance between competitiveness and collaboration involving the use of joint ventures, alliances and other cross-firm agreements can indeed be explained by the theory. The advantages of co-operation combined with the barriers to full merger provide a convincing rationale for the new pattern. Further, it is possible to construct dynamic explanations of continued, widened and deepened co-operative behaviour using concepts such as trust, forbearance, commitment and reputation (Buckley and Casson, 1988). This process has much further to go. The ethos of competition is so strong and so embedded in (economic) theory that a secure foundation must be found for co-operative theory. Much of the work on game theory, for instance, concerns competitive rather than co-operative games (but see Telser, 1987). It is of particular importance that analysis of Japanese companies pose a definite challenge to neo-classical theory (Aoki, 1984).

2. The political economy of deregulation, privatization and integration is currently the focus of much attention, particularly with regard to the liberalization and marketization of eastern Europe. The concepts which govern the changing boundary between market and organization are well developed in international business theory (Buckley and Casson, 1976) and are serviceable for this purpose. Again, it is essential to pay attention to the dynamics of this process. Despite all the attention paid to the Single European Market Act, 1992 is well covered by theories of economic integration (for a collection of classic papers see Robson, 1984) and of business strategy (e.g. Buckley and Artisien, 1987). The impact of political change on business strategy is best seen in terms of restructuring policies (see point 5).

3. The economics of technological change are of continuing importance in international business theory. The links between this issue and the others are very strong. The increasing cost of technological development is a fundamental reason for the growth of alliances, joint research developments and new technological strategies of firms and nations (Chesnais, 1986; Buckley, 1990b).

The imperative of technological change is not a one-way device. It has both agglomeration effects and splitting effects on organizations. The incentive to combine to create a major research initiative is true in firms (joint technological programmes) in Universities and at national level (Human Frontiers Programme in Japan, European initiatives). However technology can cause the break up of organizations – as in breakaways where individuals depart to set up their own organizations. A careful and continuing study of these developments is necessary to maintain the relevance of theory.

4. Social pressures are everywhere evident in international business. The external economies and diseconomies of business activity have long been noted as a problem for the wider policy (Coase, 1960). The desire to make the producers of social costs bear the appropriate penalty has never been stronger. Environmental issues present a test case par excellence. These issues naturally have an international dimension in that each citizen is potentialy at risk from long-term damage to the ecosystem.

Demands for regulation are therefore naturally presented at the supranational level.

5. The issue of restructuring in response to social, political, economic and technological pressure is a key question for the multinational enterprises of the 1990s. Figure 1.2 presents a schema of potential responses, drawing heavily on Enderwick's 1989 article. A variety of potential responses are listed.

- Intensification which seeks to achieve a greater productive return from existing assets without a fundamental reorganization of the work process or new investment.
- Investment and technical change involves a significant change in methods of production, a willingness to adapt and organizational flexibility.
- Rationalization involves the elimination of capacity and concentration on the most efficient sites, products and process.
- Deintegration uses externalization of function to achieve an effective division of labour outsourcing; subcontracting and homeworking are examples of the process.
- Collaboration depends on building alliances, joint venture and other co-operative modes of business, but may ultimately be a form of cartelization.
- Incremental internationalization through increased foreign investment is also a response to restructuring pressures.

Enderwick suggests that different national groups of firms are responding to restructuring pressures in identifiably different ways. It is clear that nationality of ownership is but one way in which we can identify different restructuring policies.

6. The response of multinationals from advanced countries to the Third World is currently undergoing change as a reaction to the new openness to inward foreign involvement. Although the hostility to multinationals is still differential by mode of entry (joint ventures or licensing preferred to wholly owned subsidiaries), it is now far more welcoming than any time since the 1950s (Buckley and Clegg, 1990). However this renewed partnership is very much a trial marriage. The pressures are on foreign investors to produce results in the more favourable climate now on offer in the Third World. An opportunity to meet

needs is available and it behoves multinationals to take it, for their own sake as well as for the host countries.

*Figure* 1.2   Policies of the firm in response to changes in the world economy

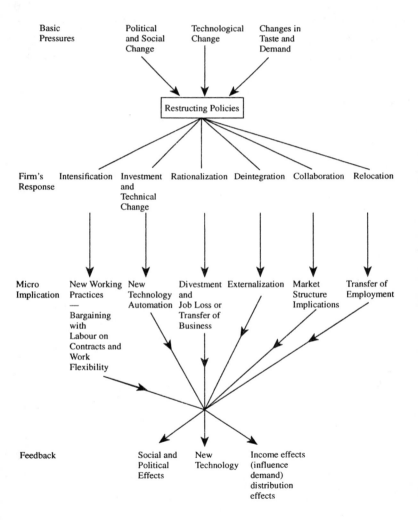

## 5  CONCLUSION

This paper has presented more problems than it has solved. This should not be surprising. The nature of such speculation is to leave unanswered questions trailing in its wake. However it is clear that international business theory is in a good position to square up to the unanswered questions while the 1990s will pose.

We should not lose sight of the considerable achievements of international business theory to date. It has moved out of a

*Figure* 1.3    The interaction between internalization decisions and market structure (After Hymer 1968)

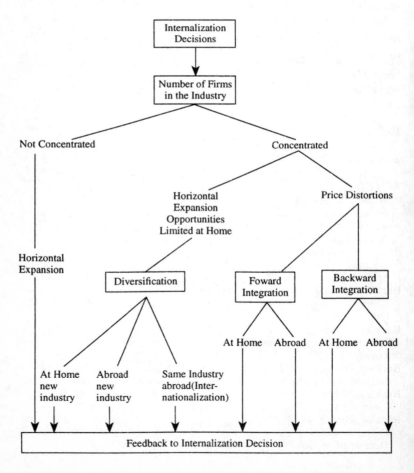

narrow economistic neo-classical format to being able to meet the challenge of a more general explanation of business behaviour. It has begun to tackle such key dilemmas as the balance between competition and co-operation and at a more micro level has begun to reconcile the welfare improving internalization economies with welfare decreasing market power effects. Indeed Casson's rediscovery of a 1968 paper by Hymer, as developed by Buckley (1990a) shows that the market power and internalization models are themselves complementary, not mutually exclusive. Figure 1.3 illustrates the interaction between the two processes.

Moreover, as Figure 1.1 showed, international business theory is able to combine a general theory of the growth of firms with special explanations of great explanatory power.

The widening and deepening of this conceptual structure by introducing such concepts as culture, trust and reciprocal relationships give the approach a broader base from which to tackle the explanation and prediction of the key phenomena of the world economy.

## References

Aliber, Robert Z. (1970), 'A Theory of Foreign Direct Investment', in: *The International Firm*, Kindleberger, C. P. (ed.), Cambridge Mass, MIT Press.

Aliber, Robert Z. (1991), 'The Multinational Enterprise in a Multiple Currency World', in: *The Multinational Enterprise*, Dunning, John H (ed.), London, George Allen & Unwin.

Aoki, Masahiko (ed.) (1984), *The Economic Analysis of the Japanese Firm*, Amsterdam, North-Holland.

Brown, Wilson R. (1984), 'Firm-Like Behaviour in Markets: The Administered Channel', *International Journal of Industrial Organisation*, **12**, No. 4, pp. 263–76.

Buckley, Peter J. (1983). 'New Theories of International Business: Some Unresolved Issues', in: *The Growth of International Business*, Casson, Mark (ed.) , London, George Allen & Unwin.

Buckley, Peter J. (1988), 'The Limits of Explanation: Testing the Internationalisation Theory of the Multinational Enterprise', *Journal of International Business Studies*, **XIX**, No. 2, Summer, pp. 181–93.

Buckley, Peter J. (1990a), 'Problems and Developments in the Core Theory of International Business', *Journal of International Business Studies* (in press).

Buckley, Peter J. (1990b), *Alliances, Technology and Hierarchies: A Cautionary Tale*, University of Bradford, *mimeo*.

Buckley, Peter J. and Artisien, Patrick F. R. (1987), 'Policy Issues of Intra-EC Direct Investment', *Journal of Common Market Studies*, **XXVI**, No. 2, December, pp. 207–30.

16 *Theory*

Buckley, Peter J. and Casson, Mark (1976), *The Future of the Multinational Enterprise* , London, Macmillan.

Buckley, Peter J. and Casson, Mark (1981). 'The Optimal Timing of a Foreign Direct Investment', *Economic Journal*, **92**, No. 361, March, pp. 75–87. Reprinted in: Buckley, Peter J. and Casson, Mark (1985), *The Economic Theory of the Multinational Enterprise,* London, Macmillan.

Buckley, Peter J. and Casson, Mark (1988), 'A Theory of Co-operation in International Business', in: *Co-operative Strategies in International Business,* Contractor, Farok J. and Lorange, Peter (eds), Lexington, Mass, Lexington Books D. C. Heath & Co.

Buckley, Peter J. and Casson, Mark (1990). 'The Multinational Enterprise in Less Developed Countries: Cultural and Economic Interactions', in: Buckley and Clegg (eds), *op. cit.*

Buckley, Peter J. and Clegg, Jeremy (eds) (1990), *Multinational Enterprises in Less Developed Countries,* London, Macmillan.

Buckley, Peter J., Pass, C. L. and Prescott, Kate (1990), 'Foreign Market Servicing by Multinationals: An Integrated Approach', *International Marketing Review,* **7**, No. 4, pp. 25–40.

Casson, Mark (1981), 'Foreword' to: Rugman, Alan M., *Inside the Multinationals* London, Croom Helm.

Casson, Mark (1982), *The Entrepreneur: An Economic Theory,* Oxford, Martin Robertson.

Casson, Mark (1990), *Internalisation Theory and Beyond*, University of Reading, *mimeo.*

Chesnais, Francois (1986) 'Science, Technology & Competitiveness', *STI Review,* No. 1, Autumn, pp. 85–129.

Coase, Ronald (1960), 'The Problem of Social Cost', *The Journal of Law and Economics*, **3**, October, pp. 1–44.

Enderwick, Peter (1989), 'Multinational Corporate Restructuring and International Competitiveness', *California Management Review,* **32**, No.1, Fall, pp. 44–59

Hymer, Stephen H. (1968), 'The Large International "Corporation": An Analysis of Some Motives for the International Integration of Business'. Original version in: *Revue Economique*, **19**, No. 6 pp. 949–73. English version in: *The Multinational Enterprise: Selected Readings*, Casson, Mark (ed.) (1990), Cheltenham, Edward Elgar.

Jorde, Thomas M. and Teece, Donald J. (1989), 'Competition and Co-operation: Striking the Right Balance', *California Management Review*, **31**, No. 3, pp. 25–37.

Kindleberger, Charles P. (1988), 'The "New" Multinationalization of Business', *ASEAN Economic Bulletin*, **5**, November, pp. 113–24.

Robson, Peter (ed.) (1984), *The Economics of International Economic Integration* (2nd edition), London, George Allen & Unwin.

Telser, Lester G. (1987), *A Theory of Efficient Co-operation and Competition*, Cambridge, Cambridge University Press.

Weinshall, Theodore D. (ed.) (1977), *Culture and Management*, Harmondsworth, Penguin.

# 2 Barriers to Internationalization*

The argument of this chapter is that internationalization is a special case of the growth of the firm. Consequently, many of the concepts that have proved serviceable in analyzing the growth of the firm domestically can prove useful in the case of internationalization. However, there are extra dimensions to international expansion that need to be delineated.

Internationalization is defined here as establishing operations outside the home country. Therefore, exporting from a domestic base is excluded from consideration, but the establishment and development of agencies, licensing arrangements, sales and production subsidiaries, and joint ventures all fall within the definition.

However, models based on economics tend to be comparative static and to ignore processes. Change elements are often disregarded or underplayed. Indeed, change itself is often seen as costless. This chapter attempts to introduce dynamic elements into the calculus, and it argues that examining internationalization has forced unorthodox elements into theories of the growth of the firm, notably the importance of management decisions and processes. These two elements are interrelated. In order to have a theory of management, it is essential to move away from comparing states to company processes – in particular to contrast management processes with market processes. This is a recurring theme in this chapter.

## THE GROWTH OF THE FIRM

Several key forces are crucial in the growth of the firm. Among them are: (1) meeting demand; (2) capitalizing technology;

* L. Zan, S. Zambon and A. Pettigrew (eds) *Perspectives on Strategic Change*, Kluwer, Norwell, Mass, 1993 (reprinted by permission of Kluwer Academic Publishers).

(3) financing expansion; (4) expanding the management team; (5) recruiting resources (particularly labor); (6) competitive pressure; (7) information barriers; (8) external, particularly governmental, regulations; (9) intraorganizational constraints, perhaps rising from the historical evolution of the company; and (10) pressure from suppliers, buyers, joint venture partners, and other external bodies.

These factors are interrelated. The interaction of several of these factors may be construed as a 'barrier.' In different circumstances one, or more, of these forces may be a constraint on growth. A number of authors have concentrated on one of these forces as crucial: for instance, Penrose's classic (1959) exposition of underutilized resources (notably management) and its corollary that the expansion of the management team may be a crucial constraint on growth. Other authors, in examining the competitive process, have pointed to a concatenation of forces as barriers. Porter's pressures from suppliers, buyers, new entrants, and substitutes as well as existing rivals (1985, p. 6, Fig. 1.2) may well be construed as a comprehensive catalog, derived from industrial economics, of external barriers.

Special categories of firms may also be subjected to particularly strong barriers to growth. Particular attention has been paid to small firms, for whom some of the normal environmental and internal pressures may be barriers to growth. This may be particularly true when a number of barriers are simultaneously operative. Two crucial internal shortages, of capital and of management time, are central to this thesis (Buckley, 1989). The difficulty of expanding the management team in a small firm with the consequent loss of control by the existing managers and of raising capital for expansion are interrelated. The difficulty of capitalizing knowhow, raising funds while not losing control of key competitive advantages, compounds the difficulties. While a large, specialized literature has developed on small firms, it is essential to emphasize one key point: the relationship between firm size and market size. Two situations can be envisioned; a small firm attempting to grow in a 'large firm' industry, that is, an industry where optimal scale is large relative to market size, versus an industry with few economies of scale where many small firms exist. Industries requiring a wide range of specialist intermediate inputs, in particular, present a small firm in equilibrium with a small market. The role of small firms to fill a market niche has been noted, for instance, in the analysis of Third World foreign investors, whose main skill is as versatile users of flexible equipment (Wells, 1983). Because of their relative vulnerability to changes in demand, technology, and competition arising from their lack of diversification or reserves, small firms may succumb to external changes rather more quickly and more often than large firms.

## SPECIAL FACTORS IN INTERNATIONALIZATION

While the general analysis of the growth of the firm serves well in its application to internationalization, a number of key factors also apply. Crudely, these are: (1) the imposition of a second (or multiple) set of government restrictions; (2) cultural differences between nations; (3) the role of multinationality itself; and (4) differences arising from the comparative advantage of firms in different locations.

Each of these requires separate analysis.

The international expansion of the firm requires it to come under the jurisdiction of more than one sovereign government, with all that that implies in terms of different tax regimes, standards, and regulatory machinery. As well as the additional impact of complying with the 'new' government's legislation, there will be an interactive effect of the bilateral relations between the two governments. This causes problems from the mechanical (different accounting regimes) to the philosophical (questions of allegiance). It also presents opportunities, notably for reducing the tax bill through the manipulation of transfer prices.

Differences in culture between nations pose many problems of adjustment, particularly for first-time foreign entrants. The concept of psychic distance has been utilized in an attempt to convey the notion that cultural distance is relative and can be measured between any two points (Hallen and Weidersheim-Paul, 1979). It can be argued that cultural differences exist within a nation. Firms from Lombardy investing in Sicily, for instance, may be journeying further in cultural distance (and physical distance) than if they invested in Switzerland. However, there are aspects of culture that are national, and many cultural barriers such as language and attitudes to the law and government align closely with national boundaries. While concepts of culture and psychic distance must be used with discretion, they provide an extra dimension to the theorizing on internationalization.

For more established multinational firms the very fact of multinationality may be relevant in internationalization. It has been a tenet of many approaches to international business that foreign entrants are at a disadvantage relative to domestic firms because of lack of knowledge of how to do business (a strong cultural element is present in this argument) (Hymer, 1960; Kindleberger, 1969). This is only true for naive noninternationalized companies. It may well be easier for an established multinational to enter its $(n + 1)$th market and grow to a certain size than for a local firm to grow beyond its current size in that market. Multinationality may also improve informational diffusion for the firm, making it easier for a multinational firm not present in a particular market to spot an opportunity in that market faster than a local firm (Buckley and Dunning, 1976).

It may further be suggested that firms are highly stimulated by their local environment and are more likely to innovate when their immediate surroundings are more conducive to the creation of (particular) new techniques or products. This is the basis of the product cycle model (Vernon, 1966, 1974, 1979). For internationalization to occur, these innovations must be transferable to other economies. In adapting to its market, the firm (in the product cycle model) moves through stages from innovation to standardization and maturity according to the developing forces of supply and demand for its product. This model of taking sequential decisions has had a great influence on internationalization theory.

## APPROACHES TO INTERNATIONALIZATION

When considering the entry of a particular firm into a particular foreign market, it is essential to distinguish between initial entry and subsequent market development. Several studies have examined the firm's first foreign direct investment (Aharoni, 1966; Buckley, Newbould, and Thurwell, 1988). A recent wide-ranging review builds this distinction into its title (Young et al., 1989). While a firm's first foreign direct investment does represent a crucial threshold in its international development, here we must concentrate on the whole of the internationalization process and not become too concerned with changes of state (for instance, from nonforeign investor to foreign investor) except as markers on the growth process. Indeed, the significance of changes of state as indicators of process development in the stages approach to internationalization are subject to controversy. What is particularly at issue is the sequential and orderly internationalization that may have been (inadvertently) implied by some of the earlier studies of internationalization. A number of seemingly distinct lines of development include: (1) the international product cycle and its derivatives; (2) the stages approach to internationalization; (3) foreign market servicing models and the analysis of switches of mode of foreign market servicing; (4) transactions cost approaches; (5) business strategy analyses; and (6) models of cooperation, alliances, and the network approach.

## The International Product Cycle

The influence of Raymond Vernon's (1966) original model goes way beyond its original application to the development of U.S. foreign direct investment in Europe and in the cheap labor countries and beyond his reappraisal of its usefulness (1979) in response to critics (e.g., Giddy, 1978). The dynamic of the model lies in the interaction of the evolving forces of demand (taste) patterns and production possibilities. In some ways, its powerful, yet simple, dynamic resting on the interaction of demand and supply over time has never been bettered. The model also contains a clear cost-based switch point:

Invest abroad when $MPCX + TC > APCA$

where    $MPCX$ is the marginal cost of production for export;
           $TC$ is transport cost;

*APCA* is average cost of production in the foreign market.

This rationale for internationalization following cost changes is followed through in stage III investment which is entirely cost based as the market becomes homogeneous and supply costs dominate.

The twin rationales of cost imperatives and market pull are simply expounded in Vernon's model. Its programmatic nature, however, may have straight-jacketed further analyses into a unilineal internationalization path. Its attention, to discrete decisions rather than the management of the internationalization process further limits its general applicability.

## Stages of Involvement Approaches

The process of gradually increasing involvement in foreign markets has been a widely noted phenomenon especially in Scandinavian (mostly Swedish) studies. There are two types of increasing involvement that often seem to be implied. First is increasing involvement in any one foreign market. An orderly process of exporting, agency establishment, sales subsidiary, and finally production subsidiary with the possible intervention of a licensing or other contractual form also being included may be implied. Second is orderly stepwise penetration of different foreign markets beginning with the closest market in terms of psychic distance (Hallen and Weidersheim-Paul, 1979) and often physical distance, gradually extending to more distant and therefore more difficult markets.

These stages are often tied to hypotheses on the learning of firms. At each stage the firm acquires knowledge of the market, or it can transfer lessons learned in one foreign market to another one. Observations of three types have been made by Johanson and Weidersheim-Paul (1975) on a sample of four Swedish companies, Johanson and Vahlne (1977), and Buckley, Newbould, and Thurwell (1988, original edition 1978). This orderly process and the gradualism and risk aversion it implies have been criticized by Hedlund and Kverneland (1983) and by Turnbull (1987).

The gradual learning theory can be criticized on methodological grounds and in terms of its applicability. First, when we observe a foreign production subsidiary and look back in time over its development, many other ventures that failed before reaching this stage will not be extant. Thus a bias is induced toward success in longer establishment patterns (Buckley, 1989; Hedlund and Kverneland, 1983) (see Figure 2.1). Second, it may apply more to naive (first-time) foreign investors than to experienced companies. This is acknowledged by its proponents: for example, Johanson and Wiedersheim-Paul (1975) expect jumps in the establishment chain in firms with extensive experience in other foreign markets. Support for a more direct (less gradualist) entry route is given in Hedlund and Kverneland (1983), but the special case of Japan also induces extraordinary biases (notably the discontinuities in liberalizing entry into the market).

An important and neglected aspect of internationalization stages approaches is the attention paid to commitment. The proponents of the model hypothesize that commitment to internationalization increases with each further step into the

*Figure 2.1*    Route to a foreign production subsidiary; routes taken by two groups of direct investors in production

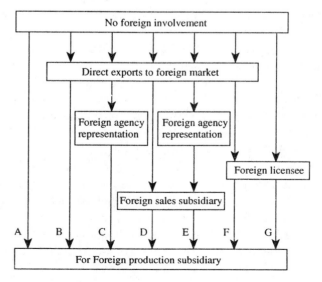

international area. There is thus a feedback relationship between level of internationalization and commitment to further internationalization. This relationship is underresearched. It is clear from many studies (longitudinal, cross-sectional, and individual cases) that a growing international awareness in managers is a major motivating force to overcoming barriers to internationalization. Psychic barriers are perceived to be lower as internationalization proceeds.

Despite these controversies, it is obvious that internationalization patterns are influenced by the previous internationalization of the company. Barriers to the internationalization of a small naive firm will be easily overcome by a well-established multinational and thus may mean that the two firms enter a market in different ways. A further issue here is the question of how far world markets are becoming more homogeneous. This is pointed up in the contrast between gradualist 'internationalization' models and more grandiose 'globalization' models which are analyzed below under business strategy models.

The key barriers in stages models are lack of knowledge (information) and of resources, notably management time. Their applicability to smaller firms is thus likely to be stronger.

## Models of Methods of Foreign Market Servicing

The stages approach finds an echo in models of foreign market servicing because such models attempt to establish the conditions under which a firm will service a foreign market by a particular method. The generic methods are exporting, licensing, and foreign direct investment; but more recent models examine the interactions of these models, their channel implications, and their context as part of the firm's strategy.

There are three generic methods by which a firm can penetrate a particular foreign market: exporting, licensing, or direct investment. Each of these methods has a variety of subtypes, and the interaction between the methods are, in practice, very important. There is a huge literature on each of exporting, licensing, joint ventures, and foreign direct investment. For a review of this literature see Young and associates (1989).

Exporting can be regarded as the most straightforward way of selling in a foreign market, avoiding, as it does, most of the costs of doing business abroad. It is separated from the other two main forms of foreign market servicing by the location factor in that the bulk of the value-adding activities take place in the home (not the foreign) market. Exporting may attract tax advantages, and the associated risks are low because usually little capital is involved. However, the fixed costs of exporting (including making contact, negotiating prices, arranging shipping, adapting product and promotion) mean that a small volume of export sales can be uneconomic. Costs of product adaptation, tariff and non-tariff barriers, and transport costs may dictate local operations rather than exporting.

International licensing appears to combine the best of both worlds – the advantage in technology and skills of the licensing multinational plus the local knowledge of the licencee. However, licensing accounts for only 7 percent of the total foreign sales of British companies (Buckley and Prescott, 1989) and approximately the same proportion in the other major trading nations. The reasons lie in the costs and difficulties of designing and maintaining contractual arrangements. These transaction costs center on the identifiability of the advantage, policing costs (constraining the licencee from using the knowledge in 'ways which have not been paid for'), the danger of creating a competitor, problems, in the market for licenses (including the buyer uncertainty problem: that the buyer does not know what to pay for the knowledge until he/she has it, when he/she has it he/she has no need to pay for it!), and the search costs in bringing buyer and seller together (Buckley and Davies, 1981). In other instances, the market structure may militate in favor of licensing as a form of market entry – cross-licensing in oligopolistic industries may be preferable to head-to-head competition. Licensing may also be a second best choice when exporting or direct investment is ruled out by government policy, intrafirm scarcities, or risk profiles. Licensing also be useful to extend the life of an idea or technology or to reach small or difficult foreign markets. In the theory of international business, the choice between licensing and direct investment is crucial in illustrating the choice between a market (external) solution – licensing – and an internal solution – direct investment (Buckley and Casson, 1976, 1985).

The foreign investment decision is a crucial step in internationalization. In fact, foreign direct investment is often treated as if it were synonymous with internationalization. Just as there are many forms of contractual arrangements for conducting international business, of which licensing is just one (Buckley, 1983) so are there many forms of foreign direct investment. The major motives for conducting foreign direct investment are market oriented, cost oriented, and for control of key inputs (see Table 2.1).

A recent attempt to integrate approaches to the foreign market servicing decisions of multinational firms is made in Buckley, Pass, and Prescott (1990). Foreign market servicing decisions concern the choice of which production or service facility should cover which particular foreign market and the means by which this should be performed. Thus the mode of servicing (exporting, licensing, investment) and the channel decisions need to be integrated. The article deals with a wider range of functions than is usual and presents some strong propositions on the form and development of foreign market servicing channels, focusing on the key choices of location and of internal versus external control systems. The simple choice of exporting, licensing, or investment is too crude a division because it ignores the crucial issues of channel management and the flows of information within the firm. The management of information and choice of form link this theoretical piece with the internationalization approach and provide testable propositions for empirical work (see Figure 2.2).

Market servicing models again are largely comparatively static. They ignore the costs of switching modes and the process aspects of the change. Management is assumed to choose the lowest cost method of doing business abroad and to implement this decision costlessly. The considerable difficulties of computing the least-cost method in a situation of extreme uncertainty are excluded. Consequently these models are seemingly at variance with decisions observed in the real world, based on 'rules of thumb', 'guesstimates,' and 'hunches.' However, they do provide rational guidelines for management decision makers.

Table 2.1 A typology of international cooperation modes

| Form of Cooperation | Equity or Nonequity | Time Limited or Unlimited | Space Limited | Transfer of Resources & Rights | Mode of Transfer |
|---|---|---|---|---|---|
| 1. Wholly owned foreign subsidiaries | Equity | Unlimited | At discretion of MNE | Whole range | Internal |
| 2. Joint ventures | Equity | Unlimited | Agreed | Whole range? | Internal |
| 3. Foreign minority holdings | Equity | Unlimited | Limited | Whole range? | Internal |
| 4. 'Fadeout' agreements | Equity | Limited | Nature of agreement | Whole range for limited period | Internal changing to market |
| 5. Licensing | Nonequity | Limited by contract | May include limitation in contract | Limited range | Market |
| 6. (Franchising) | Nonequity | Limited by contract | Yes | Limited + support | Market |
| 7. Management contracts | Nonequity | Limited by contract | May be specified | Limited | Market |
| 8. 'Turnkey ventures' | Nonequity | Limited | Not usually | Limited in time | Market |
| 9. 'Contractual joint ventures' | Nonequity | Limited | May be agreed | Specified by contract | Mixed |
| 10. International subcontracting | Nonequity | Limited | Yes | Small | Market |

*Figure 2.2*    A schematic diagram of the key constituent elements of the firm's activities

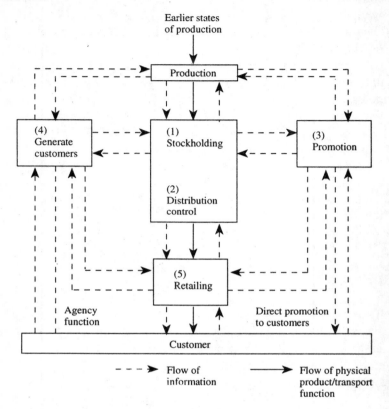

*Source*: Developed from Buckley and Casson (1976, p. 51)

## Transaction Cost Models

Given the dominance of transaction cost-based models of the multinational enterprise (Buckley and Casson, 1976), it is not surprising that internationalization should be seen in the light of transaction cost minimization. An attempt to relate transaction costs to mode of foreign entry has been made by Anderson and Gatignan (1986). This model explains the mode of foreign market servicing and therefore the pace and direction of internationalization by the tradeoff between control (of foreign operations) and resource commitment (and therefore risk). Key variables in this approach are: (1) transaction specific assets that are specialized in few uses, including proprietary technology, user-customized products, and new products; (2) external uncertainty, including political risk; (3) internal uncertainty, including principal – agent problems, which significantly may be related to international experience and psychic distance; and (4) free-riding potential, the agent's ability to receive benefits without bearing the associated costs.

This approach generates a number of hypotheses on internationalization relating product characteristics to type of market servicing and identifying the influence of political stability and environmental conditions in the host country. A cost-benefit calculus can thus, in theory, be generated so as to help determine the direction of internationalization.

**Business Strategy Models**

The business strategy approach to internationalization emphasizes planning within the company. At the extreme, 'globalization' models seem to imply that the external barriers to internationalization are minimal – (all that a firm has to do in order to internationalize is to put this in the strategic plan!)

The range of application of the globalization model, like the stages of involvement approach, may be circumscribed (Porter, 1986). In its pure form, the existence of a 'global product,' standardized marketing techniques, and centralized planning and control, the answer is that not many sectors, products, and industries conform to a homogeneous worldwide strategy. The model is thus an idealized view of the organization of firms at the opposite end of the size spectrum from naive first-time investors. National markets are firmly idiosyncratic in many areas. Psychic distance or cultural difference still exist. There are many instances of the failure of multinationals to impose a uniform product on an unwilling national market. However, the existence of market niches leaves global marketeers vulnerable to competition from nonstandardized products.

Consequently, a more cautious version of the globalization model is now the norm. Porter's model (1986) suggests that there is not a single global strategy (Young, 1987). Rather, strategy is constrained by the value chain (vertical integration imperatives), configuration (location costs of interrelated activities internalized within the firm), and coordination issues. This leads to a typology of global strategies. A related categorization by White and Poynter (1984) distinguishes the types of integration among networks of foreign affiliates (miniature replicas, marketing satellites, rationalized manufacture, product specialist, strategic independent). This has much in common with Casson's typology (1986) which relies on an extended version of the product life cycle to analyze changes in the international division of labor. Concentrating on intermediate goods flows, Casson provides a typology of industries: new product industries, mature product industries, rationalized product industries, resource-based industries, trading, and nontradeable service industries.

Again, the nature of the industry and its competitive dynamics are essential external constraints on the internationalization process.

## Models of Organizational Development

An archetypal stages model of the organizational development of multinational enterprises is given by John Stopford's research on U.S. multinational enterprises. The path of development moves through the international division stage to either area division or worldwide product division to a global matrix or grid. It is generally agreed that such models either as description or prescription are oversimplifications of a much more complex process (Bartlett, 1981). This is often connected with explicit or implicit assumptions on centralization versus decentralization. Nevertheless, the complexity of the task of description and prescription should not deter all attempts, and it is ironic that most of the severe critics of stages models of organization often offer modified stages models. An example is Millington and Bayliss (1990, p. 159) which does 'not support a narrowly incremental view of the process of internationalization, a step-wide inter-

nationalization process being the exception rather than the rule'
but 'these results support a life cycle model which is based on
the international development of the firm... In the early stages of
international development the firm relies on market experience
and incremental adjustment. As the degree of international
experience increases, this process is superseded by formal planning and systematic search. In the final *stages* of development
international experience may be transferred across market and
between products, thereby enabling firms to leapfrog the incremental process within markets' (p. 159, emphases added). In
fact, Millington and Bayliss examine only quoted companies, the
smallest of which had a turnover of £10 million – coincidentally
the upper limit on the Buckley and associates (1988) study. The
Millington and Bayliss study examines only the final stage of the
internationalization process – the establishment of a production
subsidiary in the market and the firm's immediately prior
arrangement. This cannot rule out an incremental sequence up to
the stage of sales subsidiary (for instance) for those firms with
that arrangement immediately proceeding production. Moreover,
the study gives no indication of the timing in stage changes, that
is, how long the firm persisted with an agent or sales subsidiary
before switching to a manufacturing venture. Stage models
usually have explicit or implicit assumptions on durations of
stages.

Often organizational transformation costs are entirely omitted
from such models. Firms are not completely flexible, nor can
flexibility be achieved at zero cost! It is crucial to remember that
the organization structure at one given moment of time is a snapshot of a dynamic process (Brooke, 1984; Buckley, 1988).

## Cooperation, Alliances, and the Network Approach

Any study of internationalization cannot ignore 'the dense
network of cooperation and affiliation by which firms are interrelated' (Richardson, 1972, p. 833). The role of cooperation
between firms in international business is an area of current
research interest (Contractor and Lorange, 1988), and it has
separated strands in the work on networks of firms (Johanson

and Mattsson, 1988) and work on strategic alliances (Hamel, Doz, and Pralahad, 1989; Porter, 1986).

Work on joint ventures and other collaborative modes has been a staple of the field of internationalization for a considerable period (for a review, see Buckley, 1983). Recently the focus has shifted to strategic alliances, implicitly between large multinational firms. Networking is seemingly less aggressive (and reprehensible in competitive terms) but amounts to the same thing – long-term agreements between firms to achieve certain goals.

The network approach also takes up Richardson's point on cooperation and affiliation between firms. The model describes (industrial) markets as networks of relationship between firms. The belief of the proponents of such models is that the network model, 'being superior to some other models of 'markets', makes it possible to consider some important interdependencies and development processes on international markets' (Johanson and Mattsson, 1988, p. 237).

The virtue of the network approach is indeed the ability of observers to study interactions over time between network members and to race interdependences. What is now necessary is to show how far these interdependences affect managerial behavior. It is unclear how much an individual manager would prefer to deal with a network member rather than an outsider. Is it the case that network members prefer to deal with each other even if an outsider could offer a service at a lower price? If so, this implies nonrational behavior from the point of view of the individual firm (unless the network, an informal group, is the focus for profit maximization, which seems unlikely). It may be that networks create noncompeting groups. For instance, an outsider may not be able to tender for a particular product or service because the specifications are not released outside network members. In this case, networks are anticompetitive cartels and their members would be subject to antitrust legislation in many national jurisdictions. While it is undeniable that network behavior is observed in terms of the frequency of transactions between certain firms, it is unclear how much this is due to processes other than normal market behavior and managerial choice.

## SYNTHESIS: BARRIERS TO INTERNATIONALIZATION

Several key issues must be present in any approach to internationalization. These include: (1) the relationship between the firm and the market; (2) the relationship between the firm and its industry; (3) internal planning and resource availability; (4) external constraints; and (5) the historical, time dimension.

The relationship between the firm and the market provides a context for internationalization. The market is the ultimate constraint on the ability of any firm to internationalize. The ability of the firm to overcome (or appropriate) transaction costs will determine the direction of its growth and may keep it confined to a particular national market or markets, or to a small or low-growth product segment.

The relationship of the firm and its industry is also significant. Cost imperatives, technological imperatives, and competitive pressure and exit barriers from the firm's particular industry group (Caves and Porter, 1979) confine and direct the direction of expansion. Industry dynamics as modeled in the product life cycle also have a determining effect on internationalization.

Resource availability and planning are internal constraints. Of particular importance here is the ability of the firm to augment its management team.

External constraints are often taken for granted in the internationalization literature. However, government regulations, particularly local ownership requirements, local content specifications, differential taxes, and tariffs, clearly alter (*distort* in the loaded term of economists) internationalization patterns.

The time dimension, too, is crucial. The historical evolution of the company cannot be ignored. Studies of first-time foreign investors cannot be read across to established multinational firms, nor vice versa. Decisions at time $t$ will be affected by those at $(t - 1)$. Sequential decision making may look rational post hoc but may be far more contingent than an outsider can know. (The role of risk clearly varies over time; entry into the $n$th market may well change in both ease and riskiness after $n$ surpasses a certain number (5, 10, 15?).)

However, while this list represents the main focus of research to date, it is in fact too limited. Despite attention to the history of firms, too little attention has been paid to management processes versus market processes in internationalization and to the non-costless management of change. The move from one state to another is frequently assumed by a comparison of objective costs. This is too large an assumption to swallow in situations of uncertainty about levels of costs, outcomes, and the range of choice. Bounded rationality has a greater role to play in barriers to internationalization than has so far been granted. Cost comparisons only become meaningful when grounded in uncertainty. It is management's role to respond to uncertainty; those analyses based on a description of what managers do in internationalizing their companies (e.g., Aharoni, 1966) show far greater reliance on heuristic processes than careful cost computations. Internationalization is not a single unilineal process. It interacts with the development of the organizational structure, with organizational commitment, and with management development. The interactions between these elements have been inadequately spelled out, and so the literature features single barriers rather than nexuses of obstacles.

## CONCLUSION

Internationalization may well need to be understood by situational logic. The principles may be well established, but the conditions under which those principles operate may be so varied and variable that general rules are hard to follow. Barriers to internationalization clearly change over the life of the firm and the industry. Internationalization is a dynamic process and is not easily understood within a (any) static framework (e.g., the eclectic approach: Dunning, 1991). However, the general case of the growth of the firm is a useful overarching viewpoint from which to establish the particular features of international expansion. Despite the wild statements on globalization to which some analysts and businessmen are prone, there do remain significant international barriers to growth, and these are ignored by firms, of whatever size and scope, at their peril.

The study of internationalization as a process is thus at a crossroads. Many single barriers to internationalization are well understood, described and analyzed. The formidable task that remains is the formulation of internationalization as a process, where change is not costless, feedback relationships between key variables are fully specified, and management is formulated – not as point of time decision making, but as sequential development.

## Acknowledgment

The author is grateful to Professor Pervez Ghauri for comments on an earlier draft.

## References

Aharoni, Y., 1966, *The Foreign Investment Decision Process,* Boston, MA.: Graduate School of Business Administration, Harvard University.

Anderson, E., Gatignan, H., 1986, 'Modes of Foreign Entry: A Transaction Cost Analysis and Propositions,' *Journal of International Business Studies,* 17, 3, pp. 1–26.

Bartlett, C. A., 1981, 'Multinational Structural Change: Evolution versus Reorganization,' in Otterbeck, L. (ed.), *The Management of Headquarters – Subsidiary Relationships in Multinational Corporations,* Aldershot: Gower.

Brooke, M. Z., 1984, *Centralization and Autonomy,* Eastbourne: Holt, Rinehart and Winston.

Buckley, P. J., 1983, 'New forms of International Industrial Cooperations: A Survey of the Literature,' *Aussenwirtschaft,* 38, 2, pp. 195–222. (Reprinted in Buckley and Casson, 1985.)

Buckley, P. J., et al., 1988, 'Organizational Forms and Multinational Companies,' in Thompson, S., Wright, M. (eds), *Internal Organization, Efficiency and Profit,* Oxford: Philip Allan.

Buckley, P. J., 1989, 'Foreign Direct Investment by Small and Medium Sized Enterprises: The Theoretical Background,' *The Multinational Enterprise: Theory and Applications,* London: Macmillan.

Buckley, P. J., Casson, M., 1976, *The Future of the Multinational Enterprise,* London: Macmillan.

Buckley, P. J., Casson, M., 1985, *The Economic Theory of the Multinational Enterprise,* London: Macmillan.

Buckley, P. J., Davies, H., 1981, 'Foreign Licensing in Overseas Operations: Theory and Evidence from the UK,' in: Hawkins, R. G., Prasad, A. J. (eds), *Technology Transfer and Economic Development,* Greenwich, CT.: JAI Press.

Buckley, P. J., Dunning, J. H., 1976, 'The Industrial Structure of US Investment in the UK,' *Journal of International Business Studies,* 7, 2, pp. 5–13.

Buckley, P. J., Newbould, G. D., Thurwell, J., 1988, *Foreign Direct Investment by Smaller UK Firms,* London: Macmillan. (Previously published in 1978 as *Going International: The Experiences of Smaller Firms Overseas.*)

Buckley, P. J., Pass, C. L. Prescott, K., 1990, 'Foreign Market Servicing by Multinationals: An Integrated Approach,' *International Marketing Review*, 7, 4, pp. 25–40.

Buckley, P. J., Prescott, K., 1989, 'The Structure of British Industry's Sales in Foreign Markets,' *Managerial and Decision Economics*, 10, 3, pp. 189–208.

Casson, M., and Associates, 1986, *Multinationals and World Trade*, London: George Allen & Unwin.

Caves, R. E., Porter, M. E., 1979, 'From Entry Barriers to Mobility Barriers: Conjectural Variations and Contrived Deterrence to New Competition,' *Quarterly Journal of Economics*, 9, pp. 241–261.

Contractor, F., Lorange, P. (eds), 1988, *Cooperative Strategies in International Business*, Lexington, MA.: Lexington Books, D.C. Heath & Co.

Dunning, J. H., 1991, 'The Eclectic Paradigm of International Production: A Personal Perspective,' in: Pitelis, C. N. and Sugden, R. (eds), *The Nature of the Transnational Firm*, London: Routledge.

Giddy, I. H., 1978, 'The Demise of the Product Cycle Model in International Business Theory,' *Columbia Journal of World Business*, 13, pp. 90–97.

Hallen, L., Weidersheim-Paul, F., 1979, 'Psychic Distance and Buyer–Seller Interaction.' *Organization, Markand och Samhalle*, 16, 5, pp. 308–324.

Hamel, G., Doz, Y., Prahalad, C. K., (1989), 'Collaborate with Your Competitors – and Win,' *Harvard Business Review*, January–February, pp. 113–139.

Hedlund, G., Kverneland, A., 1983, 'Are Establishments and Growth Strategies for Foreign Market Changing,' paper presented at the 9th European International Business Association Conference, Oslo, December 18–20, 1983.

Hymer, S. H., 1976, *The International Operations of National Firms: A Study of Direct Investment*, Cambridge, MA.: MIT Press. (Previously unpublished doctoral dissertation, 1960.)

Johanson, J., Mattsson, L. G., 1988, 'Internationalization in Industrial Systems – A Network Approach,' in: Hood, N. and Vahlne, J. E. (eds), *Strategies in Global Competition*, London: Croom-Helm.

Johanson, J., Vahlne, J. E. 1977, 'The Internationalization Process of the Firm – A Model of Knowledge Development and Increasing Foreign Market Commitments,' *Journal of International Business Studies*, 8, 1, pp. 23–32.

Johanson, J., Vahlne, J. E. 1990, 'The Mechanism of Internationalization,' *International Marketing Review*, 7, 4. pp. 11–24.

Johanson, J., Wiedersheim-Paul, F., 1975, 'The Internationalization of the Firm – Four Swedish Cases,' *Journal of Management Studies*, October, pp. 305–322.

Kindleberger, C. P., 1969, *American Business Abroad*, New Haven, CT.: Yale University Press.

Luostarinen, R., 1979, *The Internationalization of the Firm*, Helsinki: Acta Academia Oeconomica Helsingiensis.

Millington, A. I., Bayliss, B. T., 1990, 'The Process of Internationalization: UK Companies in the EC,' *Management International Review*, 30, 2, pp. 151–161.

Penrose, E., 1959, *The Theory of the Growth of the Firm*, Oxford: Basil Blackwell.

Porter, M. E., (1985), *Competitive Advantage*, New York: Free Press.

Porter, M. E., (ed.), 1986, *Competition in Global Industries*, Boston, MA.: Harvard Business School Press.

Richardson, G. B., 1972, 'The Organization of Industry,' *Economic Journal*, 82, pp. 883–896.

Turnbull, P., 1987, 'A Challenge to the Stages Theory of the Internationalization Process,' in: Rosson, P. J., Reid, S. D. (eds), *Managing Export Entry and Expansion*, New York: Praeger.

Vernon, R., 1966, 'International Investment and International Trade in the Product Cycle,' *Quarterly Journal of Economics*, 80, pp. 190–207.

Vernon, R., 1974, 'The Location of Economic Activity,' in: Dunning J. H. (ed.), *Economic Analysis and the Multinational Enterprise*, London: George Allen & Unwin.

Vernon, R., 1979, 'The Product Cycle Hypothesis in a New International Environment,' *Oxford Bulletin of Economics and Statistics*, 41, pp. 255–267.

Wells, L. T., 1983, *Third World Multinationals: The Rise of Foreign Investment from Developing Countries*, Cambridge, MA.: MIT Press.

White, R. G., Poynter, T. A. 1984, 'Strategies for Foreign Owned Subsidiaries in Canada,' *Business Quarterly*, 49, 2, pp. 59–69.

Young, S., 1987, 'Business Strategy and the Internationalization of Business, Recent Approaches,' *Managerial and Decision Economics*, 1, pp. 31–40.

Young, S., *et al.*, 1989, *International Market Entry and Development Strategies and Management*, Hemel Hempstead: Harvester Wheatsheaf.

# 3 Kojima's Theory of Japanese Foreign Direct Investment Revisited*

## I. INTRODUCTION

Two recent publications by Kiyoshi Kojima (1989) (1990) present an opportunity to assess the development of his thought and to contrast it with developments in the mainstream or core theory of international business and the multinational enterprise (Buckley, 1990). *Japanese Direct Investment Abroad* represents a compilation of Kojima's thought up to the end of 1987 and the 1989 article extends his work. It also contains further criticisms of the theory of internalisation.

Old arguments do not need to be rehearsed. My view, expressed in earlier articles (Buckley, 1983a 1985 and 1989) that Kojima's basic approach is unduly narrow in its assumptions, inapplicable to most (Japanese) direct investment, lacks attention to the form of investment, is unduly static and relies on key concepts from the internalisation rubric, remain unchanged. Essentially, the general stance of criticism made here is that Kojima misrepresents internalisation theory in two ways. (1) His criticism attacks certain elements of internalisation theory which he believes to be implicit in the theory, but actually are not. (2) He often restates internalisation theory as if it were an integral part of the Kojima approach. However, with the adoption of 'agreed specialisation' as a response to scale economies and the evaluation of internalisation theory by Kojima, there does seem to be more hope for fruitful dialogue and perhaps even convergence. This article largely follows Kojima's (1989) in its structure.

*An earlier version of this paper was presented as a response to Kojima to the Conference *MNEs and 21st Century Scenarios* organised by The Workshop for the Studies of Multinational Enterprise, Tokyo, 4–6 July 1990. I am grateful to the participants for their constructive comments and for later comments from Mark Casson, Hafiz Mirza and John Stopford.

*Hitotsubashi Journal of Economics*, Vol. 32, No. 2, December 1991, pp. 368–74 (reprinted by permission of the Hitotsubashi Academy, Hitotsubashi University).

## II.  KOJIMA'S THEORISING

It is essential to make a distinction between firm level economies of scale and plant level economies of scale. Kojima's discussion (1989, pp. 66–70) seems to concern plant level economies. In establishing production plants abroad it is essential to take into account the fixed costs of establishing the plant. This was explicit in Vernon's (1966) celebrated switching point in the product cycle model:

Invest abroad when $MPC_x + TC > APC_A$
where   $MPC_x$ is marginal cost of production for export
$TC$ is transport cost to target market
$APC_A$ is average cost of production abroad

The Buckley and Casson development of this model (1981) refined this point by postulating two types of fixed costs. (1) A non recoverable set up cost, which is a once-for-all cost incurred as soon as the mode is adopted. (2) A recurrent fixed cost, independent of the rate of output, which results from indivisibilities in the factor inputs hired in connection with the market servicing activity. The introduction of economies of scale into the model provides a valuable service as the original mode of doing so ('production with large plant' versus 'production with small plant') was admittedly crude. However to do so whilst ignoring fixed costs and set up costs of any kind is to devalue the model and to make nonsense of the decision rules. Of course, plants with lowest average minimum cost will be most efficient in the absence of any balancing fixed costs. The concept of economies of scale at plant level used by Kojima may be becoming obsolete in the presence of changing demand conditions flexible manufacturing techniques, robotization and just-in-time inventory control. Although the imperative to achieve minimum efficient scale may have shifted to component suppliers rather than assemblers.

However, some of the major gains from multinational operations arise in the area of firm level economies of scale. These economies, through the operation of internal markets, allow the more efficient coordination of functions within the firm (Buckley and Casson, 1976; Buckley, Pass and Prescott 1990).

Coordination of functions such as production, R&D, finance and marketing and their subfunctions (distribution, inventory control, production promotion) allows costs to be decreased across the firm through the flow and control, not just of products, but of information. These gains will not show up as lower average costs of production but as dynamic gains in innovation and as lower selling costs, more rapid new production introductions, increased product variety, and in increased demand for the company by meeting the customers' needs more closely. The increasing capital intensity of production means that financing costs weigh more heavily (e.g. fixed costs in plant establishment') and the variable costs of labour inputs declines – in many cases to a negligible part of total costs. Recent studies have shown falling plant level economies of scale. Baden-Fuller *et al.* (1988) show that, when reductions in minimum efficient scale at the plant level occur with local consumer demand shifts for greater variety, the benefits of international cost reducing investments are eroded and sometimes eliminated. To deal with such conditions, the form of the foreign investments necessary to coordinate supplies is shifting the order to achieve improvements in relative quality, as measured by variety, service and product reliability, rather than achieving lower relative costs (Stopford, 1990).

## III.  THE GAINS FROM INTERNATIONALIZATION

It has been explicit in the internalization approach that in every cost of internationalization of a market, the benefits should be set against the costs of internalization (Buckley and Casson, 1976, pp. 37, 41–44). Indeed it has often been necessary to re-emphasise costs to reduce the ardour of the over zealous (Buckley, 1983b, 1990) and, whilst the decision-making firm will consider the decision in terms of its effect on long run profits, the welfare effects of the contrary pressures of cost and benefits have been frequently explicated (e.g. Buckley, 1987, p. 24, quoted by Kojima, 1989, p. 75).

Kojima's points on gains through internalization hardly represent refutation of this position. The original examples of the advantages of the firm (or organization) over the market were presented by Coase (1937), largely in terms of the benefits of a longer run flexible labour contract versus the costs of constantly hiring workers on short run contracts. The transaction cost reductions of the substitution of entrepreneurial control of workers' time rather than exceedingly detailed labour contracts are well known. Of course this is not to deny the benefits of part-time workers and subcontracting, particularly in times of turbulence. The limit to internalization of workers' contracts is set by the firm's judgement of the benefits given by control and direction of full-time internal workers, plus the dynamic learning, loyalty and trust effects to which Kojima [(1981), p. 71] alludes, versus the flexibility and speed of adjustment to change. Modern corporations, including Japanese ones, use a combination of these means of filling labour needs with a core, tenured or permanent staff being complemented by a periphery of more causal contracted labour.

The issues of licensing-in versus developing technology and the optimal strategy of the licensor are key elements in the internalisation approach (Buckley and Casson, 1976, Casson, 1979). There is no suggestion that internal development of technology is always superior to licensing in. Indeed, the dangers of innovating a radical breakthrough have also been dealt with (Buckley, 1983b). The choice of research expansion paths is crucial too, because as Kojima says, (1979, p. 72) 'it is too expensive to innovate every kind of technology the firm needs'. Licensing in technology may also provide a faster route to market as Japanese firms have proved repeatedly. The costs of innovation are high and rising, but what is crucial is the link between R&D and production, marketing, finance and the other functions of the firm through internal markets. In this way, dynamic welfare benefits through innovation can occur. To continue the quote which Kojima attenuates (Kojima 1989, p. 75, note 7, quoting Buckley, 1987, p. 24) 'It is important to see also the dynamic elements. The multinational's internal market allows greater inter-plant and function cooperation (e.g. between production, marketing and R&D) and in the long run this will stimulate the undertaking of R&D and its effective implementation in production and marketing and improving welfare.' Follower advantages are undeniably often strong, and part of the fascination of business strategy lies in the ability of followers to capitalise on their position, of which one area of strength is not to bear the huge financing costs of innovation.

It is essential to emphasise revenues as well as costs. Many of the dynamic gains arise from higher revenues, not reduced costs. Further, it is important to distinguish on the cost side between production costs and transaction costs.

Location endowments are not under the control of multinationals. Location decisions of multinationals, including the foreign direct investment decision, are designed to take advantage of differences in location endowments – immobile factors such as labour and raw-materials – and to use the mobile assets of the firm to exploit protected markets, financing ability and the use of internal transfer pricing to reduce the impact of government intervention. The effects of the latter group of motives have welfare implications for host and source countries and the world economy which do not satisfy first-best comparisons. Free trade would be a more welfare enhancing solution, but often the motives for foreign direct investment are complex.

In examining the role of transfer pricing it is necessary to distinguish two types of internal prices. One use of transfer pricing is to minimise government interference, notably taxation. Another theoretical possibility is that transfer prices are market perfecting, that is, such prices are shadow prices approximating to the perfect market solution rather than the external imperfect market prices. It is possible that transfer prices following this rule lead to welfare enhancement through improved resource allocation.

## IV.  MONOPOLY OR COMPETITION

It is nonsense to state that the theory of internalisation justifies monopolistic behaviour (Kojima, 1989, p. 75). The costs and benefits of internalisation are spelled out in the quote from Buckley (1987) and its continuation. Of more interest is the interaction between internalization decisions and market struc-

*Figure 3.1* The interaction between internalization decisions and market structure (after Hymer, 1968)

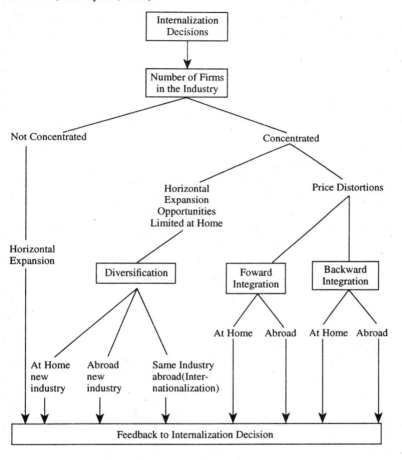

ture. A recent article (Buckley, 1990) drawing on Hymer's (1968) article in Casson (1990) attempts to integrate internalization decisions with market structure. This interaction is illustrated in Figure 3.1. A satisfying model can thus be derived.

It is insufficient to specify multinational firms as monopolists. The nature of monopoly must also be specified. Much of the 'justification' of monopoly practices which Kojima perceives actually relate to attempts made by multinational firms to capture part of the social gain of innovation as private rents in a situation of defective property rights. Other types of monopoly produce different welfare outcomes. The use of scale as a barrier to entry does indeed constitute a welfare loss rather than an issue of appropriation of benefits.

## V. CONCLUSION

Despite moves to incorporate elements of the internalization approach in his thinking, Kojima's theory is seriously flawed. First, it represents a special case because of its restrictive assumptions and lack of general applicability. The incorporation of entrepreneurial advantages reduces it to a special case of a special case (Kojima, 1990). It cannot be generalized beyond an explanation of a particular type of investment (Japanese?) in a particular host country (less developed). Second, it is outdated. The emphasis on plant level economies of scale ignores flexible manufacturing techniques, computer controlled manufacturing and inventory control, all of which require a radical re-evaluation of economies of scale. Further, the impact of increasing auto-mation and robotization on relative costs suggest that pace Kojima, fixed costs are rising and variable costs decreasing (labour costs in some cases falling asymptotically towards zero). Third, the competitive process is ignored. Special skills of com-panies – firm specific advantages in the short run – are ignored, together with the whole phenomenon of imperfect competition dynamics. Quality and variety competition, innovation strategy and barriers to entry are all conflated into economies of scale and the reduction of variable costs. As part of this process, economies of scale may be traded off for local customer services. Competition is not based solely on the reduction costs. Fourth, the role of services is ignored. This is true both for service pro-duction and for the increasingly important phenomenon of the internal flow of services in the modern corporation. Fifth, and surprisingly, Kojima ignores the role of national, regional and local culture, which provides an important explanatory factor in outward foreign investment and its preferred destinations (Buckley and Casson, 1990).

The welfare effects which Kojima emphasises are indeed important. Protected markets may induce inward investors to produce behind tariff walls with plants of less than efficient scale. Free trade here would be the best solution. Whilst the switch to foreign production may be below the minimum efficient scale, there may be other reasons for this shift – to supply more adequately local demand, for instance. It is arguable that the Single European Market Act 1992 has had just such an effect on (potential) Japanese investors.

The danger of Kojima's approach is that it leads into a conceptual 'cul de sac' (Mirza, 1989) from which its proponent finds it increasingly difficult to re-emerge. The way out is clear. It is represented by a more wholehearted acceptance of internalisation concepts and integration with the strategic trade approach of modern international economies.

# References

Baden-Fuller, Charles, John M. Stopford and Phaidon Nicholaides (1988) 'Globale o nazionale: scelte strategiche e performance delle imprese nell'industrial europa degli elettrodomestici branchi,' *L'industria* **IX**, No. 2 (April–June).

Buckley, Peter J. (1983a) 'Macroeconomic versus International Business Approach to Direct Foreign Investment: A Comment on Professor Kojima's Interpretation,' *Hitotsubashi Journal of Economics* 24, No. 1 (June).

Buckley, Peter J. (1983b) 'New Theories of International Business: Some Unresolved Issues', in: Mark Casson (ed.), *The Growth of International Business,* London, George Allen & Unwin.

Buckley, Peter J. (1985), 'The Economic Analysis of the Multinational Enterprise: Reading versus Japan?,' *Hitotsubashi Journal of Economics* 26, No. 2 (December).

Buckley, Peter J. (1987), *The Theory of the Multinational Enterprise,* Uppsala, Studia Oeconomiae Negotiorum.

Buckley, Peter J. (1989), *The Multinational Enterprise: Theory and Applications,* London, Macmillan.

Buckley, Peter J. (1990), 'Problems and Developments in the Core Theory of International Business,' *Journal of International Business Studies* 21 (4).

Buckley, Peter J. and Mark Casson (1976), *The Future of the Multinational Enterprise,* London, Macmillan.

Buckley, Peter J. and Mark Casson (1981), 'The Optimal Timing of a Foreign Direct Investment,' *Economic Journal* 91 (March).

Buckley, Peter J. and Mark Casson (1990), 'Multinational Enterprises in Less Developed Countries: Cultural and Economic Interactions', in: Peter J. Buckley and Jeremy Clegg (eds), *Multinational Enterprises in Less Developed Countries,* London, Macmillan.

Buckley, Peter J., C. L. Pass and Kate Prescott (1990), 'Foreign Market Servicing by Multinationals: An Integrated Treatment,' *International Marketing Review*, 7 (4).

Casson, Mark (1979), *Alternatives to the Multinational Enterprise*, London, Macmillan.

Casson, Mark (ed.) (1990) *Multinational Corporations*, Aldershot, Edward Elgar.

Coase, Ronald (1937), 'The Nature of the Firm,' *Economica*, 4 (November).

Hymer, Stephen H. (1968), 'The Large Multinational Corporation: An Analysis of Some Motives for the International Integration of Business', in: Casson (ed.) (1990) op cit. Original version in French in *Revue Economique* 19 (6).

Kojima, Kiyoshi (1989), 'Theory of Internalisation by Multinational Corporations,' *Hitotsubashi Journal of Economics* 30, No. 2 (December).

Kojima, Kiyoshi (1990), *Japanese Direct Investment Abroad*, Tokyo, International Christian University Social Science Research Institute Monograph Series, No. 1.

Mirza, Hafiz (1989), 'Professor Kojima's Macroeconomic Theory of Foreign Direct Investment and Recent Japanese FDI in Europe: A Critical Analysis', in: Joop A. Stam (ed.). *Industrial Cooperation between Europe and Japan*, Rotterdam, Erasmus University.

Stopford, John M. (1990), 'Multinationals' Strategy: Competition for Resources,' paper given to Conference MNEs and 21st Century Scenarios, Tokyo, 4–6 July.

Vernon, Raymond M. (1966), 'International Investment and International Trade in the Product Cycle,' *Quarterly Journal of Economics* 80, pp. 190–207.

# 4 The Role of Management in Internalization Theory*

## INTRODUCTION AND STATEMENT OF THE ISSUES

Previous writings on international business theory based on the internalization paradigm have prescribed only a minor role for management decision making in determining outcomes. This is a largely a function of the provenance of internalization theory from the neo-classical theory of the firm. A great deal of progress has been made in combining institutionalist arguments into the theory of the multinational firm through the central concept of internalization but this apparently leaves management decision making to play a minor role. The following section of this paper examines the role of management in the internalization approach. The third section critically examines the criticisms of the internalization approach and finds that it is capable of considerable extension. This is exemplified on pp. 55–7 by focussing on innovation in multinational firms.

## THE ROLE OF MANAGEMENT IN INTERNALIZATION THEORY

As the internalization theory of the multinational firm plays a central role in international business theory it is worth examining its premises on the role of management. Put simply, this approach hypotheses that firms grow by replacing imperfect (or non-existent) external markets by internal ones. When combined with locational variance in the prices of spatially fixed inputs (non tradeables), the theory can predict the pattern and direction of growth of multinational enterprises (Buckley and Casson, 1976, 1985; Hennart, 1982; Rugman, 1981; Casson, 1987;

---

*Management International Review, Vol. 33, No. 3, 1993, pp. 197–207 (reprinted by permission).

Buckley 1988). This approach needs to be combined with market power considerations deriving from Hymer (1968) to give a satisfying picture of the rate and direction of growth of multinationals (Buckley 1990).

In order to appreciate the bearing of the internalization approach on management decision making, it is essential to keep in mind the premises of the approach's purview.

1. The firm performs other functions than routine production. The coordination of these functions requires management decision making and intermediate markets in knowledge and expertise. These alternatives (management and the market) may in certain circumstances be complementary means of solving allocation problems. Communications costs within and outwith the firm are crucial in coordination and may be operated upon by cultural differences.

2. Most multinational firms are also multi-product firms, giving rise to economies of scope as well as economies of scale. Coordination across product groups yields significant returns to effective management of joint inputs and joint products.

3. Multinational firms are, by definition, multi plant (or multi unit) enterprises. The minimisation of transaction costs between plants owned and controlled by the same entity presents a major answer to the dilemma posed by the ability of below optimal scale multiplant units being able to outcompete unitary firms (Scherer, 1975). Again, the management role in reducing such costs is vital.

4. It is possible, by using financial markets and markets for factor services, to achieve a separation of functions within the firm (Casson, 1985). Thus, for example, the funding, ownership and utilization of foreign assets can be carried out by different bodies. There is no necessity for these to be combined in a single multinational firm. Management judgement on the scope of functional separation in international capital markets is like any other internalization decision, a question of betting on beating the market outcome. This provides a direct link between the internalization approach and one based on internal competences.

5. The internalization approach is not identical to a view of the multinational enterprise which is always and everywhere market-perfecting. The firm can, and will, invest in erecting barriers to entry and other forms of rent seeking behaviour. It will further use its external influence to have others erect protective devices (notably governments). These points are developed below.

6. Crucially, the orthodox approach is rooted in a view of the world which incorporates limited information. Management decision taking in this context is perforce plagued with errors (ex post) and unintended consequences.

However the picture given is of firms driven by external circumstances. Firms, even the most powerful and dominant, are perceived as responding to changes in their environment.

In the simple approach, the role of management is confined to three key areas. First, managers make internalisation decisions which determine the scale and scope of the firm. These 'buy' or 'build' decisions determine the interface between the firm and the market and the degree to which horizontal and vertical integration proceeds (Casson, 1987). Second, managers, in making internalisation decisions, choose the direction of growth of the firm by identifying market imperfections and seeking opportunities to profit by appropriating rent. Third, managers can play a proactive role in contriving market imperfections in order to maximise opportunities for growth. The role of management as conventionally portrayed thus is the sequential identification, exploitation and creation of profitable market imperfections as opportunities for growth.

It is however possible to go further than these basic propositions and to suggest a fourth management strategy which lies within the conventional purview. This strategy is to seek to raise the transactions costs of competitors. In this context, internalisation is a strategic weapon. Two types of this strategy can be identified. The first is to achieve exclusive access to key inputs. One example is to achieve a 'corner' in key resources. Another is to secure key factor inputs by the designs of exclusive contracts whose purpose is to keep managers and other key personnel tied into particular firms for long periods of time. Such contracts (enhancing pensions, loyalty bonuses, provision of complementary resources, penalties for contract breaking) are observed not only for managers but also for key R & D workers, salespeople, designers and production engineers. The second strategy is to achieve competitive advantage in the market for final goods by tying in customers. This covers strategies from building brand loyalty and awareness to the provision of a full range of products so that customers are not obliged to seek a product outside the firm's range. Such strategies raise the cost to the consumer of a product switch and increase the transactions costs of competitors.

We can thus see that the internalization approach, despite its limitations, is capable of extension beyond its traditional confines to encompass management strategies. The following section examines the areas where the approach is said to be lacking.

## A CRITICAL VIEW OF CRITICISMS OF THE INTERNALIZATION THEORY OF THE MULTINATIONAL ENTERPRISE

There must be a sense of irony in the thrust of this paper. The internalization approach is based on the substitution of management processes for market processes. For many managers this implies a (largely) fixed investment in human resources. The scope and functions of the people employed are obviously crucial elements in this decision. However, there are several key points of criticism of the theory which can be articulated as a means for 'putting management back in'.

First, the dynamics of the process of growth of firms are neglected. Without the addition of specific propositions the theory faces us with comparative static choices. In fact, the theory is more dynamic than it is given credit for and is actually better developed in this direction than competitor paradigms (Buckley, 1983). However much of the dynamic content is derived from supporting propositions which leave much to be desired – for instance the assumption of exogenous market growth in models of the growth of the multinational firm which give the switch point in Buckley and Casson's model (1981) and the income related (trickle down) model in Vernon's justly celebrated product cycle model (1966).

A strict interpretation of the orthodox theory of the multinational firm makes it possible to predict, in principle, the organisational choice between firm and markets. However, this choice is assumed to take place in a purely neoclassical world in which all the relevant information about the environment is encompassed in freely available market prices. In such a neoclassical world, the invisible hand of the market does practically all the management required. It is not possible to have an economic theory of the multinational firm which includes both the neoclassical theory of location and a realistic theory of management (Casson, 1987, p. 40).

To incorporate a theory of management, it is essential to move away from a comparison of *states* to a comparison of *processes* and, in particular, to contrast management processes with market processes. A third type of process, that of market making may also be required (Casson, 1987). Such an approach needs the fusion of economic method with that more traditionally associated with organizational sociology and social anthropology. Point-of-time ahistorical comparisons need to be combined with longitudinal observation. Progress can be made by comparisons of the changing balance of the boundary between 'firm' and 'market' and intermediate states over given time periods and by identification of the key factors which move this boundary.

Second, the theory fails to address the issue of why one firm is more successful than other. The internalization approach has as its central point of explanation the question of the growth of the firm relative to the market, not relative to another firm. As the relative success of individual firms is a central issue in the business policy/corporate strategy literature, it may be possible to seek interfaces with this literature, which the following section seeks to do. However a rephrasing of the issue may help. We may ask 'why is one firm more successful than another *for a time*?' The inclusion of the time dimension focuses attention to issues of team building, paradigm technologies and situational advantages, all of which can be integrated with the core propositions of existing theory (Buckley, 1983). Such an approach is consistent with the view that restrictions are being placed on a general theory. Essentially, the internalization approach is concerned with the long run development of the firm. Imposing a shorter run constraint on this model allows several basic propositions to be included. These may be along the lines that technology is partially tacit, content specific and tied to local skills and routines (Cantwell, 1989; Nelson and Winter, 1982; and Kogut and Zander, 1992). Such shorter term elements will constrain the growth and the direction of growth of the firm. Such propositions require explicit hypotheses on the time needed to build teams (particularly management teams), on the creation, utilisation and diffusion of technology and on the sequential creation of competitive advantages. It is doubtful that hypotheses of this kind can have a great deal of generality across industries, countries and even specific firms.

However, propositions can be formed that firms became 'locked into' particular technologies and fail to appreciate the development of radical shifts in technology which arise outside their traditional area of operation (industrial or spatial). Indeed firms may make radical innovations which it is impossible for them to absorb internally. Consequently such technologies are often 'spun off' or 'bought out' by the personnel who created them. The ability of firms to appropriate such developments may be restricted and a key determinant of this ability will be the rigidity or flexibility of management.

Further, firms can become dependent on particular cultural attributes derived largely (but not necessarily) from their home countries. Such 'cultural advantages' may atrophy over time as changing socioeconomic and political changes occur (Jones, 1991). They may turn out to be non transferable from the home country or to have hidden costs in a new environment. The extent to which cultural advantages exist and how far they can be transformed from a country specific advantage to a firm specific advantage is a matter of current controversy. Integration of cultural perspectives with corporate strategy is a most promising avenue of research in the internalization tradition (*vide* Casson, 1991). The theory of teams and team-building is likely to become a major plank in this type of theorising. The ability of management to build and hold together viable teams is a key factor in creating competitive advantage and propositions can be derived on this ability which suggest direction of growth for firms and classes of firms. Teambuilding in R & D and innovation has already been identified as a key skill of management (Casson (ed.), 1991) which differs spatially, in time and by ownership. The rise and fall of competitive groups can thus begin to be built into the theory of the multinational firm.

Third, the issue of the success of firms focuses attention on the process of international competition, largely excluded from the central paradigm. Indeed, Graham (1992) has described the basic received approach as a theory of international monopoly. The view which Graham puts is that the orthodox internalization approach is closely connected with 'old' industrial organization in many treatments of the subject and that 'new industrial organisation' provides a way of moving to a framework which deals more directly with the structures of international competition. The methodology involved relies on the application of non-cooperative game theory to oligopolistic moves. There is something of a tradition of this type of work in international business, dating back to Knickerbocker's (1973) book. Moving in this direction helps to tie international business research more closely with frontier work in international trade theory. Rivalry between firms, e.g. in seeking new rent yielding assets by innovation is an obvious application of this approach. There is however something of a dissonance between this view of the firm and the view which emerges from executive interviews, which only infrequently give the view that strategic moves are predicated on matching those of competitors. Leader–follower models are also notoriously weak in predicting the behaviour of the leader.

Fourth, the relationship between the firm and its environment is capable of a more complex solution than the firm as automaton. However, efforts are currently being made to provide a more satisfactory view of the firm's relationship with its environment. A great deal of work of this kind has been conducted in research on the political behaviour of firms (see the summary in Boddewyn, 1992). Boddewyn traces three stages of development of this research: (1) political actors (notably Governments) seen as *constraints* on the objectives, strategies and operations of

multinational firms, (2) *conflict and bargaining* between multinationals and government and (3) international political behaviour examined in *strategic* terms. Boddewyn further
differentiates the final phase as firm-against-government in
strategy formulation and firm-with-government, whereby companies use governments to acquire and maintain competitive
advantages over their competitors. The role of the state as patron,
sponsor and defensive shield for firms is an important dimension
often omitted from analyses of corporate strategy. The use of
government and its agencies to create market imperfections to
which the multinational can then respond is a further dimension
of potential. This argument can also be extended to the regional
level where groups of cooperating governments (e.g. the
European Community) are pitted against other groups.

Fifth, the internalisation approach has neglected to develop its
implications for relationships *within* the firm. A number of
avenues are available to meet this challenge. They include an
examination of the knowledge base of the firm (Kogut and
Zander, 1992), learning process within the firm (Lyles, 1988),
analyses of commitment building (Johanson and Vahlne, 1977,
1990) and principal-agent problems (as now widely applied in
the analysis of joint ventures). Pfeffer (1992) in an analysis of
power in organizations, places emphasis on method rather than
structure in internal processes.

Again, however, solutions are being sought within the orthodox
paradigm. Hennart (1991), for instance, has examined the roles of
price and management fiat in allocation problems within firms.

As Langlois (1992) has recently re-emphasised, the tradition
begun by Edith Penrose (1959) was to regard the firm as a pool
of resources. More particularly, it is the intangible resources
which are crucial. This leads to the capabilities view of the firm
based on shared knowledge within the firm, unavailable (or
available at a finite cost) to outsiders. The protection and
replenishment of this pool of intangible assets is at the root of
strategy formulation as conceptualised by amongst others,
Marshall (1921), Chandler (1977), Teece (1976).

On this view there is a great deal of scope for meeting the
challenge of 'putting management back in' from approaches
entirely *within* the current framework.

## THE MANAGEMENT OF RESEARCH AND DEVELOPMENT

David Teece (1992) has suggested that 'earlier work on a foreign direct investment ... may have missed an issue which is becoming increasingly important ... – the role that direct foreign investment can play in technological accumulation and business development'. This is because 'it is not monopoly rents which are at issue in foreign direct investment, rather it is the Ricardian and Schumpeterian rents flowing from the gradual transfer of firm specific capabilities in production and innovation' (p. 102). At face value, this is an unfair criticism, because it was precisely the internal absorption of the fruit of R & D in firm-specific developments which gives the multinational firm its dynamic in Buckley and Casson's (1976) model. However what is perhaps underemphasised is the use of foreign direct investment as a means to acquire previously external technology as in Teece's case studies of foreign investment in Silicon Valley. Teece is correct in this emphasis on corporate capabilities in analysing foreign direct investment for technology acquisition as his cases show the importance of complementary assets in the acquiring company. These usually take the form of distribution networks, existing high value brand names and different (foreign) management perceptions of the value of the technology. On this reading, technology is simply one of several packaged assets leading acquirers, who cannot buy the technology unpacked, to acquire the whole firm. Foreign investment is the means to do this, and, in principle, this is not different from a technology intensive firms buying up a preassembled distribution network.

Or is it? The crux of the matter lies in assumptions (prejudices?) on the valuing of technology. If a foreign acquiror pays 'over the odds' for a distribution network (in the USA or elsewhere) then arguments can be put forward on the 'correct value' of the network. One element in this is the value to whom? The purchaser may invest the newly acquired network with complementary assets and the joint value increase (synergy) justifies the higher price – or may do so if the managerial judgement is correct. Why should this argument differ when technology is the packaged asset acquired? Only because of implicit normative judgements. Views of the judgement of the value of technology are invested with a (national) strategic concern which transcends business valuation. We should, the argument goes, be more concerned that Japanese companies buy 'our' indigenous technology creators than when they buy mere artifacts such as distribution networks. It is at least arguable that the most effective Japanese incursions into foreign markets have been precisely where they have bought distribution networks rather than technology creators. Is there then a simple assumption that the foreign investors (higher) valuation of technology creating firms is always correct (or overwhelmingly more correct than the market value)? Why are market values *before* foreign incursion systematically undervaluing technology creating firms? It seems unlikely that nearly every national capital market should undervalue its technology creating firms.

This brings us back to the complementary assets view of technology-acquiring foreign direct investment. The premium comes from the foreign management's judgement of its net return from acquired assets in combination with its existing corporate strengths. There is no magic and no special case.

The approach to innovation in multinational firms in Buckley and Casson (1992) is centered on breaking up the process of innovation into distinct stages. These stages are: project formulation, project selection and implementation. The key inputs into each stage are: research/imaginative synthesis, general managerial judgement and structural flexibility. The process is then examined by analysis of the firm's internal knowledge market' which requires an efficient 'internal venture capital market' whose purpose it is to select and back winners. This judgement is no different in principle from any decision of the firm which is to back its view of the world against that of the market. Otherwise, there is no need for firms to exist, except where market transaction costs are prevalent.

It is, of course, the case that some firms (and perhaps national groups of firms) are better at managing this process than are others. Management must analyse not only the internal/external balance of activities but also the company culture, which must be formulated so as to allow personal responsibility to individual technocratic entrepreneurs. Such a structure – individuals and small teams backed by the resources of a large organization –

resolves the Schumpeterian dilemma of individual incentive versus scale in stimulating innovative activity. Part of the organizational design necessary is to achieve the integration of the R&D department with the rest of the firm. The interfaces with production and marketing are crucial (Buckley and Casson, 1976).

It may well be possible to generalise these arguments. The internalization approach has, to this point in time, concentrated on the selling and output functions of the firm. International purchasing and supply have been neglected as sources of raw data on sourcing strategies. Much can be learned by examining the management processes involved in purchasing.

## CONCLUSION

This paper has shown that there is a role for management and management decision making in international business theory based on the internalization framework. The narrow view that managers simply make 'buy or build' decisions or sequentially identify, exploit and create profitable market imperfections needs to be extended. Strategic behaviour can be identified within the internalisation framework by firms securing exclusive access to key inputs and tying in customers. Extensions to the basic model include dynamic elements and internal growth strategies such as team building, internal knowledge accretion and learning.

## Notes

The author would like to thank Mark Casson, Jeremy Clegg, Peter Enderwick, Neil Hood and the journal's reviewers for comments on an earlier version.

## References

Boddewyn, J. J. 1992. Political behaviour research, in: P. J. Buckley: (ed.), *New Directions in International Business: Research priorities for the 1990s.* Aldershot: Edward Elgar.

Buckley, P. J. 1983. New theories of international business: Some unresolved issues, in M. C. Casson (ed.) *The Growth of International Business*. London: George Allen & Unwin.

Buckley, P. J. 1988. The limits of explanation: Testing the internalisation theory of the multinational enterprise. *Journal of International Business Studies*, 2, Summer, pp. 181–193.

Buckley, P. J. 1990. Problems and developments in the core theory of international business. *Journal of International Business Studies*, 4 Winter, pp. 657–665.

Buckley, P. J. and M. Casson 1976. *The Future of the Multinational Enterprise*. London: Macmillan.

Buckley, P. J. and M. Casson 1981. The optimal timing of a foreign direct investment. *Economic Journal*, 1, March, pp. 70–87.

Buckley, P. J. and M. Casson 1985. *The Economic Theory of the Multinational Enterprise*. London: Macmillan.

Buckley, P. J. and M. Casson 1992. Organising for innovation: The multinational enterprise in the twenty-first century, in: P. J. Buckley and M. Casson, (eds) *Multinational Enterprises in the World Economy: Essays in honour of John Dunning*. Aldershot: Edward Elgar.

Cantwell, J. 1989. *Technological Innovation and Multinational Corporations*. Oxford: Basil Blackwell.

Casson, M. 1985. The theory of foreign direct investment, in: P. J. Buckley and M. Casson, *The Economic Theory of the Multinational Enterprise*. London: Macmillan.

Casson, M. 1987. *The Firm and the Market*. London: Basil Blackwell.

Casson, M. (ed.) 1991. *Global Research Strategy and International Competitiveness*. Oxford: Basil Blackwell.

Casson, M. 1991. *The Economics of Business Culture: Game theory transaction costs and economic performance*. Oxford: Oxford University Press.

Chandler, A. 1977. *The Visible Hand: the managerial revolution in American business*. Cambridge, Mass: Harvard University Press.

Graham, E. M. 1992. The theory of the firm, in: P. J. Buckley (ed.) *New Directions in International Business: Research priorities for the 1990s*. Aldershot: Edward Elgar.

Hennart, J. F. 1982. *A Theory of Multinational Enterprise*. Ann Arbor: University of Michigan Press.

Hennart, J. F. 1991. Control in multinational firms: The role of price and hierarchy. *Management International Review*, Special Issue, pp. 71–96.

Hymer, S. H. 1968. *The International Operations of National Firms: a study of direct foreign investment*. Cambridge Mass: MIT Press. Published 1976.

Johanson, J. and J.-E. Vahlne. 1977. The international process of the firm – a model of knowledge development and increasing foreign market commitments. *Journal of International Business Studies*, 1, Spring/Summer, pp. 23–32.

Johanson, J. and J.-E. Vahlne. 1990. The mechanism of internalisation. *International Marketing Review*, 4, pp. 11–24.

Jones, G. 1991. British multinational banking strategies in historical perspective, in: H. Cox (ed.) Changing patterns of international business: short and long run perspectives. Proceedings of UK AIB Conference 1991. South Bank Polytechnic, London.

Knickerbocker, F. T. 1973. *Oligopolistic Reaction and Multinational Enterprise*. Cambridge, Mass: Harvard University Press.

Kogut, B. and U. Zander 1992. Knowledge of the firm, combinative capabilities, and the replication of technology. *Organization Science*, 3, August, pp. 383–397.

Langlois, R. N. 1992. Transaction-cost economics in real time. *Industrial and Corporate Change*, 1, pp. 99–128.

Lyles, M. A. 1988. Learning among joint venture-sophisticated firms, in: F. J. Contractor and P. Lorange (ed.) *Cooperative Strategies in International Business,* Lexington, Mass: Lexington Books.

Marshall, A. 1921. *Industry and Trade*. London: Macmillan, 3rd edn.

Nelson, R. R. and S. G. Winter 1982. *An Evolutionary Theory of Economic Change*. Cambridge, Mass: Belknap Press.

Penrose, E. T. 1959. *The Theory of the Growth of the Firm*. Oxford: Basil Blackwell.

Pfeffer, J. 1992. Understanding power in organizations. *California Management Review*, 2, Winter, pp. 29–50.

Rugman, A. M. 1981. *Inside the Multinationals*. Croom Helm: London.

Scherer, F. M. *et al.* 1975. *The Economics of Multi-plant Operation: an international comparisons study*. Cambridge, Mass: Harvard University Press.

Teece, D. J. 1976. *The Multinational Corporation and the Resource Cost of International Technology Transfer*. Cambridge, Mass: Ballinger.

Teece, D. J. 1992. Foreign investment and technological development in Silicon Valley. *California Management Review*, 2, Winter, pp. 88–106.

Vernon, R. 1966. International investment and international trade in the product cycle. *Quarterly Journal of Economics*, May, pp. 190–207.

# 5 International Business versus International Management?*

## 1. INTRODUCTION

The purpose of this paper is to compare and contrast two important literatures: international business theory, drawing on the internalization approach, and international strategic management. These literatures intersect and overlap. They are both complementary and competitive, although not mutually exclusive. They are drawn from somewhat different disciplinary bases. International business theory is heavily dependent on economics whilst international management draws on business policy and strategic management, which themselves derive strength from core concepts in organization behaviour, marketing, economics and psychology. The literatures are based within (an aimed at) different journals exemplified by *Journal of International Business* and *Strategic Management Journal*, although these journals and approaches are not mutually exclusive and interpenetration occurs. In a sense the final target audience differs; mainly academics for international business with managers-secondary, 'written primarily for managers' (Bartlett and Ghoshal, 1989: x) for international management. Essentially this amounts to two 'camps' of academic strength, not always mutually comprehensible.

It is possible to overstate the differences. Much cross-fertilization occurs and the rival camps are not overtly antagonistic. Each is liable to draw on the ideas of the other. As this paper goes on to show, there is much in common across the approaches. Further, there is much to gain from more effective cross fertilization.

* *International Journal of the Economics of Business*, Vol. 1, No. 1, 1994, pp. 95–104 (reprinted by permission of Carfax Publishing, Company, PO Box 25, Abingdon OX14 30E England).

In attempting to evaluate and reconcile two literatures, it is essential that the position of the author is unequivocal. The current author is firmly in the international business-internalization camp and the standpoint of this article is to review the international strategic management literature from the standpoint of international business theory. The bias is stated, but bias it remains.

The provenance of much of the work on business strategy is in the context of the development of teaching tools to enable practicing managers to structure the business world and their decisions within it. Many such managers find standard economic models to be over-determined. Specifically, given the fixed parameters of an economic model, there is only one 'right' outcome. In practice, however, the role of the manager is often to discover the extent and strength of the constraints present in the environment and the degree to which these impinge upon immediate objectives. Managers thus are in the process of learning about the environment and in ascertaining the 'company's' immediate objectives. This may be described as fine tuning decision making in areas where there can be some deviation from strict profit maximization – where, for instance, there is an area of discretion given by imperfect competition or deviations from full contestability. Because of the tendency for markets to become more contestable in the longer run, the proper home for strategy is in short and medium term decision making and evaluations of outcomes. As, to quote Keynes' dictum, 'in the long run we are all dead', this leaves considerable scope and importance for the strategy domain. If this view is a correct one, then the prescriptive nature of business strategy writings is an essential feature of its distinctive contribution.

In contrast, the basis of international business writings, as exemplified by Dunning (1958, 1977) Buckley and Casson (1976) and other writers in the eclectic and internalization schools, is built on a tradition centred on the economic theory of the firm enhanced by Coasian and Williamsonian perspectives. The main influences on this tradition have been Coase (1937) Williamson (1975) and models of the growth of the firm, following Kaldor (1934) and Penrose (1959). This approach has been judged successful in explaining and predicting the growth and pattern of multinational firms, although somewhat at the expense of dealing with management decision making within the firm over anything except the long run. Attempts have been made to deal with this by incorporating firm-specific advantages, although these variables currently sit rather awkwardly within the theory (Buckley, 1983, 1990). Attempts to focus on technological advance within the firm (Cantwell, 1989), on research and development as an engine of growth (Casson, 1991a; Buckley and Casson, 1992), on knowledge advances (Kogut and Zander, 1992) and on (management) learning (Lyles, 1988) all may be seen as attempts to 'put management back in' to economic models.

## 2. THE CHALLENGE OF INTERNATIONAL STRATEGIC MANAGEMENT

The theoretical base of international strategic management can be traced back to the strategy–structure–conduct–performance model, mediated via the work of Alfred Chandler (1962, 1977). To this framework has been added the perspectives of organizational theorists; Burns and Stalker (1961) and Lawrence and Lorsch (1967) have been particularly influential. Finally, the product cycle hypothesis, developed in an international context by Raymond Vernon (1966), has been a key element giving an underlying dynamic (or sequence) to the analysis. Hedlund and Rolander trace these elements in a research programme which they label 'structure follows strategy' (1990: 16).

This combination of influences is acknowledged in the preface to Bartlett and Ghoshal's influential 1989 book *Managing Across Borders: The Transnational Solution*. Earlier generations of Harvard based work are highly important, including business policy research (Bower, Andrews and Christensen), the international business project led by Ray Vernon, and the organisation behaviour research of Lawrence and Lorsch which are the three streams of writing that intersect to produce the book's theoretical underpinnings (Bartlett and Ghoshal, 1989: ix). Similar antecedents formed an earlier generation of international business strategy writings from Harvard, exemplified by Stopford and Wells (1972).

It is important at this stage to note parallels between the intellectual traditions resulting in the internalization approach to international business and the international strategic management stream. The work of Chandler explicitly acknowledges the centrality of the 'make or buy' internalization decision. Indeed, the title of Chandler's 1977 book *The Visible Hand* contrasts managerial decision making with the invisible hand of the market. The contribution of international strategic management is to shed light on managerial decisions, most notably those within the firm. Often this is by (excessive) concentration on the formal structure of the firm as an intermediate variable. Hedlund and Rolander (1990) are among many who point out that informal structures are more important in actual decision making.

A second key point of similarity between the two approaches is the attention given to the interaction between locational variables and organizational variables. This is expressed very formally in the internalization approach whereas the interaction is richer, more complex but often more diffuse in the international strategic management literature where concepts such as 'flexibility' express the potential for differentiated and specialised roles of subsidiaries.

Third, internal control mechanisms are seen as crucial in both approaches. Again, this is dealt with in a formal fashion by internalization researchers who seek to strike a balance between internal pricing (shadow prices) and management fiat as methods of internal coordination (Buckley and Casson, 1976; Brown, 1984; Hennart, 1986, 1991; Buckley, 1983). Work in international strategic management here is much more discursive and shades into discussions of international human resource management.

The work of Michael Porter on international management (1980, 1985, 1986) is significant, not least for his brilliant deconstruction of standard industrial economics. The reconfiguration of the classic concepts from Joe Bain (1956) onwards into a prescriptive programme for managers is justly lauded. Porter's work enables bridges to be built between mainstream economics and management strategy. Similar effects can now be observed between 'new' industrial economics based on game-modelling of company behaviour and business strategy (Graham, 1991).

However, it is the work of Bartlett and Ghoshal which is best taken as an exemplar of international strategic management. Their advice on building the transnational involves combining the cardinal virtues of three earlier (less complete or less effective) models of organisation. The 'transnational' combines the responsiveness of the multinational (typically observed in branded packaged products) with the efficiency of the global firm (consumer electronics as a case) and the ability to transfer knowledge and competences of the international firm (observed in the telecommunications switching industry). The organisational characteristics of the transnational thus are: a configuration of assets and capabilities which is dispersed, interdependent and specialised; foreign operations which represent differentiated contributions by national units to an integrated world-wide operation and knowledge developed jointly between units of the firm and shared worldwide (Bartlett and Ghoshal, 1989).

For the internalization theorists, this model suggests several key propositions. These are best expressed in normative terms although this is not the normal language of internalization theory.

H1: Multinational firms are best organised where foreign subsidiaries have considerable managerial autonomy and play a differentiated role within the organisation. (Responsiveness).

H2: Multinational firms must capture global economies of scale by integrating activities located so as to minimise overall costs. (Efficiency).

H3: Specialized units of the firm should develop research and development capabilities, the results of which are diffused through the firm. (Transfer of knowledge and competences).

The first two hypotheses are currently at the forefront of research developments in internalization theory but the last deserves extended treatment. The third section of this paper contrasts Bartlett and Ghoshal's own development of this theme with that of internalization theorists.

**Constraints**

Several important constraints on achieving 'transnational status' are developed by Bartlett and Ghoshal.

1. History matters. The administrative heritage or organisational history of the company often increases the costs of change. This is an important counter-weight to a historical economic theory and, in practice, represents an often insuperable barrier to progress.

2. Many companies are bound by a culturally influenced management philosophy. Such a philosophy might well constrain international success if it 'does not travel well' to other cultural settings. Inappropriate rigidities can inhibit adaptation to foreign markets and methods of production. This aspect of business behaviour has been much studied in the generally assumed success of Japanese management philosophies (Pascale and Athos, 1982; Buckley and Mirza, 1986).

3. Company norms and values and modes of leadership may also be a constraint on achieving international success. There is a close link between this view and much of the work being developed on culture and international business (Casson, 1991b).

International management attempts to attack one area which currently presents problems for international business theory – the interactions which the company faces across its various markets. International business theory is very successful in describing, predicting and to a limited extent prescribing foreign market entry and development strategies (Young *et al.*, 1989). However, in general, this works best when a single foreign market is being examined. Interaction or knock-on effects between markets are largely unexamined and inadequately modelled.

The international management literature attempts to cast this problem in terms of not structure but process. As in-depth examination of decision processes, concentrating on information needs and flows is at the core of this issue. Attention to processes is an important development for internalization theory which must be addressed.

## 3.  THE MANAGEMENT OF RESEARCH AND DEVELOPMENT

The management of R & D in multinational firms is currently being researched extensively. The purpose of this section is not to review this literature but to contrast the approach to R & D management in internalization theory and in international strategic management.

Bartlett and Ghoshal (1990) examine innovation in the transnational company by close attention to processes in their nine target companies. The key factor in their discussion is the balance between local market sensitivity and global coordination of research effort. Of particular interest to internalisation theorists is their fascinating discussion of Matsushita which combines internal market mechanisms and fierce competition between rival projects and research groups (1990: 225–9). Matsushita's pioneering of centralised innovation processes contrasts with Philips' championing of local innovations. Bartlett and Ghoshal's response to the diversity which they find is to advocate an allocation of differentiated roles based on the importance of the level of local resources and capabilities versus the strategic importance of the local environment. This yields a two-by-two table with subsidiaries being classified as strategic leader, contributor, implementor or sensor (black hole) (1990:244). The units so designated can then be allocated resources in order to play their role more effectively. The authors take the view that increased spending on R & D is not necessarily the solution to problems of lack of innovation in companies. The divorce of R & D from other specialized functions is a major source of problems and seeing R & D as a separate and separable function can lead to a loss of synergy.

The contrast with the internalization approach to the same problem is instructive (Buckley and Casson, 1992). The approach here abstracts completely from individual firm cases and from industry examples, although much supporting empirical evidence can be found in Casson (1991a). The analysis is centred on breaking up the process of innovation into distinct stages (project formulation, project selection, implementation) and examining the key (internal) inputs into each stage viz:

research/imaginative synthesis, general managerial judgement and structural flexibility. The process is then examined by analysis of the firm's 'internal knowledge market' which requires an efficient 'internal venture capital market' whose purpose it is to select and back winners. This requires an analysis not only of the internal/external balance of activities but also of the company culture which ideally should allow personal responsibility decentralised to individual entrepreneurs who are supported by the resources of the large organization (thus resolving the Schumpeterian dilemma of incentive versus scale in stimulating innovative activity). In a much earlier work, Buckley and Casson (1976:34) emphasised the importance of the integration of R & D with the marketing and production functions; the 1992 paper extends this finding to the organisational context.

It is perhaps the similarities in the results of these two investigations of innovation in multinational firms which stands out. Both emphasise local versus firm wide conflicts, the integration of R & D with the other activities of the firm, the importance of selection mechanisms and the internal competition of rival projects.

There remain important differences in emphasis. The contrast in the nature of the supporting evidence is stark. Bartlett and Ghoshal rely on small numbers of closely worked case studies, Buckley and Casson on generalities and appeals to a wider literature. The prescriptions, too, differ; Bartlett and Ghoshal see organizational change as the key to improvement while Buckley and Casson point to process improvements and the creation of more perfect internal markets.

## 4. POTENTIAL BRIDGES BETWEEN THE TWO APPROACHES

Several means may be suggested towards bridging the gap between internal business theory and international strategic management. Among these potential bridges are the behavioural theory of the firm, approaches to the internationalization process including evolutionary models and work on the internal organization of multinational enterprises.

## The Behavioural Theory of the Firm

Cyert and March's behavioural theory of the firm (1963) was a response to the lack of fit between the basic profit maximizing assumptions of orthodox economics and the 'lived reality' (Buckley and Chapman, 1993) of corporate life. Part of this dysfunction was attacked by the notion of 'bounded rationality', derived from the work of Simon (1957), and relates to issues of the imperfection of information within the corporation, tackled below. The notion of 'behaviour' was an attempt to include the reality of managers making decisions under uncertainty and bounded by constraints in receiving and processing information. Aharoni's (1966) work on the foreign investment decision *process* is very much in this tradition, with its emphases on the costs of information collection, the distortion of information within the firm, the crucial role of uncertainty and the inertia of management within the firm.

## The Internationalization Process

Some students of international business, including many who have contributed to both schools surveyed here, have subscribed to an implicit or explicit evolutionary approach to internationalization. This has been in terms of a 'stages' model (Johanson and Wedersheim-Paul, 1975; Johanson and Vahlne, 1977) and models based on the seminal product cycle analysis (Vernon, 1966) or as the outcome of empirical tracking of the internationalization of small firms (Buckley *et al.*, 1983, 1988).

Rigid 'stages' models have been criticised as over deterministic (Turnbull, 1987; Hedlund and Kverneland, 1983) and defended (Welch and Luostarinen, 1988) as introducing much needed dynamic elements into dangerously static theorising. Their virtues, for the purposes of this article, are that they have focused attention on management processes and, in particular, on management learning. Kogut (1983), for example, developed an argument that foreign direct investment is a sequential process and in distinguishing between initial foreign direct investment and subsequent incremental investment flows, built up a notion of momentum in internationalization. The notion of management learning suggests that in an integrated multinational firm, experiences from one geographic area (or division or function) of the firm can be transferred to another thus obviating the need for incremental expansion in all markets. In other words, experienced firms can 'jump' stages.

## *The Organizational Development of Multinational Firms*

Linking behavioural theories and internationalization models are writings on the organizational development of multinational firms. The work owes its inspiration to Alfred Chandler whose work on changes in organizational form through multifunction operation to divisionalization (1962) and the growth and effect of management hierarchies (1977), spawned a number of studies on the organizational development of multinational firms of different origins (see Buckley, 1986). The framework taken by later authors is (implicitly at least) evolutionary. The conventional approach is a stages model, running from an autonomous subsidiary stage, followed by an international division, then an international organisation structure (based on either geographical area or product or occasionally function as the key organising principle) and finally a global matrix approach. This rigid evolutionary typology is now outdated. More apposite is a view of organisational structure as a means of resolving internal tensions and external pressures. Organizational structure at any one point of time is a snapshot of a dynamic process which can revert to 'earlier' stages in the crude typology.

The issues of centralization versus decentralization are also crucial in the organization of diversified multinational firms. Here, the 'modern' literature on international strategic management has a lot to offer. The empirical work including case studies can, with sensitive interpretation, illuminate some key issues. Among these issues are the companies' responses to principal-agent problems – motivating managers and workers and providing an appropriate balance of incentives and orders (Jensen and Meckling, 1976).

Internalization theory has a great deal to offer in this area. Much play has been made by Rugman (1981 among others) of internalization enabling centralization of activities. In fact, it is possible to envisage a situation where the firm operates as closely as possible to the actions of a perfect external market. By transmitting a set of shadow price signals to decision makers (in foreign subsidiaries) acting as cost or profit centres, the firm mimics the market mechanism and enables the plans of each decision maker to be meshed and optimum coordination to be achieved (Buckley, 1983, 1988). The observations of international strategic management researchers also enable testing of hypotheses derived from tournament theory (Nalebuff and Stiglitz, 1983) which emphazises that agency costs may be reduced where managers compete for prizes, such as a limited number of promotions, because each employee knows that his or her performance is being judged against that of others. There is much scope for building of bridges between the two research traditions in these areas.

## *Models of Internationalization as a Learning Process*

A recent paper by Casson (1993) attempts to unify internationalization processes with internalization theory and globalization models by specifying the conditions under which sequential internationalization rather than simultaneous entry to foreign markets will be undertaken. Casson's model introduces set up costs which derive from the acquisition of information about a market and shows that the sequential approach relies on the exploitation of systematic similarities between markets. In this case the main advantage of sequential entry is that it exploits economies of scope in knowledge. This knowledge is a particular type. It is knowledge of how to diagnose the state of a market not knowledge of the state of the market itself; know how rather than factual knowledge. The economies of scope are culture-bound in that what is learnt about the investigation of a society of one (cultural) type cannot necessarily be applied to one of a different type. International expansion thus is a process of know how acquisition and accumulation but it is possible to economise on information processing by foregoing investigation and learning from experience instead – the cost of this economy is the mistakes that will be made. However the converse of this is that mistakes can be an economy because they avoid investigation costs.

## Summary: The Importance of the Generation, Transmission and Use of Internal Knowledge in Multinational Firms

All the above bridges between international business theory and international management have, at their core, issues of the generation, transmission and use of knowledge within the firm. There are many areas where this issue is at the forefront of current research, including management accounting practices, the role of research and development within the firm and issues of functional integration (between production, marketing, R & D and their constituent activities).

International business theory has concentrated on specifying the formal problems of information flows and feedbacks. The diagrams in Buckley and Casson (1976:34) and Buckley (1990:37) are instructive of this approach. Functional integration is effected by the *two-way* flow of information within the firm which cannot be replicated perfectly if the relationship specified between production, marketing and R & D or within the marketing function is market based.

The role of information management has not been fully addressed within mainstream books on international management perhaps because it has become a semi-detached sub-discipline (Roche, 1992). Managers are often assumed to have access to all relevant information and, if they haven't, this is the fault of the information system of the firm!

## 5. CONCLUSION

The internalization approach to the multinational enterprise can be contrasted with the literature on international strategic management. The different emphasis of the international strategic management literature, its prescriptive nature and its attention to individual cases differentiate its focus. However, the two approaches have much in common, including joint elements of intellectual heritage, which are shown clearly when the two approaches are applied to a common research problem such as the management of innovation. This paper has sought to build bridges between the approaches and in particular highlighted the important linking role intra-company information flows may play in future research.

## References

Aharoni, Yair, *The Foreign Investment Decision Process*. Boston: Graduate School of Business Administration, Harvard University, 1966.

Bain, Joe S., *Barriers to New Competition*. Cambridge, MA: Harvard University Press, 1956.

Bartlett, Christopher and Ghoshal, Sumantra, *Managing Across Borders: The Transnational Solution*. Boston: Harvard Business School Press, 1989.

Brown, Wilson B., 'Firm-like Behaviour in Markets – The Administered Channel,' *International Journal of Industrial Organisation*, 1984, 2, 263–76.

Buckley, Peter J., 'New Theories of International Business: Some Unresolved Issues,' in Mark Casson, (ed.), *The Growth of International Business*. London: George Allen & Unwin, 1983.

Buckley, Peter J., 'Organisational Forms and Multinational Companies,' in Steve Thompson and Mike Wright (eds.), *Internal Organisation, Efficiency and Profit*. Oxford: Philip Allan, 1988.

Buckley, Peter J., 'Problems and Developments in the Core Theory of International Business,' *Journal of International Business Studies*, 4, Winter 1990, 657–65.

Buckley, Peter J. and Casson, Mark, *The Future of the Multinational Enterprise*. London: Macmillan, 1976.

Buckley, Peter J. and Casson, Mark., 'Organising for Innovation: The Multinational Enterprise in the 21st Century,' in: Peter J. Buckley and Mark Casson (eds.), *Multinational Enterprises in the World Economy: Essays in Honour of John H. Dunning*. Aldershot: Edward Elgar, 1992.

Buckley, Peter J. and Chapman, Malcolm, 'The Management of Cooperative Strategies,' University of Bradford, mimeo, 1993.

Buckley, Peter J. and Mirza, Hafiz, 'The wit and wisdom of Japanese management: an iconoclastic analysis,' *Management International Review*, 25(3), Spring 1986.

Buckley, Peter J., Berkova, Zdenka and Newbould, Gerald D., *Direct Investment in the UK by Smaller European Firms*, London: Macmillan, 1983.

Buckley, Peter J., Newbould, Gerald D. and Thurwell, Jane, *Foreign Direct Investment by Smaller UK Firms*, London: Macmillan, 1988.

Buckley, Peter J., Pass, C. L. and Prescott, Kate, 'Foreign Market Servicing by Multinationals: An Integrated Treatment,' *International Marketing Review*, 7 (4), 1990, 25–40.

Burns, T. and Stalker, G. M., *The Management of Innovation*. London: Tavistock, 1961.

Cantwell, John, *Technological Innovation and Multinational Corporations*. Oxford: Basil Blackwell, 1989.

Casson, Mark, *Global Research Strategy and International Competitiveness*. Oxford: Basil Blackwell, 1991a.

Casson, Mark, *The Economics of Business Culture: Game Theory, Transaction Costs and Economic Performance.* Oxford: Oxford University Press, 1991b.

Casson, Mark, 'Internationalisation as a Learning Process: A Model of Corporate Growth and Geographical Diversification,' University of Reading, mimeo, 1993.

Chandler, Alfred, *Strategy and Structure.* Cambridge, MA: MIT Press, 1962.

Chandler, Alfred, *The Visible Hand: The Managerial Revolution in American Business.* Cambridge, MA: Harvard University Press, 1977.

Coase, Ronald, 'The Nature of the Firm,' *Economica*, 4, 1937, 386–405.

Cyert, R. and March, J., *The Behavioural Theory of the Firm.* Englewood Cliffs, NJ: Prentice-Hall, 1963.

Dunning, John H., *American Investment in British Manufacturing Industry.* London: George Allen & Unwin, 1958.

Dunning, John H., 'Trade, Location of Economic Activity and the Multinational Enterprise: The Search for an Eclectic Approach,' in: B. Ohlin, P. O. Hessleborn and P. M. Wijkman, (eds.), *The International Allocation of Economic Activity.* London: Macmillan, 1977.

Graham, E. M., 'The Theory of the Firm,' in: Peter J. Buckley, (eds.), *New Directions in International Business: Research Priorities for the 1990s.* Aldershot: Edward Elgar, 1991.

Hedlund, G. and Kverneland, A., 'Are Entry Strategies for Foreign Markets Changing? The Case of Swedish Investment in Japan,' Stockholm School of Economics, 1983. Reprinted in: Peter J. Buckley and Pervez N. Ghauri, (eds.), *The Internationalisation of the Firm.* London: Academic Press, 1993.

Hedlund, Gunnar and Rolander, Dag, 'Action in Heterarchies: New Approaches to Managing the MNC,' in: C. A. Bartlett, Y. Doz and G. Hedlund, (eds.), *Managing the Global Firm.* London: Routledge, 1990.

Hennart, Jean-Francois, 'What is Internalization?,' *Weltwirtschaftliches Archiv*, 122, 1986, 791–8.

Hennart, Jean-Francois, 'Control in Multinational Firms: the Role of Price and Hierarchy,' *Management International Review*, special issue, 1991, 71–96.

Jensen, M. C. and Meckling, W. H., 'The Theory of the Firm: Managerial Behaviour, Agency Costs and Ownership Structure,' *Journal of Financial Economics*, 3, 1976, 305–66.

Johanson, Jan and Vahlne, Jan-Erik, 'The Internationalisation Process of the Firm – A Model of Knowledge Development and Increasing Foreign Market Commitments,' *Journal of International Business Studies*, 8(1), 1977, 23–32.

Johanson, Jan and Wiedersheim-Paul, Finn, 'The Internationalisation of the Firm – Four Swedish Case Studies,' *Journal of Management Studies*, October 1975, 305–22.

Kaldor, Nicholas, 'The Equilibrium of the Firm,' *Economic Journal*, March 1934.

Kogut, Bruce, 'Foreign Direct Investment as a Sequential Process,' in: C. P. Kindleberger and David Audretsch, (eds.), *Multinational Corporations in the 1980s.* Cambridge, MA: MIT Press, 1983.

Kogut, Bruce and Zander, Udo, 'The Knowledge of the Firm in the Choice of the Mode of Technology Transfer,' *Working Paper* 12.02, Reginald H. Jones Centre for Management Policy, Strategy and Organisation, the Wharton School: University of Pennsylvania, 1992.

Lawrence, P. R. and Lorsch, J. W., *Organisation and Environment*. Boston: Harvard Business School, 1967.

Lyles, Majorie A., 'Learning among Joint Venture – Sophisticated Firms,' in: Farok J. Contractor and Peter Lorange (eds), *Cooperative Strategies in International Business*. Lexington, MA: Lexington Books, 1988.

Nalebuff, B. and Stiglitz, J., 'Prize and Incentives: Towards a General Theory of Compensation and Competition,' *Bell Journal of Economics*, 13, 1983, 21–43.

Pascale, Richard T. and Athos, Anthony G., *The Art of Japanese Management*. Harmondsworth: Penguin Books, 1982.

Penrose, Edith T., *The Theory of the Growth of the Firm*. Oxford: Basil Blackwell, 1959.

Porter, Michael E., *Competitive Strategy*. New York: Free Press, 1980.

Porter, Michael E., *Competitive Advantage*. New York: Free Press, 1985.

Porter, Michael E. ed., *Competition in Global Industries*. Boston, MA: Harvard Business School Press, 1986.

Roche, Edward M., *Managing Information Technology in Multinational Corporations*. New York: Macmillan, 1992.

Rugman, Alan M., *Inside the Multinationals*. London: Croom Helm, 1981.

Simon, H., *Models of Man*. New York: Wiley, 1957.

Stopford, John M. and Wells, Louis T., *Managing the Multinational Enterprise*. London: Longmans, 1972.

Turnbull, Peter W., 'A Challenge to the Stage Theory of the Internationalisation Process,' in P. J. Rosson and S. D. Reed, (eds), *Managing Export Entry and Expansion*. New York: Praeger, 1987.

Vernon, Raymond, 'International Investment and International Trade in the Product Cycle,' *Quarterly Journal of Economics*, 80, May 1966, 190–207.

Welch, Lawrence S. and Luostarinen, Reijo, 'Internationalisation: Evolution of a Concept,' *Journal of General Management*, 14(2), 1988, 14, 2, 36–64.

Williamson, Oliver E., *Markets and Hierarchies*. New York: Free Press, 1975.

Young, Stephen *et al.*, *International Market Entry and Development*. Hemel Hempstead: Harvester Wheatsheaf, 1989.

# Part II

# The Foreign Market Servicing Strategies of Multinational Enterprises

# 6 The Structure of British Industry's Sales in Foreign Markets*

(*with* Kate Prescott)

## INTRODUCTION

This paper examines the macro level picture of structure of British industry's sales in foreign markets. The structure of sales is given by the division between exports from the UK, sales licensed abroad by British firms and the sales arising from British foreign direct investment. Our concern is with British-owned industry, hence we exclude the exports of foreign-owned companies based in the UK. Thus total foreign sales (*TFS*) equals exports (*X*) plus licensed sales (*L*) plus sales from foreign investment (*I*), i.e. $TFS = X + L + I$.

The next section of this paper examines some of the relevant theoretical literature on the structure of foreign sales by examining the literature on foreign market servicing policies (the choice between export, licensing and foreign investment) and its particular application to British firms. The third section presents the methodology by which the components *X*, *L* and *I* are calculated. The fourth section presents the results of the calculations for the period 1975–84 across industries and individual foreign markets. The analysis also examines the time series trends in world market servicing by British firms and in key industries and markets. It then goes on to use ratio analysis to illuminate the structure of Britain's foreign trade. The paper concludes by identifying key elements in Britain's foreign sales and suggesting how these may affect competitiveness.

*Managerial and Decision Economics*, Vol. 10, No. 3, September 1989, pp. 189–208 (reprinted by permission of John Wiley and Sons Ltd).

## THEORY: FOREIGN MARKET SERVICING

The foreign market servicing strategies of companies have been analysed by Buckley and Pearce (1979, 1981, 1984) and by Buckley (1989). The three forms of market servicing can be analytically separated by the operation of the location effect and the internalization effect (Buckley and Casson, 1976, 1985).

At its most simple, $X$ can be differentiated from the other two methods by the location effect, as with exports the bulk of value-adding activity takes place in the home country, whilst the other two methods transfer much of value-adding activity to the host country. Similarly, $L$ can be differentiated from $X$ and $I$ by the externalization effect. $L$ represents a market sale of intermediate goods or corporate assets by the firm. In licensing the firm sells right and the use of assets to a licensee. In $X$ and $I$ such activities are internalized (Buckley and Casson, 1976, 1985a). This has important implications. Broadly, then, the internalization and location effects separate the three generic forms of market servicing:

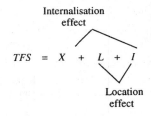

$$TFS = X + L + I$$

These simple differentiations are, in practice, highly complex. First, comparative costs are not easily calculable or obvious. In multiproduct, process and functional firms the internal division of labour and the costs associated with each activity are difficult to assess accurately. Further, there are many complex interactions between the activities involved. Location abroad of some activities will have knock-on effects on home costs and on those of third countries within the firm's international network. Second, the costs and benefits of internalization are nebulous and difficult to measure. Both sets of complication are entirely contingent on circumstances. The difficulties (and intellectual excitement) of these calculations is that the situation is dynamic and the determinants of choice of optimal market servicing strategies are continually shifting.

Cross-section analyses of market servicing are snapshot pictures at a moment in time of a continually changing process. The make-up of total foreign sales into $X$, $L$, $I$, at the macro level can give us a crude picture (Buckley and Davies, 1980) but this pattern is continually changing as the nature of international competition alters. A major complicating factor in the analysis of foreign market servicing policies is that the forms are often complements, not substitutes. This fact means that a careful analysis of the relationship between modes is essential. For instance, Hood and Young (1979) point to the existence of 'anticipatory exports' (goods exported from the source country in anticipation of building the foreign plant), 'associated exports' (complementary products exported by the parent after establishment of the subsidiary) and 'balancing exports' which result when the first plant built abroad is operating at capacity. Foreign direct investment also has a dynamic effect in maintaining the worldwide competitive position of the investing firm (Hood and Young, 1979: 313–15).

This suggests that a dynamic analysis is essential. Assumptions in modelling which do not allow for changes in demand conditions – for instance, the existence of a 'presence effect' which results in an increased demand after the establishment of an investment presence (Buckley *et al.*, 1988) – are clearly inappropriate. Similarly, models which ignore the competitive process, in particular the role of 'defensive investment' established to protect a market share, are unlikely to capture the nuances of strategy. Models must be organic rather than static and capable of specifying the relationship between exports, licensing and foreign direct investment.

In the following section the existing literature is reviewed in order to draw up a series of hypotheses on the foreign market servicing decision. It is then our intention to narrow down the number of variables in order to focus upon the key determinants of market servicing at the macro level.

**Hypotheses Arising from the Literature**

The literature yields a rich variety of hypotheses on market
servicing, as Table 6.1 shows. These hypotheses operate at different levels: macro (national), industry and firm. The literature
consists of comparative static analyses of switches in foreign
market servicing modes[1], models of the timing of switches in
mode, analyses of shifts within types of foreign market servicing, extensive discussions of the location decisions of multinational firms, the influence of the nature of the industry
'internationalization' models[2] and 'globalization' models and
strategy considerations.[3] The key hypotheses deriving from each
identified branch of the literature are shown in Table 6.1. The
remainder of the paper examines the macro level picture for
Britain's foreign sales and attempts to narrow the range of
uncertainty on the applicable hypotheses. Thus the theoretical
literature provides a preliminary list of key determinants, and an
examination of the data allows pointers to the importance of
these variables in practice.

**Empirical Studies of Foreign Market Servicing by British
Firms**

The Reddaway Report (1967 and 1968) was an inquiry into the
effects of UK direct investment overseas, concentrating mainly
on the effects on the British economy rather than the efficacy of
direct investment as a method of market servicing. However, the
basic market servicing assumption was that had the UK firm not
established production abroad then a rival would have taken the
opportunity instead. In the case of actual foreign investment
therefore, exports of finished products from Britain were not
assumed to be a feasible alternative. Estimates were made of the
impact on associated capital goods exports following the investment (1967: 182) but associated exports of intermediate goods to
foreign subsidiaries were found to be small (1967: 63–69). Given
the time span since this Report was compiled, considerable
changes in technique, market structure and international management have taken place.

*Table* 6.1  Hypotheses from the literature: a summary of key macro factors

| Author/source | Key factors |
|---|---|
| *Comparative static analyses* | |
| Vernon (1966) | Relative location costs |
| | Stage of development of the industry/product |
| Hirsh (1976) | Relative production costs |
| | Relative marketing costs |
| | Capitalization of firm-specific knowhow |
| Horst (1971, 1972) | Tariffs and taxes |
| | Demand conditions (price elasticities) in markets |
| | Market size |
| | Industry-specific influence (R&D intensity concentration, resource control) |
| | Firm size |
| *Models of the timing of switches in mode* | |
| Aliber (1970) | Exchange rates |
| | Capitalization of patents |
| | Costs of doing business abroad |
| | Market growth |
| Buckley and Casson (1985a) | Market growth and demand conditions |
| | Cost structure (fixed and variable) |
| *Shifts within market serving mode* | |
| Rosson et al. (1987) | Changes in foreign intermediaries |
| Nicholas (1986) | Transaction costs |

25

*Table* 6.1 Contd.

| Author/source | Key factors |
|---|---|
| *Location decisions of multinationals* | |
| Dunning (1972a) | Product adaptation costs |
| | Product and process structure of firms |
| | Tariffs, transport costs |
| | Output quantities |
| | Elasticities of demand and supply |
| | Availability of inputs |
| | Government policies |
| Buckley and Artisien (1987) | The Nature of integration within the firm |
| | Costs of labour |
| | Government policies |
| | Market growth and elasticities of supply and demand |
| | Macroeconomic environment |
| Casson (1985) | Comparative labour costs |
| | Technical progress (effect on transport costs/division of labour/economies of scale) |
| *The nature of the industry* | |
| Casson (1986) | Barriers to entry arising from proprietary technology |
| | Trade structure of industry |
| | Maturity of industry |
| *Internationalization* | |
| Swedish School | Evolutionary market penetration – history of involvement |
| Buckley *et al.* | Risk profile of modes of market servicing |

*Table* 6.1  Contd.

| Author/source | Key factors |
|---|---|
| *Globalization* | |
| Porter *et al.* | Standardized marketing strategy |
| | Vertical integration |
| | Location costs |
| | Co-ordination issues |
| | |
| *Strategy models* | |
| Knickerbocker (1973) | Competitor reaction |
| Porter (1986a) | (1) Industry concentration |
| | (2) Industry stability |
| | (3) Number of alternatives firm has Decision-making Structure of the firm Cooperative strategies |

A study of British manufacturing investment overseas by Shepherd *et al.* (1985) examined 23 firms in seven very broad manufacturing industries. In the main, the study concentrates on the decision to set up manufacturing abroad but the preliminary list of key factors (p. 82) encompasses the market-servicing decision. A number of factors were felt to be important: the way the firm perceives its production advantages, its ability to bear risk, the attraction of overseas markets and various locational considerations. The nature of the industry, of the firms' products and of the competitive environment were important determinants. Market size and market growth were, unsurprisingly, the key attraction of foreign markets in general. The decision to invest in the market was determined by (in order of importance): proximity to the market, formal and informal trading restrictions and transport costs. These determinants emerged from questionnaires to individual firms. In most cases the firms felt that they did have a choice of method: 50% felt that they could have exported and 60% could have licensed in the absence of the direct investment. Exporting continued to be an important method of market servicing even among highly dynamic foreign investors. The history of the company was important in determining a 'national' geographic pattern for future production in which overseas manufacture was a key element. In general, it was well-established, standardized products incorporating relatively low value added and comparatively low technology which constituted the bulk of foreign manufacturing investment. Trade restrictions also played an important role in the choice of investment.

## METHODOLOGY

### Exports

#### Exports by Country

Data for UK exports by country are taken from *External Trade Statistics*. In order to standardize all the data certain countries values were summated to obtain figures for areas – compatable with data for licensing and FDI.

*Exports by Industry*

Data for exports by industry are drawn from the *Business Monitor MQ10* series, which presents data according to the Standard Industrial Classification (SIC). However, as a result of alterations made in the SIC code in 1980, certain adjustments were necessary. Consequently some product groups are re-allocated to different industry sectors for 1983 and 1984 when the changes take effect.

As a result of the focus of the research being British industries' sales in foreign markets, export data are also adjusted to remove exports from subsidiaries of foreign companies based in the UK. Consequently, the data were reduced by the percentage of foreign exports which were presented in the *Business Monitor MA4* up to 1981. From 1975 to 1981, therefore, percentage figures for each year are taken. For 1982 and 1983 an average figure is used as no clear trends are apparent.

The data also allow a distinction to be made between industries, although the relative percentages of foreign subsidiary exports to different countries is not available.

## Licensing

*The Calculation of Sales Arising from Foreign Licensing*

The calculation of British licensed sales abroad is derived from basic data in *Business Monitor MA4* (and its predecessor *M4*) Overseas Transactions. The figures given in the *Business Monitor* provide a summary of royalty receipts from British companies by country/area and by industry, and an estimate of all receipts in each year. They are classified into 'related' and 'unrelated concerns'. Unrelated concerns refer to transactions with organizations not owned or controlled by the UK parent company. It is these figures which form the basis of the calculation of licensed sales abroad. A classification of technological and mineral royalties is also provided, which excludes receipts on printed matter, sound recordings and performing rights. Further, the proportion of royalties from manufacturing can be calculated which excludes distributive trade and 'other activities'. The latter is thought to include consulting, management contracts, research co-operation and turnkey operations. Our concern is to estimate sales from unrelated manufacturing concerns which are technological and mineral.

Our methodology is an improvement on that used by Buckley and Davies (1980) to calculate sales from foreign licensing because Buckley and Davies took a standard 20% figure for royalties from non manufacturing companies. Our figures recalculate this proportion for each year covered.

## Licensed Sales Abroad by Industry

Licensed sales abroad by industry are calculated from the raw data (summary of receipts and estimate of total receipts) by the following procedure:

(1) The summary of receipts is multiplied by 20 on the assumption that receipts average out at a 5% royalty on sales;

(2) The sales figures are 'grossed up' according to the proportion of total returns received for all activities with unrelated concerns to the estimates for all business transactions with unrelated concerns, technological and mineral. This gives an estimate for licensed sales (technological and mineral) by unrelated concerns in each industry group. This proportion of returns received: estimates for all business is recalculated for each year covered.

## Licensed Sales Abroad by Country

The calculation of licensed sales by country and/or area is rather more complex and requires even more assumptions:

(1) From the summary of receipts, the proportion which accounts for unrelated concerns in each country/area is calculated for all years;

(2) The value of technological and mineral royalties given for each area is multiplied by the proportion of unrelated concerns to give a value for receipts for technological and mineral royalties from unrelated concerns;

(3) The proportion of manufacturing royalties to total receipts is calculated for each year and is applied to (2) above. This gives the proportion of manufacturing technological and mineral royalties from unrelated concerns;

(4) The above royalty value for each country/area is multiplied by 20 on the assumption that royalties average 5% on sales;

(5) Estimated sales are grossed up according to the proportion of the summary of world returns for technological and mineral royalties from unrelated concerns to the estimated total value of receipts for technological and mineral unrelated concerns presented for that year in *Business Monitor*.

## Foreign Direct Investment

### The Calculation of Sales from Foreign Direct Investment

The calculation of sales from British foreign direct investment is based on the only available estimate – the book value of foreign UK direct investment published in *Business Monitor M4* and subsequently *MA4* supplements *Census of Overseas Assets*. Book value figures are drawn from surveys which were only undertaken in 1978, 1981 and 1984. Houston and Dunning (1976) estimate the foreign sales arising from foreign direct investment by assuming an output: net assets ratio of 2:1 based on the United Nations' Department of Economic and Social Affairs' *Multinational Corporations in World Development* (1973). They say that these estimates 'should be regarded as no better than guesses' (p. 10). The same methodology was used by Buckley and Davies (1980) following Polk *et al.* (1966). Indeed, Belli (1970) found a ratio of 2.189:1 for US multinationals in 1965. However, such a method is crude and takes no account of the large industry variation in output: sales ratios.

Consequently a sales: total assets ratio was calculated for each industry and country using data from the *Survey of Current Business* (1985), which presents data of US foreign affiliates from a survey conducted in 1982. Ratios are applied to UK foreign investment in the absence of UK data of sales: assets. The industry and country breakdown was generally comparable with those used in our survey. Where aggregations of industry groups and countries is necessary a weighted average is used to estimate the ratio. The calculated ratios fall far short of 2:1, averaging out at approximately 1.4:1.

This method is felt to be superior for our purposes, than the approach taken by Clegg (1987), which is to apply the domestic capital: output ratio for each domestic industry to the foreign investment position. Clegg's method assumes that foreign investment replicates the domestic position whilst ours assumes that the comparability of UK foreign investment is closer to US foreign investment than home investment in terms of capital: output ratios. There is considerable evidence that sub-sectors of industry are much more internationally orientated than widely defined ones, and that these pockets of internationalization spread across national differences in ownership (Knickerbocker, 1973; Buckley and Casson, 1985a).

*Foreign Sales Arising from British Outward Direct Investment: Survey Years*

Calculations proceed from the book value figures for outward direct investn.ent provided for each survey year.

*By area/country*

(1) The proportion of foreign direct investment in manufacturing industries is calculated for each major area.
(2) The book value figure for each country/area is multiplied by the relevant proportion represented by manufacturing to give an estimate of book value in manufacturing activities.
(3) The estimated book value for manufacturing activities in each country is multiplied by the US ratio for that country as calculated. UK direct investment in North America is allocated the world average ratio value as no alternative data exist. This gives an estimate of sales from foreign direct investment in manufacturing.

*By Industry*

The book value for each industry is multiplied by the corresponding US ratio within that sector to give an estimate of sales.

## Sales Arising from British Outward Direct Investment: Non-survey Years

In non-survey years it is necessary to first estimate book value before applying other assumptions. The estimating procedure is shown in Appendix 1. The procedure, although exceedingly crude, gives a fair estimate for 1982 based on successive addition of net foreign investment figures to the 1978 book value – through 1979, 1980 and 1981. The estimated book value differed from the actual by 5.8%. This was felt to represent a fair test of overall adequacy of the estimated procedure in the absence of alternative estimates. Net foreign investment figures are drawn from the 1984 and 1981 *Business Monitor*, which each provide data for several years. There is some discrepancy in overlapping years as a result of subsequent adjustments.

### By Area

(1) The book value of outward direct investment in survey years is taken as the base. An estimate for the next year is calculated by adding the value of net investment in each area to survey book value. This proceeds on an incremental year-by-year basis, the estimated book value becoming the basis for additions.

(2) The proportion of manufacturing for non-documented years is taken as an average of data presented in the surveyed years before and after. Such averages are calculated for all major areas.

(3) The proportion of manufacturing is applied to estimate book value to give estimated book values in manufacturing.

(4) The estimated book values then have the country/area's calculated ratio applied to give estimated sales arising from foreign direct investment in each area.

### By Industry

As above, each industry group is grossed up by net foreign investment in each year and the relevant industry's sales: total assets ratio is applied.

## RESULTS: EXPORTS, LICENSED SALES AND SALES ARISING FROM DIRECT INVESTMENT

### By Area/Country

The period 1975–83 has shown a general increase in exports and sales arising from foreign direct investment. The trend in licensed sales has also been upwards, although the rate of growth is significantly slower and more erratic than the incremental growth of exports and FDI. (Fig. 6.1)

Exports of British companies are the dominant form of foreign market servicing in EC countries, EFTA and Other Western Europe, and the Rest of the World. (Figs 6.2 and 6.3). Sales

*Figure 6.1*  World: absolute data 1975–83. In this and in the other figures in this chapter the following key is used: —— investment; ------ exports; – – – – – – licensing.

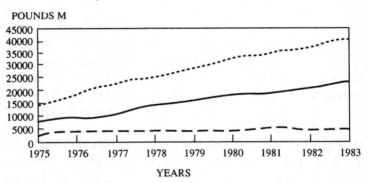

*Figure 6.2*  EC: absolute data 1975–83

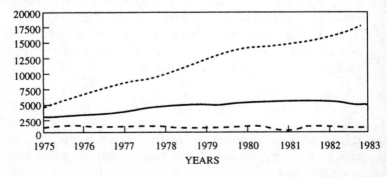

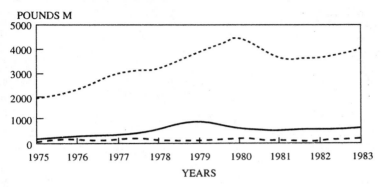

*Figure 6.3*    EFTA: absolute data 1975–83

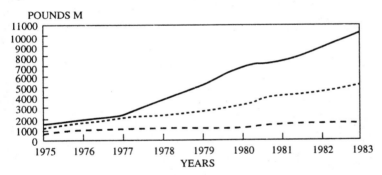

*Figure 6.4*    USA: absolute data 1975–83

arising from foreign direct investment is the predominant form
of market servicing in North America and other Developed
Countries. (Fig. 6.4) (see Appendices 2 and 3).

Licensing in general is much the smallest percentage of total
foreign sales but in certain markets it assumes great importance.
In Japan it is the most important component of Britain's sales,
(Fig. 6.5). Spain and Italy are important countries for licensed
sales and in developing countries *en bloc*, licensing accounted
for 13.5% of total sales in 1983 (see Appendix 4).

Sales arising from FDI are showing an increased importance
in manufacturing (Fig. 6.6). In the early part of the period which
we examine, direct investment sales in the EC were a more
significant proportion of total sales than latterly (Fig. 6.7). The

*Figure 6.5*   Japan: absolute data 1975–83

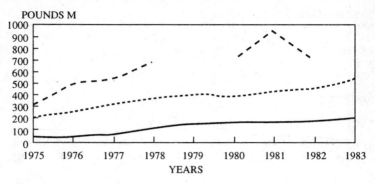

*Figure 6.6*   World: percentage data 1975–83

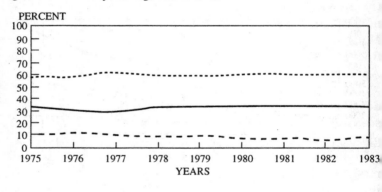

*Figure 6.7*   EC: percentage data 1975–83

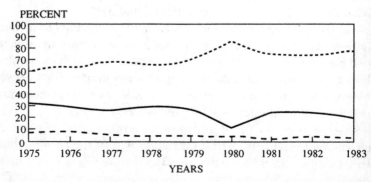

*Figure 6.8*    USA: percentage data 1975–83

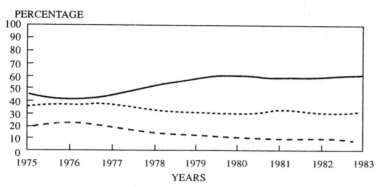

growth of exports to the EC, in line with the hypotheses above (notably Buckley and Artisien, 1987), have grown rapidly. The next major wave of foreign direct investment was directed to North America, notably the USA, where direct investment financed sales reached over 58% in 1983 (Fig. 6.8) (see Appendices 5 and 6).

The major host countries for FDI sales are predominantly developed countries. This can be explained by the similarity of sociocultural structures resulting in similar consumer tastes, organizational and consumer buying behaviour, responses to advertising and promotion, channels of distribution, marketing requirements and managerial structures. Management, marketing, distribution, buyer and product knowledge from the home market could, therefore, be more easily transferred and more effectively implemented by subsidiary companies in host countries. 'Follow the leader' – style strategic approaches may also play a part in the location of FDI. Multinational corporation management may minimize risks by investing in countries where other multinationals have been successful, learning from others' mistakes and following strategies that have yielded profitable results. Added to this, good trade relations forged by early investors and licensors may make subsequent business easier for other companies.

Licensing seems to be extensively used in markets which are difficult to penetrate by the other, more generally favoured means of market servicing. Barriers to import prevent export sales and government regulations make direct investment difficult. Difficulties arising from cultural differences and the high expense of direct investment make investment unfeasible except perhaps at a high degree of market penetration. Japan provides the most obvious example of this (Fig. 6.9), and consequently licensing is the most important component of Britain's sales, always exceeding 50% of total sales in years where the figure is available (51.5% in 1982). With such constraints, licensing may be the only option available, even if considered as a 'third-best' alternative. (Fig. 6.10) (see Appendix 7).

The trends in licensed sales, exports and sales arising from FDI over the ten-year period all show a high level of correlation. This is particularly evident between exports and FDI, which yields a 0.99 correlation coefficient. This suggests that improve-

*Figure 6.9*   Japan: percentage data 1975–83

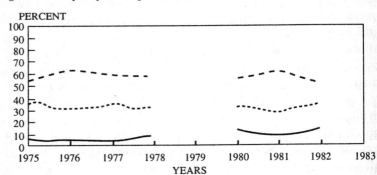

*Figure 6.10*   All manufacturing: absolute data 1975–83

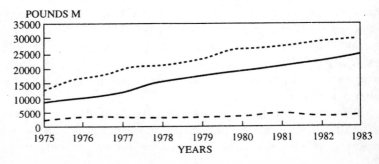

ment in sales performance in different countries/areas is complementary between the three different servicing strategies.

Licensing and FDI activities are concentrated in a small number of countries: 65.5% of licensed sales may be attributed to 11.4% of countries and 75.3% of sales from foreign direct investment are in 9.6% of countries. The formation of barriers to these forms of market servicing in only a small number of countries could, therefore, have a detrimental effect on British foreign sales.

## By Industry

An aggregation of all manufacturing reflects the picture of world manufacturing presented in the previous section, exporting being the dominant form of market servicing (Fig. 6.10). At particular industry levels foreign direct investment is the major form of overseas business in paper, printing and publishing, food, drink and tobacco, and more recently has become so in chemical and allied industries (Figs 6.11 and 6.12). This could be explained by protection of technology in rapidly developing engineering manufacturers and the locational advantage of positioning near to raw materials in the chemical and food sectors. With food, drink and tobacco, there is also the factor of perishability of goods (see Appendices 8 and 9).

Licensing is the least important form of market servicing in all industries, with the exception of shipbuilding (see Appendix

*Figure 6.11*     Food, drink and tobacco: absolute data 1975–83

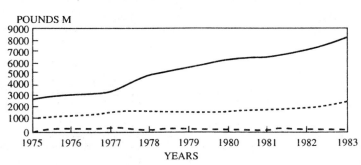

*Figure 6.12*  Chemical and allied industries: absolute data 1975–83

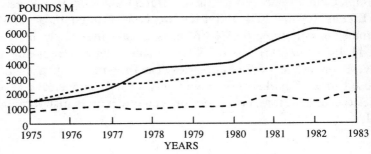

10). In this sector licensing rose above exporting in 1980 and 1981, although by 1983 the level had fallen to 20.5% as opposed to 69.5% exports. Absence of data prevents a trend being established, although the available figures suggest a recent trend towards exporting in this sector.

The increased importance of sales arising from foreign direct investment in manufacturing is mirrored in the industry data (Fig. 6.13). This is more marked in some sectors than others. In chemical and allied industries, levels of foreign investment sales and exports were comparable at the outset of the period. However, in 1978 there was a sharp increase in sales arising from foreign direct investment to 50.1% (Fig. 6.14), a level which has been sustained up to 1983. The year 1978 also witnessed an increase in Foreign Investment in the Food, Drink and Tobacco industries, which again has been maintained up to 1983 (Fig. 6.15) (see Appendices 11 and 12).

*Figure 6.13*  All manufacturing: percentage data 1975–83

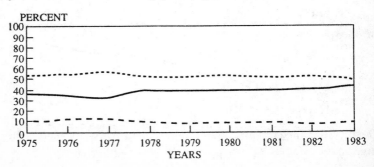

*Figure 6.14*   Chemical and allied industries: percentage data 1975–83

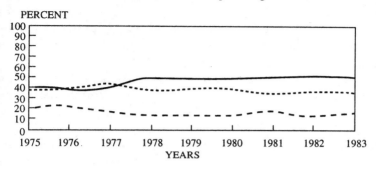

*Figure 6.15*   Food, drink and tobacco: data 1975–83

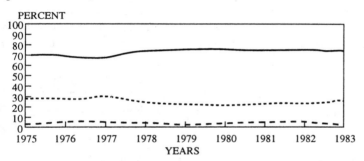

The proportion of licensed sales generally falls below 10%, except in Chemical and Allied Industries and Other Manufacturing. The level of licensed sales in Chemical and Allied industries has, however, declined over the period from 20.5% to 12.7%. Other Manufacturing, which incorporates varied industries, shows much fluctuation in the proportion of sales arising from different forms of servicing which prevents trends being established (see Appendix 13).

OVERVIEW

Despite the fact that we are dealing with market servicing at a high level of aggregation and with all the defects of the data, it is possible to draw several illuminating insights. It must not be forgotten, however, that our data represent snapshot pictures of dynamic phenomena, and that many of the processes examined in earlier sections are, to some degree, masked by aggregation and cross-section analysis at a point in time.

The first and most obvious point to make about the structure of Britain's foreign sales is that its make up differs greatly by country (market) and by industry, as Appendices 3 to 8 show. Overall, exports are the dominant form of market servicing in the period studied, but the proportion of sales arising from foreign direct investment varies greatly. Licensing is generally a small proportion of total sales except in certain countries and industries, where it can assume the major role.

Second, when we examine trends we can see that the growth rate of exports in the period 1975–84 is 2% and the growth rate of direct investment sales in the same period is 2%. Licensing is generally slow growing, with erratic jumps.

There remains a final point to note. Despite the possibility of substituting one form of foreign market servicing for another alluded to in the literature, in practice there appears to be a high degree of complementarity between forms of market servicing. In the overall figures the correlation between exports and sales arising from direct investment is 0.99 across industries and 0.98 across countries. It remains to be seen whether this is true within individual firms or whether it arises because different firms selling to the same country (and/or in the same industry) deal with the market in different ways.

This paper has shown that the structure of British industry's sales in foreign markets differs markedly by industry and by target country. Despite being cast at a high level of aggregation, it allows the key determinants of the structure to become clear. It serves as a backdrop for more micro level analysis of the firm and the industry.

## Acknowledgements

This chapter was part of a three-year project at the University of Bradford Management Centre, 'The Foreign Market Servicing

Strategies and Competitiveness of British Firms', sponsored by the Economic and Social Research Council (ESRC) in the Competitiveness and Regeneration of British Industry Research Programme (Grant No. F. 20250027). Previous versions were given to staff seminars at the University of Bradford Management Centre and the Department of Economics, University of Reading, and at a meeting of the internationalization group of ESRC's Competitiveness Initiative at the University of Bradford Management Centre. The authors are grateful for the constructive comments made. We are particularly grateful to John Cantwell and Bob Pearce of the University of Reading and to the anonymous referees.

APPENDIX 1:   ESTIMATION OF BOOK VALUE OF BRITISH OUTWARD DIRECT INVESTMENT FOR NON-SURVEY YEARS

| | Book value survey years | Previous year book value | Net + investment flow | = Estimated book value |
|---|---|---|---|---|
| 1974 | 10 117.8 | 10 117.8 | | |
| 1975 | | 10 117.8 | + 1171.2 | = 11 289 |
| 1976 | | 11 289 | + 2144.8 | = 13 433.8 |
| 1977 | | 13 433.8 | + 1884.8 | = 15 318.6 |
| | | 15 318.6 | + 2709.7 | = (18 028.3) |
| 1978 | 19 107.7[a] | (1079.4) | (5.6%) | |
| 1979 | | 19 107.7 | + 3034.6 | = 22 142.3 |
| 1980 | | 22 142.3 | + 3390.7 | = 25 533 |
| | | 25 533 | + 4671.2 | = (30 204.2) |
| 1981 | 28 545.1[b] | (1659.1) | (5.8%) | |
| 1982 | | 28 545.1 | + 2396.0 | = 30 941.1 |
| 1983 | | 30 941.1 | + 3312.5 | = 34 253.6 |

[a] Calculated value for 1978 = 1079.4, which = 5.6% error.
[b] Calculated value for 1981 = 1659.1, which = 5.8% error.

# APPENDIX 2: FOREIGN DIRECT INVESTMENT BY COUNTRY 1975–83

| | 1975 | 1976 | 1977 | 1978 | 1979 | 1980 | 1981 | 1982 | 1983 |
|---|---|---|---|---|---|---|---|---|---|
| Western Europe | 2478.0 | 3047.5 | 3518.1 | 4761.8 | 4966.1 | 5326.2 | 5285.4 | 5362.1 | 5282.6 |
| EC | 2311.7 | 2804.7 | 3179.0 | 4401.2 | 4466.1 | 4875.0 | 4936.4 | 4866.3 | 4645.4 |
| Belgium AND Lux. | 291.6 | 372.4 | 436.2 | 611.7 | 569.1 | 586.6 | 443.1 | 439.3 | 499.7 |
| Denmark | 95.1 | 100.8 | 115.9 | 163.6 | 163.8 | 186.7 | 156.2 | 159.8 | 168.8 |
| France | 586.5 | 673.9 | 782.9 | 898.3 | 962.2 | 1096.0 | 1083.6 | 1146.5 | 1267.5 |
| FR. of Germany | 900.3 | 1007.8 | 1189.6 | 1693.1 | 1647.0 | 2060.8 | 1628.3 | 1704.6 | 1701.2 |
| Greece | 11.3 | 12.1 | 16.7 | 23.4 | 27.1 | 27.0 | 31.5 | 39.3 | 38.5 |
| Irish Republic | 219.9 | 246.1 | 281.9 | 381.5 | 407.1 | 446.9 | 440.0 | 473.5 | 477.8 |
| Italy | 198.1 | 241.1 | 288.3 | 308.2 | 366.2 | 417.9 | 391.3 | 414.6 | 445.2 |
| Netherlands | 249.0 | 325.6 | 267.8 | 598.9 | 566.6 | 387.7 | 1052.0 | 770.1 | 310.9 |
| EFTA | 222.3 | 305.7 | 388.8 | 517.5 | 939.9 | 569.0 | 459.0 | 519.2 | 574.9 |
| Austria | 33.3 | 41.9 | 52.9 | 43.8 | | | 28.2 | 29.2 | 28.4 |
| Finland | 16.9 | 18.7 | 20.0 | | | | 17.8 | | |
| Norway | 5.1 | 5.2 | 6.6 | 8.2 | | | | | |
| Portugal | 29.1 | 29.9 | 34.5 | 33.3 | 71.3 | 50.9 | 63.2 | 70.9 | 87.3 |
| Sweden | 65.6 | 81.3 | 103.7 | 96.6 | 198.1 | 125.6 | 118.5 | 118.2 | 131.4 |
| Switzerland | 69.8 | 91.1 | 136.0 | 326.1 | 541.8 | 316.8 | 203.7 | 266.7 | 291.0 |
| Other W. Europe | 103.7 | 122.2 | 138.8 | 145.1 | 300.8 | 211.0 | 227.0 | 271.3 | 304.7 |
| Spain | 77.0 | 92.0 | 107.3 | 108.4 | 222.6 | 157.4 | 170.8 | 209.2 | 239.6 |
| North America | 2 232.0 | 2747.7 | 3251.8 | 4600.3 | 5953.7 | 7620.5 | 8261.9 | 9528.1 | 10989.2 |
| Canada | 666.7 | 903.6 | 885.8 | 916.0 | 1026.6 | 1129.8 | 1259.2 | 1298.0 | 1445.2 |
| USA | 1535.2 | 1917.2 | 2376.1 | 3791.3 | 5117.7 | 6812.5 | 7291.6 | 8625.7 | 10006.2 |
| Other DC | 2798.1 | 3153.9 | 3438.9 | 3782.6 | 3819.4 | 4176.5 | 4398.7 | 4721.0 | 5209.5 |
| Australia | 1349.2 | 1478.2 | 1618.9 | 1882.9 | 1912.5 | 2025.5 | 2258.9 | 2371.9 | 2554.2 |
| Japan | 45.0 | 45.9 | 63.5 | 117.1 | 149.0 | 163.4 | 174.1 | 186.7 | 210.4 |
| New Zealand | 142.3 | 163.0 | 174.1 | | | | 201.5 | 206.9 | 325.5 |
| South Africa | 999.1 | 1177.0 | 1269.0 | | | | 1349.5 | 1521.5 | 1745.0 |
| Rest of World | 1355.9 | 1581.1 | 1821.2 | 2270.3 | 2378.8 | 2712.3 | 2910.5 | 3078.2 | 3553.9 |
| Africa | 525.8 | 601.9 | 755.9 | 858.1 | 864.7 | 969.7 | 974.6 | 1108.8 | 1147.8 |
| Asia | 687.3 | 781.5 | 908.9 | 1187.8 | 1199.7 | 1313.3 | 1556.9 | 1411.3 | 1681.8 |
| Middle East | 33.6 | 46.6 | 57.2 | 141.8 | 149.3 | 162.5 | 110.6 | 130.7 | 117.0 |
| Other Asia | 782.7 | 876.7 | 1015.2 | 1233.2 | 1226.4 | 1343.9 | 1719.7 | 1511.8 | 1861.3 |
| Carribbean, Central and South America | 258.8 | 341.3 | 319.5 | 456.5 | 539.1 | 665.6 | 654.6 | 785.8 | 968.9 |
| World | 7796.2 | 9277.3 | 10579.0 | 14307.8 | 15822.8 | 18245.0 | 19387.8 | 21015.2 | 23265.0 |
| Developing | 1571.1 | 1855.8 | 2107.3 | 2428.6 | 2695.9 | 3074.0 | 3523.6 | 3726.7 | 4302.4 |
| Oil exporting | 270.0 | 350.1 | 482.8 | 645.7 | 679.1 | 774.7 | 749.1 | 896.9 | 897.4 |

APPENDIX 3: UK EXPORTS BY COUNTRY 1975-83

| | 1975 | 1976 | 1977 | 1978 | 1979 | 1980 | 1981 | 1982 | 1983 |
|---|---|---|---|---|---|---|---|---|---|
| Western Europe | 6 752.3 | 9 273.9 | 11 938.0 | 13 459.5 | 17 839.0 | 19 404.3 | 18 947.6 | 20 267.1 | 20 498.6 |
| EC | 4 427.9 | 6 326.1 | 8 206.9 | 9 577.3 | 11 976.6 | 13 951.3 | 14 572.2 | 15 724.0 | 18 025.9 |
| Belgium and Lux. | 636.6 | 966.3 | 1 251.2 | 1 495.9 | 1 653.1 | 1 757.8 | 753.5 | 1 570.5 | 1 750.7 |
| Denmark | 306.1 | 451.5 | 545.0 | 570.2 | 681.3 | 688.2 | 728.7 | 746.8 | 788.3 |
| France | 803.0 | 1 179.1 | 1 463.4 | 1 715.6 | 2 056.6 | 2 452.2 | 2 501.9 | 3 054.4 | 3 842.3 |
| FR. of Germany | 899.3 | 1 265.4 | 1 707.3 | 2 109.9 | 2 837.2 | 3 423.2 | 3 806.0 | 3 680.4 | 4 126.7 |
| Greece | 81.0 | 102.9 | 149.9 | 145.5 | 183.3 | 153.6 | 175.3 | 173.5 | 190.5 |
| Irish Republic | 625.8 | 859.9 | 1 114.9 | 1 388.7 | 1 711.5 | 1 783.3 | 1 941.0 | 1 964.8 | 2 077.6 |
| Italy | 388.5 | 569.5 | 667.4 | 763.8 | 984.1 | 1 272.8 | 1 202.3 | 1 376.5 | 1 549.8 |
| Netherlands | 768.7 | 1 034.2 | 1 457.7 | 1 533.2 | 2 052.8 | 2 573.8 | 2 773.4 | 3 144.9 | 3 699.9 |
| EFTA | 1 815.3 | 2 255.6 | 2 942.9 | 3 166.0 | 3 851.2 | 4 515.5 | 3 537.8 | 3 617.9 | 3 997.3 |
| Austria | 113.9 | 146.5 | 171.4 | 163.1 | 173.7 | 187.1 | 170.4 | 170.5 | 186.2 |
| Finland | 182.5 | 199.3 | 235.3 | 237.3 | 275.2 | 352.2 | 362.3 | 349.0 | 367.0 |
| Norway | 268.9 | 326.6 | 526.0 | 442.1 | 491.2 | 529.7 | 605.1 | 635.1 | 563.8 |
| Portugal | 108.1 | 154.0 | 203.7 | 194.7 | 206.2 | 261.3 | 230.0 | 291.4 | 270.0 |
| Sweden | 576.4 | 721.1 | 814.0 | 797.5 | 1 032.8 | 1 092.2 | 1 104.8 | 1 316.2 | 1 623.6 |
| Switzerland | 555.2 | 690.0 | 965.7 | 1 301.1 | 1 612.9 | 2 061.4 | 1 006.4 | 813.1 | 942.3 |
| Other W. Europe | 488.0 | 636.5 | 788.2 | 716.2 | 850.1 | 937.5 | 837.7 | 925.1 | 1 107.0 |
| Spain | 203.3 | 253.2 | 315.5 | 320.6 | 382.4 | 474.2 | 511.1 | 592.6 | 767.3 |
| North America | 1 608.8 | 2 138.9 | 3 251.0 | 2 917.7 | 3 240.7 | 3 664.5 | 4 920.3 | 4 543.0 | 6 457.1 |
| Canada | 371.4 | 433.8 | 477.2 | 502.7 | 514.0 | 508.4 | 351.1 | 976.5 | 1 035.8 |
| USA | 1 225.6 | 1 688.8 | 2 077.7 | 2 396.3 | 2 712.5 | 3 140.2 | 4 173.3 | 4 504.4 | 5 098.1 |
| Other DC | 1 296.6 | 1 341.1 | 1 431.2 | 1 584.5 | 1 659.3 | 1 787.6 | 2 028.0 | 2 200.1 | 2 133.0 |
| Australia | 435.9 | 474.4 | 519.0 | 580.9 | 563.3 | 547.1 | 595.9 | 708.2 | 639.6 |
| Japan | 213.6 | 248.1 | 319.7 | 368.4 | 406.2 | 400.7 | 428.0 | 463.0 | 543.5 |
| New Zealand | 175.0 | 173.3 | 195.6 | 182.1 | 209.1 | 168.2 | 162.4 | 219.2 | 194.5 |
| South Africa | 472.1 | 445.3 | 396.8 | 453.0 | 480.8 | 671.5 | 841.7 | 809.7 | 755.3 |
| Rest of World | 4 048.2 | 5 004.9 | 6 390.4 | 7 384.9 | 7 495.9 | 8 599.9 | 9 459.9 | 10 413.1 | 9 845.8 |
| Africa | 997.1 | 1 322.1 | 1 656.8 | 1 909.6 | 1 707.6 | 2 198.2 | 2 473.1 | 2 598.1 | 1 886.5 |
| Asia | 1 957.6 | 2 452.3 | 3 169.5 | 3 756.8 | 4 108.4 | 4 199.0 | 4 780.5 | 6 159.2 | 5 998.3 |
| Middle East | 878.4 | 1 214.5 | 1 639.0 | 1 852.6 | 1 909.4 | 2 130.3 | 2 540.2 | 3 627.5 | 3 120.9 |
| Other Asia | 1 079.2 | 1 237.7 | 1 530.5 | 1 904.2 | 2 199.1 | 2 068.6 | 2 240.2 | 2 531.7 | 2 877.4 |
| Caribbean, Central and South America | 644.2 | 714.2 | 939.6 | 996.1 | 971.6 | 1 389.2 | 1 461.6 | 974.4 | 1 227.5 |
| World | 13 745.8 | 11 780.9 | 23 102.5 | 25 420.0 | 28 677.5 | 33 184.6 | 35 188.7 | 37 779.3 | 41 265.3 |
| Developing | 1 575.8 | 1 963.9 | 2 530.9 | 3 109.2 | 2 867.3 | 3 544.0 | 4 015.0 | 4 023.0 | 3 826.2 |
| Oil Exporting | 1 571.4 | 2 171.2 | 2 216.2 | 3 243.1 | 2 541.0 | 3 305.1 | 4 092.7 | 4 382.7 | 4 157.0 |

# APPENDIX 4: UK LICENSED SALES ABROAD BY COUNTRY 1975–83

| | 1975 | 1976 | 1977 | 1978 | 1979 | 1980 | 1981 | 1982 | 1983 |
|---|---|---|---|---|---|---|---|---|---|
| Western Europe | 711.4 | 1 097.8 | 921.4 | 882.4 | 978.0 | 871.2 | 783.2 | 821.3 | 1 078.7 |
| EC | 507.7 | 745.6 | 639.2 | 619.0 | 694.4 | 576.0 | 447.0 | 698.7 | 698.7 |
| Belgium and Lux. | 43.4 | 88.9 | 95.2 | 75.2 | | | | | |
| Denmark | 10.3 | 11.3 | 9.5 | | 6.8 | 10.4 | 7.5 | 10.4 | 12.6 |
| France | 110.2 | 150.5 | 136.0 | 147.1 | 146.7 | 158.4 | 149.5 | 153.1 | 157.8 |
| FR. of Germany | 167.0 | 249.7 | 193.8 | 194.9 | 215.2 | 126.0 | 78.3 | 142.7 | 122.4 |
| Greece | | 4.1 | | | | | | | 21.6 |
| Irish Republic | 8.7 | 12.6 | 13.6 | 8.9 | | | | | |
| Italy | 130.3 | 191.5 | 139.4 | 133.4 | 153.2 | 151.2 | 149.5 | | 309.1 |
| Netherlands | 768.7 | 47.9 | 57.8 | 34.2 | 35.9 | 25.2 | 28.5 | 34.8 | 38.6 |
| EFTA | 1 815.3 | 150.5 | 129.2 | 112.9 | 110.8 | 122.4 | 121.0 | 114.8 | 170.7 |
| Austria | | 10.6 | | 13.7 | | | 13.5 | 13.9 | 19.3 |
| Finland | 5.0 | 20.9 | | 4.4 | | | | | |
| Norway | 15.7 | 8.9 | 9.5 | | | | | | |
| Portugal | 24.7 | 24.3 | 8.2 | 10.3 | 15.6 | 18.7 | 19.2 | | 21.6 |
| Sweden | 31.2 | 41.0 | 40.8 | 58.1 | 31.9 | 39.6 | 22.1 | 30.3 | 38.6 |
| Switzerland | | 44.5 | 44.2 | | | | | | |
| Other W. Europe | 110.2 | 205.2 | 156.4 | 150.5 | 169.5 | 194.4 | 153.1 | 160.1 | 212.5 |
| Spain | 76.8 | 126.5 | 85.0 | 112.9 | 136.9 | 136.8 | 153.1 | 132.2 | 157.8 |
| North America | 671.3 | 1 022.6 | 1 047.2 | 1 046.5 | 1 118.2 | 1 180.8 | 1 367.0 | 1 524.2 | 1 407.1 |
| Canada | 25.4 | 30.4 | 40.8 | 41.0 | 26.7 | 57.6 | 103.2 | 69.6 | 80.5 |
| USA | 651.3 | 1 022.1 | 1 020.0 | 1 019.2 | 1 091.9 | 1 126.8 | 1 260.2 | 1 451.2 | 1 320.2 |
| Other DC | 437.5 | 731.9 | 649.4 | 772.9 | 876.9 | 871.2 | 1 082.2 | 883.9 | 940.2 |
| Australia | 53.4 | 58.1 | 51.0 | 54.7 | 68.5 | 72.0 | 64.1 | 80.0 | 202.9 |
| Japan | 307.3 | 499.3 | 547.4 | 677.2 | | 709.2 | 954.1 | 689.0 | |
| New Zealand | | 17.4 | 16.7 | 15.0 | | 15.8 | | 34.8 | |
| South Africa | | 78.7 | 47.6 | 41.0 | 61.9 | 86.4 | | 83.5 | 115.9 |
| Rest of World | 497.7 | 1 049.9 | 1 132.2 | 1 101.2 | 913.3 | 1 216.8 | 1 488.1 | 929.2 | 1 465.1 |
| Africa | 43.4 | 61.6 | 47.6 | 34.2 | 45.6 | 61.2 | 64.1 | 69.6 | 122.4 |
| Asia | 153.6 | 619.0 | 438.5 | 338.6 | 378.2 | 442.8 | 131.1 | 306.2 | 309.1 |
| Middle East | 83.5 | 164.2 | 166.6 | 68.4 | 35.9 | 39.6 | 49.8 | 59.2 | 70.8 |
| Other Asia | 70.1 | 454.9 | 268.6 | 270.2 | 339.0 | 403.2 | 270.6 | 247.1 | 238.3 |
| Carribbean, Central and South America | 80.2 | 95.8 | 88.4 | 75.2 | 84.8 | 90.0 | 131.7 | 97.4 | 93.4 |
| World | 2 338.0 | 3 837.2 | 3 748.0 | 3 803.0 | 4 096.8 | 4 096.8 | 4 624.4 | 4 144.7 | 4 852.5 |
| Developing | 420.8 | 1 203.8 | 1 186.6 | 1 145.7 | 1 152.0 | 1 152.0 | 1 352.8 | 716.9 | 1 268.7 |
| Oil Exporting | 96.9 | 174.4 | 166.6 | 68.4 | 54.0 | 54.0 | 103.2 | 76.6 | 90.2 |

APPENDIX 5: PERCENTAGE OF FOREIGN DIRECT INVESTMENT BY COUNTRY 1975–83

| | 1975 | 1976 | 1977 | 1978 | 1979 | 1980 | 1981 | 1982 | 1983 |
|---|---|---|---|---|---|---|---|---|---|
| Western Europe | 24.9 | 22.7 | 21.5 | 24.9 | 20.9 | 20.8 | 21.1 | 20.3 | 19.7 |
| EC | 32.0 | 28.4 | 26.4 | 30.2 | 26.1 | 25.1 | 24.7 | 22.9 | 19.9 |
| Belgium and Lux. | 30.0 | 26.1 | 34.5 | 28.0 | | | | | |
| Denmark | 23.1 | 17.9 | 17.3 | 32.5 | 19.2 | 21.1 | 17.5 | 17.4 | 17.4 |
| France | 39.1 | 33.6 | 32.9 | 42.3 | 30.4 | 29.6 | 29.0 | 26.3 | 24.1 |
| FR. of Germany | 45.8 | 39.9 | 38.5 | | 35.0 | 36.7 | 29.5 | 30.8 | 28.6 |
| Greece | | 10.2 | | | | | | | 15.4 |
| Irish Republic | 25.7 | 22.0 | 20.0 | 21.4 | 24.4 | 22.7 | 22.4 | | 19.3 |
| Italy | 27.6 | 24.1 | 26.3 | 25.6 | 21.3 | 13.0 | 27.3 | 19.5 | 7.7 |
| Netherlands | 23.5 | 23.1 | 15.0 | 27.6 | | | | | |
| EFTA | 10.4 | 11.3 | 11.2 | 13.6 | 19.2 | 10.9 | 11.1 | 12.2 | 12.1 |
| Austria | | 21.1 | | | | | | | |
| Finland | | 7.8 | | | | | | | |
| Norway | 1.8 | 1.5 | 1.2 | 1.8 | 24.3 | 15.4 | 2.8 | 19.6 | 23.0 |
| Portugal | 19.0 | 14.4 | 14.0 | 14.0 | 15.7 | 10.0 | 20.2 | 8.1 | 7.3 |
| Sweden | 9.8 | 9.6 | 10.8 | 10.1 | | | 9.5 | | |
| Switzerland | 10.6 | 11.0 | 11.9 | | | | | | |
| Other W. Europe | 14.8 | 12.7 | 12.8 | 14.3 | 22.8 | 15.7 | | 20.0 | 18.8 |
| Spain | 21.6 | 19.5 | 21.1 | 20.0 | 30.0 | 20.5 | 20.5 | 22.4 | 20.6 |
| North America | 49.5 | 46.5 | 43.1 | 53.7 | 57.7 | 61.1 | 56.8 | 61.1 | 58.3 |
| Canada | 62.7 | 66.1 | 63.1 | 62.8 | 65.5 | 66.6 | 73.5 | 55.4 | 56.4 |
| USA | 45.0 | 41.4 | 43.4 | 52.6 | 57.3 | 61.5 | 57.3 | 59.2 | 60.9 |
| Other DC | 61.7 | 60.3 | 62.3 | 61.6 | 60.1 | 61.1 | 58.6 | 60.5 | 62.9 |
| Australia | 73.4 | 73.5 | 74.0 | 74.8 | 75.2 | 76.6 | 77.4 | 75.1 | 75.2 |
| Japan | 8.0 | 5.8 | 0.8 | 10.1 | | 12.8 | 11.2 | 13.9 | |
| New Zealand | | 46.1 | 45.1 | | | | | 44.9 | |
| South Africa | | 69.2 | 74.1 | | | | | 63.0 | 66.7 |
| Rest of World | 23.0 | 20.7 | 19.5 | 21.1 | 21.1 | 21.6 | 21.0 | 21.3 | 23.9 |
| Africa | 33.6 | 30.3 | 30.7 | 30.6 | 33.0 | 30.0 | 27.8 | 29.4 | 36.4 |
| Asia | 24.6 | 20.3 | 20.1 | 22.5 | 21.1 | 22.1 | 23.3 | 17.9 | 21.1 |
| Middle East | 3.4 | 3.3 | 3.1 | 0.9 | 7.1 | 7.0 | 4.1 | 3.4 | 3.5 |
| Other Asia | 40.5 | 34.1 | 36.1 | 36.2 | 32.6 | 35.2 | 40.6 | 35.2 | 37.4 |
| Carribbean Central and South America | 26.3 | 29.6 | 23.7 | 29.9 | 33.8 | 31.0 | 29.1 | 42.3 | 42.3 |
| World | 32.6 | 30.0 | 28.3 | 32.9 | 32.6 | 32.9 | 32.7 | 33.4 | 33.5 |
| Developing | 44.0 | 36.9 | 36.2 | 36.3 | 40.1 | 39.6 | 39.6 | 44.0 | 45.8 |
| Oil Exporting | 13.9 | 13.0 | 16.8 | 16.3 | 20.7 | 18.7 | 15.1 | 16.7 | 17.4 |

## APPENDIX 6: PERCENTAGE OF EXPORTS BY COUNTRY 1975–83

| | 1975 | 1976 | 1977 | 1978 | 1979 | 1980 | 1981 | 1982 | 1983 |
|---|---|---|---|---|---|---|---|---|---|
| Western Europe | 67.9 | 69.1 | 72.9 | 70.5 | 75.0 | 75.8 | 75.7 | 76.6 | 76.3 |
| EC | 61.0 | 64.1 | 68.2 | 65.6 | 69.9 | 85.1 | 73.0 | 73.9 | 77.1 |
| Belgium and Lux. | 65.5 | 67.7 | 70.2 | 68.5 | | | | | |
| Denmark | 74.4 | 80.1 | 81.3 | | 80.0 | 77.7 | 81.7 | 81.4 | 81.3 |
| France | 53.5 | 58.9 | 61.4 | 62.1 | 65.0 | 66.2 | 67.0 | 70.2 | 72.9 |
| FR. of Germany | 45.7 | 50.2 | 55.2 | 52.8 | 60.4 | 61.0 | 69.0 | 66.6 | 69.4 |
| Greece | | 86.4 | | | | | | | 76.0 |
| Irish Republic | 73.2 | 76.9 | 79.0 | 78.1 | 65.5 | 69.1 | 69.0 | | 67.3 |
| Italy | 54.2 | 56.8 | 60.9 | 63.4 | 77.3 | 86.2 | 72.0 | 79.6 | 91.4 |
| Netherlands | 72.7 | 73.5 | 81.7 | 70.8 | | | | | |
| EFTA | 85.2 | 83.2 | 85.0 | 83.4 | 78.6 | 86.7 | 85.9 | 85.1 | 84.3 |
| Austria | | 73.6 | | | | | | | |
| Finland | | 83.4 | | | | | | | |
| Norway | 96.4 | 95.9 | 97.0 | 97.2 | 70.3 | 79.0 | 95.1 | 80.4 | 71.3 |
| Portugal | 70.7 | 74.0 | 82.7 | 81.7 | 81.8 | 86.9 | 73.6 | 89.9 | 90.5 |
| Sweden | 86.5 | 85.5 | 84.9 | 83.8 | | | 88.7 | | |
| Switzerland | 84.6 | 83.6 | 84.3 | | | | | | |
| Other W. Europe | 69.5 | 66.0 | 72.8 | 70.8 | 64.4 | 69.8 | | 68.2 | 68.2 |
| Spain | 56.9 | 53.7 | 62.1 | 59.2 | 51.5 | 61.7 | 61.2 | 63.4 | 65.9 |
| North America | 35.7 | 36.2 | 43.1 | 34.1 | 31.4 | 29.4 | 33.8 | 29.1 | 34.2 |
| Canada | 34.9 | 31.7 | 34.0 | 34.4 | 32.8 | 30.0 | 20.5 | 41.7 | 40.4 |
| USA | 35.9 | 36.5 | 38.0 | 33.3 | 30.4 | 28.3 | 32.8 | 36.9 | 31.0 |
| Other DC | 28.6 | 25.7 | 25.9 | 25.8 | 26.1 | 26.2 | 27.0 | 28.2 | 25.8 |
| Australia | 23.7 | 23.6 | 23.7 | 23.1 | 22.1 | 20.7 | 20.4 | 22.4 | 18.8 |
| Japan | 37.7 | 31.3 | 34.4 | 31.7 | | 31.5 | 27.5 | 34.6 | 28.9 |
| New Zealand | | 49.0 | 50.6 | | | | | 47.6 | |
| South Africa | | 26.2 | 23.2 | | | | | 33.5 | |
| Rest of World | 68.6 | 65.5 | 68.4 | 68.7 | 70.7 | 68.6 | 68.3 | 72.2 | 66.2 |
| Africa | 63.7 | 66.6 | 67.3 | 68.2 | 65.2 | 68.1 | 70.4 | 68.8 | 59.8 |
| Asia | 70.0 | 63.6 | 70.2 | 71.1 | 72.3 | 70.5 | 71.7 | 78.2 | 75.1 |
| Middle East | 88.2 | 85.2 | 88.0 | 89.8 | 91.2 | 91.3 | 94.1 | 95.0 | 94.3 |
| Other Asia | 55.9 | 48.2 | 54.4 | 55.9 | 58.4 | 54.2 | 53.0 | 59.0 | 57.8 |
| Caribbean, Central and South America | 65.5 | 62.0 | 69.7 | 65.2 | 60.9 | 64.8 | 65.0 | 52.5 | 53.6 |
| World | 57.6 | 57.6 | 61.7 | 58.4 | 59.0 | 59.8 | 59.4 | 60.0 | 59.5 |
| Developing | 44.2 | 39.1 | 43.5 | 46.5 | 42.7 | 45.6 | 45.2 | 47.5 | 40.7 |
| Oil exporting | 81.1 | 80.5 | 77.3 | 82.0 | 77.6 | 80.0 | 82.8 | 81.8 | 80.8 |

# APPENDIX 7: PERCENTAGE OF LICENSED SALES BY COUNTRY 1975–83

| | 1975 | 1976 | 1977 | 1978 | 1979 | 1980 | 1981 | 1982 | 1983 |
|---|---|---|---|---|---|---|---|---|---|
| Western Europe | 7.2 | 8.2 | 5.6 | 4.6 | 4.1 | 3.4 | 3.1 | 3.1 | 4.0 |
| EC | 7.0 | 7.5 | 5.3 | 4.2 | 4.1 | 3.0 | 2.2 | 3.3 | 3.0 |
| Belgium and Lux. | 4.5 | 6.2 | 5.3 | 3.4 | | | | | |
| Denmark | 2.5 | 2.0 | 1.4 | 5.3 | 0.8 | 1.2 | 0.8 | 1.1 | 1.3 |
| France | 7.3 | 7.5 | 5.7 | 4.9 | 4.6 | 4.3 | 4.0 | 3.5 | 3.0 |
| FR. of Germany | 8.5 | 9.9 | 6.3 | | 4.6 | 2.2 | 1.4 | 2.6 | 2.1 |
| Greece | | 3.4 | | | | | | | |
| Irish Republic | 1.0 | 1.1 | 1.0 | 0.5 | | | | | |
| Italy | 18.2 | 19.1 | 12.7 | 11.1 | 10.2 | 8.2 | 8.6 | | 13.4 |
| Netherlands | 3.8 | 3.4 | 3.2 | 1.6 | 1.4 | 0.8 | 0.7 | 0.9 | 1.0 |
| EFTA | 4.4 | 5.5 | 3.7 | 3.0 | 2.3 | 2.4 | 2.9 | 2.7 | 3.6 |
| Austria | | 5.3 | | | | | | | |
| Finland | | 8.7 | | | | | | | |
| Norway | 1.8 | 2.6 | 1.8 | 1.0 | | | 2.1 | | |
| Portugal | 10.3 | 11.7 | 3.3 | 4.3 | 5.3 | 5.7 | 6.1 | | 5.7 |
| Sweden | 3.7 | 4.9 | 4.3 | 6.1 | 2.5 | 3.1 | 1.8 | | 2.2 |
| Switzerland | 4.8 | 5.4 | 3.9 | | | | | 2.1 | |
| Other W. Europe | 15.7 | 21.3 | 14.4 | 14.9 | 12.8 | 14.5 | 18.3 | 11.8 | 13.1 |
| Spain | 21.5 | 26.8 | 16.7 | 20.8 | 18.5 | 17.8 | | 14.2 | 13.5 |
| North America | 14.9 | 17.3 | 13.9 | 12.2 | 10.8 | 9.5 | 9.4 | 9.8 | 7.5 |
| Canada | 2.4 | 2.2 | 2.9 | 2.8 | 1.7 | 3.4 | 6.0 | 3.0 | 3.1 |
| USA | 19.1 | 22.1 | 18.6 | 14.1 | 12.3 | 10.2 | 9.9 | 10.0 | 8.0 |
| Other DC | 9.7 | 14.0 | 11.8 | 12.6 | 13.8 | 12.7 | 14.4 | 11.3 | 11.4 |
| Australia | 2.9 | 2.9 | 2.3 | 2.2 | 2.7 | 2.7 | 2.2 | 2.5 | 6.0 |
| Japan | 54.3 | 62.9 | 58.8 | 58.2 | | 55.7 | 61.3 | 51.5 | |
| New Zealand | | 4.9 | 4.3 | | | | | 7.6 | |
| South Africa | | 4.6 | 2.8 | | | | | 3.5 | 4.4 |
| Rest of World | 8.4 | 13.7 | 12.1 | 10.2 | 8.1 | 9.7 | 10.7 | 6.4 | 9.9 |
| Africa | 2.8 | 3.1 | 1.9 | 1.2 | 1.7 | 1.9 | 1.8 | 1.8 | 3.9 |
| Asia | 5.5 | 16.1 | 9.7 | 6.4 | 6.7 | 7.4 | 5.0 | 3.9 | 3.9 |
| Middle East | 8.4 | 11.5 | 8.9 | 3.3 | 1.7 | 1.7 | 1.8 | 1.6 | 2.1 |
| Other Asia | 3.6 | 17.7 | 9.5 | 7.9 | 9.0 | 10.6 | 6.4 | 5.8 | 4.8 |
| Carribbean, Central and South America | 8.2 | 8.3 | 6.6 | 4.9 | 5.3 | 4.2 | 5.9 | 5.2 | 4.1 |
| World | 9.8 | 12.4 | 10.0 | 8.7 | 8.4 | 7.4 | 7.8 | 6.6 | 7.0 |
| Developing | 11.8 | 24.0 | 20.4 | 17.1 | 17.2 | 14.8 | 15.2 | 8.5 | 13.5 |
| Oil Exporting | 5.0 | 6.5 | 5.8 | 1.7 | 1.6 | 1.3 | 2.1 | 1.4 | 1.7 |

APPENDIX 8: UK FOREIGN DIRECT INVESTMENT BY INDUSTRY 1975–83

| | 1975 | 1976 | 1977 | 1978 | 1979 | 1980 | 1981 | 1982 | 1983 |
|---|---|---|---|---|---|---|---|---|---|
| All Manufacturing | 8 623.9 | 10 195.6 | 11 595.7 | 15 792.3 | 17 543.5 | 19 398.5 | 21 017.0 | 25 091.0 | 22 718.2 |
| Food, Drink and Tobacco | 2 673.6 | 3 088.2 | 3 426.0 | 4 993.1 | 5 609.7 | 6 412.1 | 6 576.6 | 8 485.5 | 7 258.8 |
| Chemical and Allied Industries | 1 490.2 | 1 858.0 | 2 307.5 | 3 555.4 | 3 901.0 | 4 035.4 | 5 439.4 | 6 324.5 | 5 804.3 |
| Metal Manufacture | 271.8 | 331.4 | 381.0 | 541.5 | 598.0 | 618.8 | 320.8 | 353.8 | 345.5 |
| Mech. and Instrument Engineering | 764.8 | 934.8 | 1 037.7 | 982.5 | 1 176.7 | 1 365.3 | 1 419.9 | 1 586.9 | 1 475.2 |
| Electrical Engineering | 957.1 | 1 077.1 | 1 256.5 | 1 561.6 | 1 612.8 | 1 840.8 | 2 108.3 | 2 282.3 | 2 287.0 |
| Shipbuilding | 66.8 | 77.8 | 95.3 | 81.2 | 85.9 | 69.1 | 23.0 | 29.3 | 24.4 |
| Motor Vehicles | 234.7 | 297.3 | 325.1 | 349.6 | 316.3 | 296.6 | 852.0 | 1 137.8 | 855.2 |
| Textiles, Leather, Clothing and Footwear | 656.0 | 728.7 | 778.4 | 862.8 | 896.7 | 960.8 | 968.4 | 1 115.8 | 1 032.4 |
| Paper, Printing and Publishing | 678.6 | 817.5 | 840.6 | 1 181.9 | 1 306.2 | 1 430.4 | 1 237.2 | 1 504.3 | 1 393.3 |
| Rubber | 210.1 | 261.2 | 275.6 | 393.8 | 417.3 | 433.8 | 719.6 | 482.2 | 439.9 |
| Other Manufacturing | 791.5 | 913.8 | 1 041.6 | 1 473.7 | 1 867.4 | 2 233.4 | 1 766.5 | 2 358.7 | 2 209.2 |
| Total non-Manufacturing | 5 494.0 | 6 573.1 | 7 542.4 | 8 480.4 | 10 195.9 | 12 552.6 | 14 854.0 | 17 943.6 | 16 159.0 |
| Total All Industries | 13 454.4 | 15 984.4 | 18 246.1 | 23 057.8 | 26 389.8 | 30 458.6 | 34 254.1 | 41 104.3 | 37 129.3 |

APPENDIX 9: UK EXPORTS BY INDUSTRY 1975–83

| | 1975 | 1976 | 1977 | 1978 | 1979 | 1980 | 1981 | 1982 | 1983 |
|---|---|---|---|---|---|---|---|---|---|
| All Manufacturing | 12 714.3 | 16 662.7 | 20 300.4 | 21 461.7 | 23 519.1 | 26 842.9 | 27 621.8 | 29 166.2 | 30 212.4 |
| Food, Drink and Tobacco | 1 011.7 | 1 231.3 | 1 507.8 | 1 630.1 | 1 665.3 | 1 822.2 | 1 986.9 | 2 168.1 | 2 651.2 |
| Chemical and Allied Industries | 1 432.3 | 1 973.4 | 2 527.2 | 2 628.4 | 3 080.5 | 3 280.1 | 3 678.4 | 4 018.2 | 4 448.7 |
| Metal Manufacture | 618.7 | 766.3 | 984.7 | 1 013.3 | 1 266.3 | 1 219.8 | 1 318.8 | 1 267.4 | 1 929.9 |
| Mech. and Instrument Engineering | 2 117.5 | 2 527.2 | 2 973.1 | 3 309.8 | 3671.6 | 4 179.0 | 4 499.1 | 4 704.4 | 4 398.1 |
| Electrical Engineering | 1 047.5 | 1 391.9 | 1 736.5 | 1 905.0 | 2 116.7 | 2 318.9 | 2 581.6 | 2 978.7 | 3 908.5 |
| Shipbuilding | 221.3 | 293.2 | 316.9 | 432.4 | 478.9 | 392.1 | 316.6 | 257.6 | 203.8 |
| Motor Vehicles | 1 332.8 | 1 964.9 | 1 850.1 | 2 274.8 | 2 370.2 | 2 906.8 | 3 207.9 | 3 069.2 | 2 807.6 |
| Textiles, Leather, Clothing and Footwear | 948.1 | 1 284.2 | 1726.5 | 2 587.1 | 2 044.3 | 2138.7 | 1 943.4 | 1 948.7 | 1 795.6 |
| Paper, Printing and Publishing | 295.2 | 382.3 | 531.9 | 585.5 | 652.9 | 688.6 | 718.9 | 780.4 | 861.4 |
| Rubber | 273.9 | 345.9 | 419.2 | 468.3 | 518.4 | 586.7 | 609.7 | 624.8 | 920.2 |
| Other Manufacturing | 1 950.7 | 2 682.8 | 3 618.7 | 2 642.8 | 3 082.4 | 3 705.0 | 3 328.1 | 3 373.0 | 2 243.2 |
| Total Non-manufacturing | 1 070.1 | 1 257.4 | 2 178.0 | 4 037.8 | 5 752.3 | 7 169.8 | 8 071.2 | 9 422.0 | 11 997.5 |
| Total All Industries | 13 043.2 | 16 987.4 | 21 122.0 | 23 800.0 | 27 779.5 | 31 538.2 | 33 859.3 | 36 100.0 | 39 347.1 |

APPENDIX 10:   UK LICENSED SALES BY INDUSTRY 1975–83

| | 1975 | 1976 | 1977 | 1978 | 1979 | 1980 | 1981 | 1982 | 1983 |
|---|---|---|---|---|---|---|---|---|---|
| All Manufacturing | 2 335.1 | 3 819.9 | 3 752.0 | 3 785.2 | 3 888.2 | 3 928.1 | 4 607.2 | 4 145.9 | 4 830.5 |
| Food, Drink and Tobacco | 78.1 | 214.3 | 161.2 | 193.0 | 200.5 | 246.7 | 278.5 | 309.7 | 300.3 |
| Chemical and Allied Industries | 751.8 | 1 063.8 | 989.8 | 918.3 | 1 039.9 | 1 188.4 | 1 840.2 | 1 431.5 | 2 019.2 |
| Metal Manufacture | 41.3 | 55.8 | 73.4 | 75.5 | 44.6 | 45.9 | 50.3 | 53.7 | 48.6 |
| Mech. and Instrument Engineering | 346.2 | 313.0 | 724.1 | 606.3 | 451.0 | 547.5 | 541.4 | 432.9 | 403.3 |
| Electrical Engineering | 274.2 | 319.2 | 375.7 | 407.3 | 511.4 | 133.5 | 365.6 | 170.6 | 188.8 |
| Shipbuilding | | | | | 375.6 | 516.4 | 316.7 | 158.0 | 60.1 |
| Motor Vehicles | 34.5 | 51.4 | 49.3 | 105.0 | 75.1 | 91.8 | 96.2 | 508.8 | 703.6 |
| Textiles, Leather, Clothing and Footwear | 29.1 | 50.5 | 41.8 | 35.2 | 32.9 | 38.0 | 29.9 | 31.6 | 54.3 |
| Paper, Printing and Publishing | 148.0 | 166.7 | 161.5 | 159.0 | 146.3 | 167.9 | 179.7 | 218.0 | 220.2 |
| Rubber | 22.0 | 36.5 | 40.6 | 32.9 | 16.9 | 19.6 | 30.5 | 69.5 | 234.5 |
| Other Manufacturing | 709.6 | 1 548.2 | 1 135.6 | 1 252.7 | 993.9 | 932.0 | 978.5 | 764.7 | 594.9 |
| Total Non-Manufacturing | 684.9 | 906.7 | 1 344.7 | 1 428.1 | 861.7 | 1 050.0 | 1 150.3 | 1 557.9 | 1 636.0 |
| Total All Industries | 3 020.0 | 4 726.6 | 5 096.7 | 5 213.3 | 4 749.9 | 4 978.5 | 5 757.5 | 5 703.8 | 6 466.5 |

APPENDIX 11: PERCENTAGE OF FOREIGN DIRECT INVESTMENT BY INDUSTRY 1975–83

| | 1975 | 1976 | 1977 | 1978 | 1979 | 1980 | 1981 | 1982 | 1983 |
|---|---|---|---|---|---|---|---|---|---|
| All Manufacturing | 36.4 | 33.2 | 32.5 | 38.5 | 39.0 | 38.7 | 39.5 | 40.5 | 41.7 |
| Food, Drink and Tobacco | 71.0 | 68.1 | 67.2 | 73.3 | 75.0 | 75.6 | 74.4 | 74.6 | 74.2 |
| Chemical and Allied Industries | 40.6 | 38.0 | 39.6 | 50.1 | 48.6 | 47.5 | 49.6 | 51.6 | 49.5 |
| Metal Manufacture | 29.2 | 28.7 | 26.5 | 33.2 | 31.3 | 32.8 | 19.0 | 20.7 | 15.2 |
| Mech. and Instrument Engineering | 24.4 | 24.8 | 21.9 | 20.1 | 22.2 | 22.4 | 22.0 | 22.3 | 24.8 |
| Electrical Engineering | 42.0 | 38.6 | 37.3 | 40.3 | 38.0 | 42.9 | 41.7 | 42.1 | 35.8 |
| Shipbuilding | | | | | 9.1 | 7.1 | 3.5 | 5.5 | 10.0 |
| Motor Vehicles | 14.7 | 12.9 | 14.6 | 12.8 | 11.5 | 9.0 | 20.5 | 19.3 | 24.5 |
| Textiles, Leather, Clothing and Footwear | 40.2 | 35.3 | 30.6 | 24.8 | 30.2 | 30.6 | 32.9 | 34.3 | 37.6 |
| Paper, Printing and Publishing | 60.5 | 59.8 | 54.8 | 61.4 | 62.0 | 62.5 | 57.9 | 58.3 | 58.2 |
| Rubber | 41.5 | 40.6 | 37.5 | 44.0 | 43.8 | 41.7 | 52.9 | 38.8 | 29.5 |
| Other Manufacturing | 22.9 | 17.8 | 18.0 | 27.4 | 31.4 | 32.5 | 29.1 | 34.8 | 45.4 |
| Total Non-Manufacturing | 75.8 | 75.2 | 68.2 | 60.8 | 60.7 | 60.4 | 61.7 | 59.5 | 56.8 |
| Total All Industries | 45.6 | 42.4 | 41.0 | 44.3 | 44.8 | 45.5 | 46.4 | 47.0 | 47.3 |

110

APPENDIX 12: PERCENTAGE EXPORTS BY INDUSTRY 1975–83

|  | 1975 | 1976 | 1977 | 1978 | 1979 | 1980 | 1981 | 1982 | 1983 |
|---|---|---|---|---|---|---|---|---|---|
| All Manufacturing | 53.7 | 54.3 | 56.9 | 52.3 | 52.3 | 53.5 | 51.9 | 52.1 | 50.2 |
| Food, Drink and Tobacco | 26.9 | 27.2 | 29.6 | 23.9 | 22.3 | 21.5 | 22.5 | 22.3 | 23.2 |
| Chemical and Allied Industries | 39.0 | 40.3 | 43.4 | 37.0 | 38.4 | 38.6 | 33.6 | 35.7 | 34.8 |
| Metal Manufacture | 66.4 | 66.4 | 68.4 | 62.2 | 66.3 | 64.7 | 78.0 | 76.0 | 82.7 |
| Mech. and Instrument Engineering | 67.7 | 66.9 | 62.8 | 67.6 | 69.3 | 68.6 | 69.6 | 71.1 | 68.8 |
| Electrical Engineering | 46.0 | 49.9 | 51.5 | 49.2 | 49.9 | 54.0 | 51.1 | 54.8 | 61.3 |
| Shipbuilding |  |  |  |  | 50.9 | 40.1 | 48.2 | 58.5 | 69.5 |
| Motor Vehicles | 83.2 | 84.9 | 83.2 | 83.3 | 85.8 | 88.2 | 77.2 | 69.2 | 60.4 |
| Textiles, Leather, Clothing and Footwear | 58.1 | 62.2 | 67.8 | 74.2 | 68.7 | 68.2 | 66.1 | 64.7 | 60.5 |
| Paper, Printing and Publishing | 26.3 | 28.0 | 34.7 | 30.4 | 31.0 | 30.1 | 33.7 | 32.6 | 33.3 |
| Rubber | 54.1 | 53.7 | 57.0 | 52.3 | 54.4 | 56.4 | 44.8 | 55.1 | 56.2 |
| Other Manufacturing | 56.5 | 52.1 | 62.4 | 49.2 | 51.9 | 53.9 | 54.8 | 53.1 | 43.2 |
| Total Non-Manufacturing | 14.8 | 14.4 | 19.7 | 29.0 | 34.2 | 34.5 | 33.5 | 34.7 | 38.0 |
| Total All Industries | 44.2 | 45.1 | 47.5 | 45.7 | 47.1 | 47.1 | 45.8 | 45.7 | 45.3 |

APPENDIX 13: PERCENTAGE LICENSED SALES BY INDUSTRY 1975–83

| | 1975 | 1976 | 1977 | 1978 | 1979 | 1980 | 1981 | 1982 | 1983 |
|---|---|---|---|---|---|---|---|---|---|
| All Manufacturing | 9.9 | 12.5 | 10.5 | 9.2 | 8.6 | 7.8 | 8.7 | 7.4 | 8.0 |
| Food, Drink and Tobacco | 2.1 | 4.7 | 3.2 | 2.8 | 2.7 | 2.9 | 3.1 | 3.2 | 2.6 |
| Chemical and Allied Industries | 20.5 | 21.7 | 17.0 | 12.9 | 13.0 | 14.0 | 16.8 | 12.7 | 15.8 |
| Metal Manufacture | 4.4 | 4.8 | 5.1 | 4.6 | 2.3 | 2.4 | 3.0 | 3.2 | 2.1 |
| Mech. and Instrument Engineering | 7.9 | 8.3 | 15.3 | 12.4 | 8.5 | 9.0 | 8.4 | 6.5 | 6.3 |
| Electrical Engineering | 12.0 | 11.4 | 11.2 | 10.5 | 12.1 | 3.1 | 7.2 | 3.1 | 3.0 |
| Shipbuilding | | | | | 39.9 | 52.8 | 48.3 | 35.9 | 20.5 |
| Motor Vehicles | 2.2 | 2.2 | 2.2 | 3.8 | 2.7 | 2.8 | 2.3 | 11.5 | 15.1 |
| Textiles, Leather, Clothing and Footwear | 1.8 | 2.4 | 1.6 | 1.0 | 1.1 | 1.2 | 1.0 | 1.0 | 1.8 |
| Paper, Printing and Publishing | 13.2 | 12.2 | 10.5 | 8.3 | 6.9 | 7.3 | 8.4 | 9.1 | 8.5 |
| Rubber | 4.3 | 5.7 | 5.5 | 3.7 | 1.8 | 1.9 | 2.2 | 6.1 | 14.3 |
| Other Manufacturing | 20.6 | 30.1 | 19.6 | 23.3 | 16.7 | 13.6 | 16.1 | 12.0 | 11.4 |
| Total Non-Manufacturing | 9.4 | 10.4 | 12.2 | 10.2 | 5.1 | 5.1 | 4.8 | 5.7 | 5.2 |
| Total All Industries | 10.2 | 12.5 | 11.5 | 10.0 | 8.1 | 7.4 | 7.8 | 7.2 | 7.4 |

## Notes

1. Vernon: 'As long as the marginal production cost plus the transport cost of the goods exported from the United States is lower than the average cost of prospective production in the market of import, United States producer will presumably prefer to avoid an investment. But that calculation depends on the producer's ability to project the cost of production in a market in which factor costs and the appropriate technology differ from those at home', (Dunning, 1972b: 313).
2. A selection of references are: Carlson (1975), Johanson and Vahlne (1977), Luostarinen (1980), Welch and Wiedersheim-Paul (1980a, 1980b), Wiedersheim-Paul (1972), Cavusgil (1972), and Juul and Walters (1987).
3. References are available in Porter (1986b).

## References

Y. Aharoni (1966). *The Foreign Investment Decision Process*, Boston, Mass. Graduate School of Business Administration, Harvard University.

R. Z. Aliber (1970). A theory of foreign direct investment, in: *The International Firm*, C. P. Kindleberger (ed.), Cambridge, Mass.: MIT Press.

R. D. Belli (1970). Sales of Foreign Affiliates of US Firms 1961–5, 1967 and 1968 *Survey of Current Business*, October.

M. Z. Brooke (1984). *Centralization and Autonomy*, Eastbourne: Holt, Rinehart and Winston.

P. J. Buckley (1982). The role of exporting in the market servicing policies of multinational manufacturing enterprises: theoretical and empirical perspectives, in: *Export Management*, M. R. Czinkota and G. Tesar (eds), New York: Praeger.

P. J. Buckley (1985). New forms of international industrial cooperation, in Buckley and Casson (1985a).

P. J. Buckley (1989). Foreign Market Servicing Strategies and Competitiveness: A Theoretical Framework, in: *International Strategic Management* A. R. Negandhi and Arun Savara (eds), Lexington, Mass. Lexington Books.

P. J. Buckley and P. F. R. Artisien (1987). *North-South Direct Investment in the European Communities*. London: Macmillan.

P. J. Buckley, Z. Berkova and G. D. Newbould (1983). *Direct Investment in the UK by Smaller European Firms*. London: Macmillan.

P. J. Buckley and M. Casson (1976). *The Future of the Multinational Enterprise*, London: Macmillan.

P. J. Buckley and M. Casson (1985a). *The Economic Theory of the Multinational Enterprise: Selected Readings*, London: Macmillan.

P. J. Buckley and M. Casson (1985b). The optimal timing of a foreign direct investment, in: Buckley and Casson (1985a).

P. J. Buckley and M. Casson (1987). A theory of cooperation in international business. In *Cooperative Strategies in International Business*, F. J Contractor and P. Lorange (eds), Lexington Mass.: Lexington Books, D. C

Heath and Co. Also in *Management International Review* (Special issues on cooperative strategies in international business) (1988), 19–38.

P. J. Buckley and H. Davies (1980). Foreign licensing in overseas operations: theory and evidence from the UK, in: *Technology Transfer and Economic Development*, Greenwich, Conn.: JAI Press.

P. J. Buckley, H. Mirza and J. R. Sparkes (1984). European affiliates in Japan. *Tokyo Report to the Japan Foundation*.

P. J. Buckley, H. Mirza and J. R. Sparkes (1987). Direct foreign investment in Japan as a means of market entry. *Journal of Marketing Management* 2(3), Spring, 241–58.

P. J. Buckley, G. D. Newbould and J. Thurwell (1988). *Foreign Direct Investment by Smaller UK Firms*, London: Macmillan. 1st edn published as *Going International – The Experiences of UK Firms Overseas* (1978), London: Associated Business Press.

P. J. Buckley and R. D. Pearce (1979). Overseas production and exporting by the world's largest enterprise – a study in sourcing policy *Journal of International Business Studies*, 10(1), 9–20.

P. J. Buckley and R. D. Pearce (1981). Market servicing by multinational manufacturing firms: exporting versus foreign production. *Managerial and Economics* 2(4), 229–46.

P. J. Buckley and R. D. Pearce (1984). Exports in the strategy of multinational enterprises. *Journal of Business Research* 12(2), 209–26.

S. Carlson (1975). *How Foreign is Foreign Trade?* Uppsala: University of Uppsala.

M. Casson (1985) Multinational and intermediate product trade. In Buckley and Casson (1985a).

M. Casson (ed.) (1986). *Multinationals and World Trade*, London: Allen & Unwin.

S. T. Cavusgil (1972). Some observations on the relevance of critical variables for internationalisation stages, in: *Export Management*, M. R. Czinkota and G. Tesar (eds), New York: Praeger.

J. Clegg (1987). *Multinational Enterprise and World Competition*, London: Macmillan.

H. Davies (1972a). Technology transfer through commercial transactions. *Journal of Industrial Economics* 26(4), 161–75.

J. H. Dunning (1972a). The location of international firms in an enlarged EEC: an exploratory paper. Manchester: Manchester Statistical Society.

J. H. Dunning (ed.) (1972b). *International Investment*, Harmondsworth: Penguin.

J. H. Dunning (ed.) (1981). *International Production and the Multinational Enterprise*, London: Allen & Unwin.

J. H. Dunning and P. J. Buckley (1977). International production and alternative models of trade. *Manchester School* 65(4), 392–403.

European Management Forum (1984). *Report on Industrial Competitiveness* 1984, Switzerland: EMIF.

I. H. Giddy (1978). The demise of the product cycle in international business theory. *Columbia Journal of World Business* 13(1), 90–7.

I. H. Giddy and A. M. Rugman (1979). A model of trade, foreign direct investment and licencing. Columbia University, mimeo, New York.

J.-F. Hennart (1986). What is internalization? *Weltwirtschaftliches Archiv.* 122(4), 791–804.

114       *Foreign Market Servicing Strategies*

S. Hirsh (1976). An international trade and investment theory of the firm. *Oxford Economic Papers* **28**, 258–70.

N. Hood and S. Young (1979). *The Economics of Multinational Enterprise*, London: Longman.

T. O. Horst (1971). The theory of the multinational firm – optimal behaviour under different tariff and tax rates. *Journal of Political Economy* **79**(5), 1059–72.

T. O. Horst (1972). Firm and industry determinants of the decision to investment abroad: an empirical study. *Review of Economics and Statistics* **54**, 258–66.

T. O. Horst (1974). The theory of the firm, in: *Economic Analysis and the Multinational Enterprise*, J. H. Dunning (ed.), London: Allen & Unwin.

J. Johanson and J. E. Vahine (1977). The internationalization process of the firm – a model of knowledge development and increasing foreign market commitments. *Journal of International Business Studies* **8**(1), 23–32.

F. T. Knickerbocker (1973). *Oligopolistic Reaction and Multinational Enterprise* Cambridge, Mass: Harvard University Press.

P. R. Krugman (ed.) (1986). *Strategic Trade Policy and the New International Economic*, **27**(1), 58–66.

R. Luostarinen (1978). *Internationalization of the Firm*, Helsinki: Helsinki School of Economics.

K. Ohmae (1985). *Triad Power: The Coming Shape of Global Competition*, New York: The Free Press.

S. Nicholas (1986). The theory of multinational enterprise as a transaction mode, in: *Multinational: Theory and History*, P. Hertner and G. Jones (eds), Aldershot: Gower.

J. Polk, F. W. Meister and L. A. Veit (1966) *US Production Abroad and the Balance of Payments*. New York: The National Industrial Conference Board.

M. E. Porter (1986a). Competition in global industries: a conceptual framework, in: Porter (1986b).

M. E. Porter (ed.) (1986b). Competition in global industries. Boston, Mass.: Harvard Business School Press.

D. Shepherd, A. Silbertson and R. Strange (1985) *British Manufacturing Investment Overseas*. London: Methuen.

F. M. Sherer *et al.* (1975). *The Economics of Multi-Plant Operation – An International Comparison Study*, Cambridge, Mass.: Harvard University Press.

H. Simon and D. M. Palder (1987). Market entry in Japan – some problems and solutions. *Journal of Marketing Management* **2**(3), 225–39.

R. Vernon (1966). International investment and international trade in the product cycle. *QuarterJournal of Economics* **80**, 190–207.

L. Welch and F. Wiedersheim-Paul (1980a). Domestic expansion – internationalization at home. *South Carolina Essays in International Business* **2**.

L. Welch and F. Wiedersheim-Paul (1980b). Initial exports – a marketing failure. *Journal of Management Studies* **17**(3).

R. G. White and T. A Poynter (1984). Strategies for foreign-owned subsidiiaries in Canada. *Business Quarterly*.

F. Wiedersheim-Paul (1972). Uncertainty and economic distance. *Uppsala Studies in International Business*, Uppsala University.

S. Young (1987). Business strategy and the internationalization of business: recent approaches. *Managerial and Decision Economics* **8**(1), 31–40.

# 7 Foreign Market Servicing Strategies and Competitiveness*

(*with* Christopher L. Pass and Kate Prescott)

Firms adopt markedly different approaches in servicing their foreign markets. A subsidiary company tends to be preferred to licensing or to using agents. This is seen as the best way to get closer to customers and achieve long-term benefits.

## INTRODUCTION

The growing 'openness' of the world economy, fostered by trade liberalization programmes and the formation of various free trade blocs and common markets, together with the expansion of multinational companies (MNCs), has served to sharpen the competitive pressures facing UK companies in international markets. In this article we report the results of a study of the foreign market servicing strategies of a sample of UK manufacturing firms in their attempts to advance and protect their international competitiveness.[1]

We begin by looking at a number of general aspects of competitiveness and foreign market servicing strategy.

## (i) Competitiveness

'Competitiveness' may be defined as the ability of a firm to meet and beat its rivals in supplying a product on a sustainable (long-

* *Journal of General Management*, Vol. 17, No. 2, Winter 1991, pp. 34–46 (reprinted by permission).

term) and viable (profitable) basis.[2] In the international context, this rules out, for example, short-term 'dumping' where market share is 'bought' by selling the product at unprofitable prices. Competitive success is underpinned by the possession of firm-specific competitive advantages over rival suppliers.[3] These are of two main types – low costs and product differentiation. Low costs, particularly in the supply of standardized products, help the firm not only to survive price competition should it become fierce but often enable it to assume the role of market 'leader' in establishing price levels which ensure high and stable levels of market profitability. The sources of cost effectiveness are varied, including the exploitation of economies of scale to lower unit costs, investment in best state-of-the-art technology and preferential access to raw materials and distribution channels. Over time, investment in plant renewal, modernization and process innovation is essential to maintain cost advantages.

In the case of product differentiation a firm seeks to be unique in its market along a dimension that is valued by its customers. Product differentiation possibilities vary from market to market but are associated with the potential for distinguishing products by variations in their physical properties and attributes and the 'satisfaction' – real and psychological – imparted by the product to consumers. Again, given the dynamic nature of markets, competitive advantage in this area needs to be sustained by an active programme of new product innovation and the upgrading of existing products.

Operating internationally adds a number of other dimensions to competitiveness;[4] for example, the possibility that the advantage of low production costs deriving from centralized plants might be offset, wholly or in part, by the extra costs of physical distribution to remote markets, or negated, in price terms, by the imposition of tariffs or a currency appreciation. Likewise, in the case of product differentiation, cultural differences between countries often require firms to 'customize' their marketing efforts and modify products to meet local buyer preferences.

## (ii) Foreign Market Servicing Strategy

There are three generic strategies which may be deployed by firms in supplying their products to overseas markets – exporting, licensing and foreign direct investment.[5] The first two forms of market servicing can be used by firms operating out of a single 'home' country base, while the latter is the hallmark of a multinational company (i.e. a firm which owns income-generating assets – mines, manufacturing plants, offices, sales subsidiaries – in two or more countries).

Exporting (X) involves production in one country, with products being sold in overseas markets. This can take the form of indirect exports with the firm using various market intermediaries (agents, distributors, trading companies etc) to handle overseas sales, or direct exports handled by the firm's own export departments. Licensing (L) involves the assignment of production and selling rights by a firm to producers in target markets in return for a lump sum and/or on-going royalty payments. Foreign direct investment (FDI) involves the firm establishing its own production and selling facilities in overseas markets. This can take the form of a new greenfield investment, a merger with, or takeover of, an established supplier, or a joint-venture arrangement.[6]

At its most simple, X can be distinguished from the other two methods of market servicing by the *location effect* as with exports the bulk of value adding activity takes place in the home country, whilst the other two methods transfer all or a high proportion of value adding activity to host country markets. Similarly, L can be distinguished from X and FDI by the *exter-*

*Figure 7.1*    Foreign market servicing strategy choices

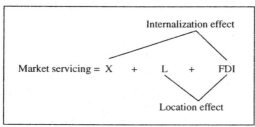

# 118 Foreign Market Servicing Strategies

*nalization effect.* In licensing, the firm sells rights and the use o
assets (know-how, production methods, brand names, etc.) to a
'outside' firm, the licensee. In X and FDI such activities ar
*internalized* and remain within the initiating firm. Broadly then
the location and internalization effects separate the three generi
forms of market servicing.

### (iii) Foreign Market Servicing Strategy and Its Impact on Competitiveness

We are now in a position to look at the *interrelationship* betwee
foreign market servicing strategy and the maintenance an
enhancement of a firm's competitive advantage.[7] In resource an
competitive terms, exporting from an established 'home' produc
tion plant is a relatively inexpensive and low risk way of servic
ing a foreign market (i.e. it obviates the need to invest i
overseas plants) and maximum advantage can be taken of cen
tralized production to secure economies of scale and thus lowe
unit costs. On the other hand, the firm could be put at a com
petitive disadvantage either because of local producers' lowe
cost structures (deriving, for example, from lower labour costs
and control of distribution channels, or because of governmenta
tariffs, quotas and other restrictions on imports as well as advers
currency movements. Moreover, in the case of indirect exportin
export performance may be retarded by a 'poor' selection o
agents and distributors (lacking commitment, motivation an
resources to provide satisfactory sales cover and marketing
Licensing may be attractive because it enables a firm, particu
larly one constrained by a shortage of management and capita
resources, to gain rapid market penetration, and because it doe
not involve direct entry into the market it thus avoids head-o
competition with local suppliers. On the other hand, the royaltie
obtained may represent a poor return on an innovative process o
product, with the ultimate danger that the technology or produc
may be 'captured' and developed further by competitors leadin
to the elimination of the firm's initial competitive advantage
Foreign direct investment can be expensive and risky, althoug
host country governments often offer subsidies etc to attra

nward investment, and investment costs can be lowered by
stablishing a joint venture with a local partner. In many cases,
owever, the 'presence' effects of operating locally (familiarity
vith local market conditions, the cultivation of contacts with
ɔcal suppliers, distributors and government agencies, and the
rovision of back-up services such as maintenance and repair)
ıay be important factors in building profitable market share over
ıe long term. Moreover, direct investment by internalizing
arious aspects of a firm's market servicing operation may
nable the MNC both to avoid the transaction costs of using the
ıarket (specifically, the costs of concluding and policing con-
racts with agents, distributors etc) and to increase its marketing
ffectiveness through a greater control of key distribution and
ıarketing functions.

In sum, the selection of an appropriate foreign maket servicing
trategy designed to enhance and protect the competitiveness of
ıe firm is dependent on an amalgam of *firm-specific factors* (e.g.
ıe nature and 'uniqueness' of the firm's competitive advantage,
nd resource availability), *industry-specific factors* in target
ıarkets (e.g. the level of market concentration and the extent of
arriers to entry), and *location/country-specific factors* (e.g. the
xtent to which products need to be adapted to meet local
ɔquirements, host government policies on tarrifs, subsidies, etc).

## ˈOLICIES ON MARKET SERVICING

˙he main proposition addressed in the study is that the inter-
ational competitiveness of a firm is dependent on the selection
f an appropriate set of foreign market servicing strategies and
ıe effective *management* of the chosen market servicing modes.
n-depth interviews were conducted with thirteen manufacturing
rms[A] (see p. 136) operating in three industry groups (scientific
ıstruments, pharmaceuticals and decorative paints) who re-
orted a total of 22 foreign market servicing mode changes
ı respect of their operations in Europe, the USA and
apan/Australia. The sampled firms varied greatly in size (and
ssociated *resources* available for international expansion) and

*experience* of international operations from 'small-sized' firms (turnover under £25 million) with only a limited international involvement, mainly exports; 'medium-sized' firms (turnover £26m–£200m) making further internationalization moves, often involving FDI for the first time; and 'large-sized' firms (turnover £201m plus), mainly established multinational concerns with extensive international operations. Thus, it is recognized that the choice of particular foreign market servicing strategies is dependent, in part, on resource constraints (financial and managerial, in particular) and 'maturity' (i.e. whether the firm is a 'first time' international operator or an experienced MNC).

## The Sample

Our sample of thirteen companies and the outcome of the investigation are shown in Tables 7.1–3. Each table lists the target market and key competitive advantages of the firms. The switch in foreign market servicing is shown in columns three and four ('before' and 'after'). The penultimate column describes the impact of the current form of foreign market servicing mode on competitiveness and the final column examines likely changes in this form.

### 1. Scientific Instruments

The scientific instruments industry is an important intermediate good industry which supplies a diverse range of low-medium-high technology products for research, healthcare, defence and industrial process control and automation. Internationally, the industry, despite the presence of a number of major multinational companies, remains fragmented. Small and medium-sized firms compete successfully with larger firms. Small firms tend to be specialized whilst the larger firms often produce instruments along with other capital goods (e.g. laboratory chemicals, diagnostic kits, etc.) or have fairly diversified instrument product lines. The major producer countries of scientific instruments globally are: USA, Japan, France, Germany, Italy, UK, Holland, Sweden, Switzerland. These same countries are the major users of instruments because of their high technology levels, the importance of their research and development sectors and their sophisticated industrial production systems.

The five firms analysed in the scientific instruments sector differ in scale, scope and product range. In the main their key competitive advantages internationally related to low cost production. Only one firm (1.4) has a high quality, research-backed product.

As Table 7.1 shows the predominant form of foreign market servicing prior to the switches in mode which were undertaken was exporting through an intermediary–an agent or distributor. In many cases this was felt to be unsatisfactory because of a lack of commitment from the intermediary, because of slow responses to customers' needs or problems related to the lack of a presence. Many of the intermediaries were deemed to be unsuccessful because of their lack of market coverage (by geographical area or product lines).

The market servicing switches were largely in changing the form of exporting either by changing the intermediary or replacing an 'arm's length' intermediary with a sales subsidiary. In general, the sales subsidiary was acknowledged to be the optimum form of foreign market servicing by the scientific instruments firms. Lack of finance and unwillingness to undertake the necessary risks prevented the firms in some situations from moving towards what they perceived to be the optimal form. In our small sample, moves towards foreign production did not prove successful.

## 2. *Pharmaceuticals*

The term 'pharmaceuticals' covers a wide spectrum of health-care products ranging from drugs used in the clinical treatment of heart, respiratory and nervous system disorders to items used to treat more minor ailments such as headaches, coughs and colds. 'Ethical' pharmaceuticals refers to the former category of drugs and forms the focus for this study.

Within the ethical pharmaceuticals sector, firms can be divided into two distinct groups: global firms specializing in research-intensive 'patented' drugs with a wide distribution network for

Table 7.1   Scientific instrument firms

| Firm Code and Market | Competitive Advantages | Previous Foreign Market Servicing Mode | Current Foreign Market Servicing Mode | Impact of Current Foreign Market Servicing Mode on Competitiveness (Defined in terms of profitable market share) | Likely Change in Foreign Market Servicing Mode to improve Performance |
|---|---|---|---|---|---|
| 1.1 USA | Low costs/prices product line depth | Exports through agents | Sales subsidiary (take-over of firm selling related spares and accessories) | Strongly positive | Would consider a manufacturing plant if exchange rates became a problem |
| Germany | | | Exports through distributor | Poor (but improving slowly) | Sales subsidiary (but held back by financial constraints) |
| 1.2 USA | Low costs/prices product quality | Exports through distributor | Direct export sales to end-users | Positive (but limited) | Sales subsidiary (but financial constraints) |

*Table* 7.1  Contd.

| Firm Code and Market | Competitive Advantages | Previous Foreign Market Servicing Mode | Current Foreign Market Servicing Mode | Impact of Current Foreign Market Servicing Mode on Competitiveness (Defined in terms of profitable market share) | Likely Change in Foreign Market Servicing Mode to improve Performance |
|---|---|---|---|---|---|
| France | | Exports through 'unknown' distributor | Exports through 'known' distributor (ex-company employee) | Positve (but distributor lacks wide market coverage and financial resources) | Buy-out the distributor (but financial constraints of their own) |
| 1.3 France | Low costs/prices product quality R&D | Exports through distributor | Joint venture with French company (1989) | Early days, sales and profits up after 'teething problems' | |
| Germany | | Exports through distributor | Wholly-owned sales subsidiary (1988) | Early days, sales and profits improving | |

*Table* 7.1  Contd.

| Firm Code and Market | Competitive Advantages | Previous Foreign Market Servicing Mode | Current Foreign Market Servicing Mode | Impact of Current Foreign Market Servicing Mode on Competitiveness (Defined in terms of profitable market share) | Likely Change in Foreign Market Servicing Mode to improve Performance |
|---|---|---|---|---|---|
| USA | | Exports through distributor, bought-out distributor and set up sales subsidiary | Wholly-owned Greenfield manufacturing plant (1988) | Negative. Currently losing money | Exit costs high; need to improve marketing |
| 1.4 USA | Product quality R&D | Sales subsidiary | Manufacturing subsidiary (take-over of firm selling complimentary product range) | Negative, acquired firm losing money – turn round still to be achieved | Sales subsidiary ideal for selling complex equipment; low technology items could be sold more effectively through a network of distributors giving wider geographic coverage |

*Table* 7.1  Contd.

| Firm Code and Market | Competitive Advantages | Previous Foreign Market Servicing Mode | Current Foreign Market Servicing Mode | Impact of Current Foreign Market Servicing Mode on Competitiveness (Defined in terms of profitable market share) | Likely Change in Foreign Market Servicing Mode to improve Performance |
|---|---|---|---|---|---|
| 1.5 France | Low costs/prices (but its products lack 'uniqueness') | | Exports through distributor | Positive, but not outstanding | Distributor has started manufacturing. Company is considering the establishment of a sales subsidiary (but financial constraints) |
| USA | | | Exports through a distributor in which it has an equity stake | Poor (ineffectual management and communication problems) | Sales subsidiary (but financial constraints) |

their products, reflecting the significance of economies of scale and the vast sums of money required to undertake risky research and development; and firms who concentrate on 'generic' drugs (i.e. drugs on which the patent rights have expired) principally in their own markets.

The main markets for pharmaceuticals are the USA (29 per cent of world sales), Japan (20 per cent), Germany (8 per cent), France (7 per cent), Italy (7 per cent) and the UK (3 per cent). Governments play a pervasive role in the industry's affairs. They are key purchasers of ethical drugs and it is important for companies to get their drugs placed on 'approved' lists. Lengthy safety and efficacy trials reduce the *effective* patent life (normally 20 years in Europe and 17 years in the USA) of most drugs by about half so that companies are under a strong imperative to recoup R&D expenses and make profits by rapid and extensive international marketing. The customary policy of many governments to place a high proportion of their orders with indigenous producers has encouraged international companies to invest in local manufacturing plant. Governments also dictate the prices of new drugs they are prepared to buy. In recent years, attempts by governments to reduce their healthcare spending has led to price cuts and lower industry margins.

Competition in the industry is focused primarily on the search for new drugs. For the leading companies research and development intensity is high (R&D expenditures typically average 10–15 per cent of company turnover), with companies operating under a constant imperative to bring out a succession of new products to augment/replace ones whose patent protection has expired or which have been made obsolete by technical advance.

Our sample includes global firms selling patented ethical drug products worldwide and smaller generic drugs producers. Naturally, their competitive advantages differ according to subsector (Table 7.2), the ethical drug producers relying on patent and R&D back-up and the desperate rush to find new drugs whilst the generic producers rely on low costs and the development of existing products and market deepening and widening.

For generic producers, the major 'switches' in foreign market servicing were into exporting from a low or zero base. The results may be characterized as 'slow progress'.

*Table* 7.2  Pharmaceutical firms

| Firm Code and Market | Competitive Advantages | Previous Foreign Market Servicing Mode | Current Foreign Market Servicing Mode | Impact of Current Foreign Market Servicing Mode on Competitiveness (Defined in Terms of Profitable Market Share) | Likely Change in Foreign Market Serving Mode to Improve Performance |
|---|---|---|---|---|---|
| 2.1 Japan | Patented drugs, R&D | Licensing of major indigenous manufacturer | 50/50 Joint venture with former licencee (local manufacturing and marketing); 'active ingredients' exported | Strongly positive | Possibly a wholly-owned subsidiary to capitalize on their 'learning experiences' of the market |
| Australia | | Exports of patented drugs through distributor | Acquired a generic manufacturing company (1974) | Poor, due to government price controls | Likely to pull out, unless government becomes more 'sympathetic' |

Table 7.2  Contd.

| Firm Code and Market | Competitive Advantages | Previous Foreign Market Servicing Mode | Current Foreign Market Servicing Mode | Impact of Current Foreign Market Servicing Mode on Competitiveness (Defined in Terms of Profitable Market Share) | Likely Change in Foreign Market Serving Mode to Improve Performance |
|---|---|---|---|---|---|
| 2.2 France | Patented drugs R&D | Direct exporting | Greenfield manufacturing/sales subsidiary (1989); 'active ingredients' exported from UK | Strongly positive | Proposes a major rethink of the location of its manufacturing/ sales subsidiaries in the light of the Single European Market 1992 initiative |
| 2.3 (General) | Generics specialist low costs/prices | | 'Incidental' exporting | Very marginal | Intends to put exporting on a firm footing in the light of the Single European Market initiative, possibly using agents or sales subsidiaries (but financial constraints are a problem) |

*Table 7.2* Contd.

| Firm Code and Market | Competitive Advantages | Previous Foreign Market Servicing Mode | Current Foreign Market Servicing Mode | Impact of Current Foreign Market Servicing Mode on Competitiveness (Defined in Terms of Profitable Market Share) | Likely Change in Foreign Market Serving Mode to Improve Performance |
|---|---|---|---|---|---|
| 2.4 USA | Patented drugs R&D | Exports through agents augmented by co-marketing with European producer's US sales subsidiary | Takeover of small manufacturing company (1974) as a prelude to establishment of major Greenfield manufacturing/sales facility; 'active ingredients' exported from US | Strongly positive | |

Table 7.2 Contd.

| Firm Code and Market | Competitive Advantages | Previous Foreign Market Servicing Mode | Current Foreign Market Servicing Mode | Impact of Current Foreign Market Servicing Mode on Competitiveness (Defined in Terms of Profitable Market Share) | Likely Change in Foreign Market Serving Mode to Improve Performance |
|---|---|---|---|---|---|
| Japan | | Exports through agent | Established 50/50 sales subsidiary with major Japanese manufacturer (1968) followed by Greenfield manufacturing plant; 'active ingredients' exported from UK | Strongly positive, but 'could do better' with more effective marketing | |
| 2.5 USA | Patented drugs and generics. Development rather than basic research | | Exports through a number of distribution selected to service particular market segments | Positive (but slow progress) | FDI operation (but financial constraints) |

The major ethical producers were predominantly concerned with a switch from either exporting or licensing to some form of local market presence, usually a manufacturing presence. For these large firms, determined entry into major markets proved highly positive. (The exception is firm 2.1 in Australia where external factors, notably the role of government, were held to be the cause of problems.) For some companies, it will be noted, production of the 'active ingredients' of their drugs (the patented element of the drug) is centralized in the UK in order to protect key proprietary know-how. Active ingredients are then exported to overseas production plants undertaking secondary manufacturing operations and packaging operations, often involving the customization of products to suit local preferences and prescription requirements.

## 3. Decorative Paint

The industry has experienced a number of competitive pressures in recent years arising from market maturity and overcapacity in some countries and the squeezing of profit margins by large retail buyers. This has led to various rationalization moves in the industry and strategic rethinks with some companies broadening their interests both in terms of geographical and product spread, while others have retrenched into specialist niche sectors.

Overall, industry concentration levels have increased, and multinational companies have come to dominate the global industry. Internationalization has come about primarily by mergers and takeovers and to a lesser extent greenfield expansion and licensing agreements. Given the nature of the product, which is bulky and expensive to transport, there is only a small volume of export trade in paint. North America is the leading market with around 31 per cent of world sales, followed by Europe (29 per cent) and the Asia/Pacific region (24 per cent).

Again the three firms analysed in this industry cover the spectrum from global players to niche marketeers (Table 7.3). Correspondingly, their competitive advantages are based either on innovative products and R&D or on low costs of production. Except for the dominant player (3.1), production is centralized in the UK and so switches in mode are confined to export switches

*Table 7.3*  Decorative paint firms

| Firm Code and Market | Competitive Advantage | Previous Foreign Market Servicing Mode | Current Foreign Market Servicing Mode | Impact of Current Foreign Market Serving Mode on Competitiveness (Defined in Terms of Profitable Market Share) | Likely Change in Foreign Market Servicing Mode to Improve Performance |
|---|---|---|---|---|---|
| 3.1 Sweden | Innovative products R&D | (Exports of industrial paints) | Exports through deal with major retailing group in Sweden in order to overcome problems of market access | Positive (knock-on effect into other markets), but potential limited by partners own scale of operations | |
| West Germany | | | Manufacturing subsidiary (1975) (takeover of number of local companies) | Limited, competitive potential impaired by integration and communication problems | Proposes a major re-think of the location of its European manufacturing/sales subsidiaries to provide a more coherent operational/strategic fit. |

*Table* 7.3  Contd.

| Firm Code and Market | Competitive Advantage | Previous Foreign Market Servicing Mode | Current Foreign Market Servicing Mode | Impact of Current Foreign Market Serving Mode on Competitiveness (Defined in Terms of Profitable Market Share) | Likely Change in Foreign Market Servicing Mode to Improve Performance |
|---|---|---|---|---|---|
| 3.2 USA | Innovative products R&D | | Exports through distributor | Positive, but potential limited by distributors size | Possibly a wholly-owned manufacturing/sales subsidiary |
| 3.3 France | Low costs/price 'own label' specialist | Exports through distributor | Sales manager (ex-buyer from French supermarket group) | Positive, steady progress | Possibly a depot/sales subsidiary (but financial constraints) |
| West Germany | | | Exports through main distributor and regional agents | Positive, but limited to date | Possibly a depot/sales subsidiary (but financial constraints) |

and, as in the case of scientific instruments, success is severely constrained by the ability, commitment and scope of the intermediary be it distributor, agent or foreign sales manager. The dominant player, having switched to production in the foreign market via the takeover route, was intending to move to a more rational location of foreign subsidiaries by a major reorganization. Similarly 3.2 saw a wholly-owned manufacturing and sales subsidiary as its ultimate aim. The low cost producer (3.3) saw a number of depot/sales subsidiaries as the best form of servicing its (European) foreign markets.

## The Three Sectors Compared

Our sample illustrates the necessity to match the foreign market servicing stance with the competitive advantages which the firm possesses relative to its competitors and to industry and market conditions.

It is generally acknowledged that, because of the need to control quality and gain economies of scale in specialist markets, core production will be centralized as in scientific instruments. There is, however, near unanimity in that industry that sales subsidiaries in foreign markets are essential to deal satisfactorily with customer needs, to respond rapidly and to control and co-ordinate marketing and production. This has something in common with the generic pharmaceutical producers who operate under similar constraints. However the imperative for patented ethical drug producers is local manufacturing largely to cater for local governmental regulations but partly for market presence and 'closeness to the customer' requirements. The decorative paint industry appears to be at the moment more like the scientific instrument pattern—relying on centralized production but with dispersed sales/depot arrangements. However, the pan-European rationalization of production which is currently underway suggests that this industry's future is much more in line with ethical drugs based on dispersed production catering for local markets, founded on a strong central core.

CONCLUSION

The selection of an appropriate foreign market servicing mode is clearly an important element of the competitiveness of a firm operating in international markets. This choice is often limited due to constraints imposed on firms by their products, host market conditions, or their own financial and managerial constraints. From our sample, a number of firms were unable to take the optimal route due to financial constraints. However, in some cases this was self-imposed (i.e. they had resources to invest but were too concerned with short-term as opposed to long-term profit returns). Even where firms were not limited financially, our sample reveals that firms show markedly different approaches to foreign market servicing. This often reflects the character of individual companies and the diverse nature of management structures and styles from which differing strategic approaches emerge.

A number of interesting considerations arise from the firms sampled. Some firms found exporting through agents/distributors to be 'unsatisfactory' and switched to alternative modes of market servicing. However, it should be emphasized that many firms have forged highly successful relationships with their agents/distributors.[8] A key factor in this respect is the selection of the 'right' intermediary (one which has the resources and incentives to promote the firm's products to the maximum effect), and the establishment of a good *two-way* dialogue and commitment between the two (or more) parties. The firms sampled generally avoided licensing because of its potential for undermining competitive advantages, although, again, it can be usefully employed by financially constrained firms or used to secure entry into 'difficult' markets.[9] There was a consensus of opinion that some form of market presence is required to service overseas markets effectively. For firms who choose not to manufacture abroad, the nature of the ideal presence is a sales/marketing subsidiary. The major benefit offered by pursuing this strategy is 'closeness to customers' which is perceived by most managers as a way of overcoming problems of cultural and business naivety when selling abroad, allowing firms a better understanding of consumers and competitors in targeted markets. Above all, even where firms have a well-defined approach to foreign market servicing the need for a *long-termist* and *flexible* outlook is considered to be particularly important. The former underpins learning curve effects[10] and encourages the firm to seek long-term rather than short-term profit returns; the latter emphasizes (given the different nuances and characteristics of different markets) the need to approach each market separately-looking to the optimum mode of servicing individual markets rather than attempting a holistic, global strategy.

## Notes

A. Coded as follows to preserve anonymity:-
   Scientific instrument firms (1.1 to 1.5).
   Pharmaceutical firms (2.1 to 2.5).
   Decorative paint firms (3.1 to 3.3).

1. This paper was part of a three-year project at the University of Bradford Management Centre 'The Foreign Market Servicing Strategies and Competitiveness of British Firms' sponsored by the ESRC in the Competitiveness and Regeneration of British Industry Research Programme (Grant No. F20250027).

2. Buckley, Peter J., Pass, C. L. and Prescott, Kate, 'Measures of International Competitiveness: A Critical Survey', *Journal of Marketing Management,* Vol. 4, No. 2, Winter 1988.

3. Porter M. E., *Competitive Advantage: Creating and Sustaining Superior Performance,* Free Press, 1985.

4. Porter, M. E., (ed.), *Competition in Global Industries*, Harvard University Press, 1986.

5. Buckley, Peter J. and Casson, M., *The Future of the Multinational Enterprise,* Macmillan, 1976.

6. Root, F. R., *Entry Strategies for International Markets,* Lexington Books 1989.

7. Willard, G. and Savara, A. M., 'Patterns of Entry: Pathways to New Markets', *California Management Review,* XXX, No. 2, 1988.

8. Anderson, E. and Coughlan, A. T., 'International Market Entry and Expansion via Independent or Integrated Channels of Distribution' *Journal of Marketing,* Vol. 51, January 1987.

9. Buckley, Peter J. and Davies, H., 'Foreign Licensing in Overseas Operations: Theory and Evidence from the UK', in *Technology Transfer and Economic Development,* JAI Press, 1980.

10. Johanson, J. and Vahlne, J., 'The Internationalisation Process of the Firm' *Journal of Management Studies,* Volume 8, Spring/Summer 1977.

# 8 UK International Joint Ventures: An Analysis of Patterns of Activity and Distribution*

(*with* Keith Glaister)

## 1 INTRODUCTION

Over the past decade or so there has been an increased interest by academic observers in inter-firm collaboration, largely fuelled by the apparent growing incidence of such collaboration as a form of corporate strategy (see, for example, the contributions to Contractor and Lorange, 1988a). Joint ventures are not in fact a new phenomenon, but have long been used by firms to move into new businesses and tap new markets, particularly where firms were expanding overseas. For instance entry by large UK or US multinational firms into overseas markets often required them to take local firms as partners. This was especially so within developing nations and socialist countries where, in order to penetrate the market, companies had to form joint ventures with domestic firms to satisfy host Government regulations. From the late 1970s, however, there has been an increased incidence of joint venture activity within industrial free market economies. Firms in Europe, the USA and Japan have formed joint ventures on a voluntary basis as a deliberate strategy in preference to undertaking an activity on their own behalf or through a fully owned subsidiary. It is increasingly the case today that companies are willing to entertain the possibility of cooperation as part of their strategic planning (Harrigan, 1988, p. 142; Lyons, 1991).

The recognition that the nature of joint venture formation has changed since the late 1970s is stressed by Viesti (1988: 1) who

* *British Journal of Management*, Vol. 5, No. 1, March 1994, pp. 33–51 (reprinted by permission of John Wiley & Sons Ltd).

has identified three principal characteristics which distinguish the new types.

(1) There has been an increase in collaboration between major firms in advanced countries and, at the same time, a significant increase in collaboration initiatives between large multinational companies and small businesses, particularly in the high-tech area.

(2) Recent joint ventures have an important technological content and often concern joint R and D projects between two or more firms.

(3) In the past the joint venture relationship has mainly involved a small company, usually acting on a sub-contracting basis, for a large purchaser (Hladik, 1985: 18) The more recent tendency has increasingly favoured balanced agreements between firms, often located at the same stages of the production cycle, which have similar products and are mutually competitive and equally strong on the market. Agreements of this type have often been described as strategic partnerships or, in cases involving two companies which are developing a common long run strategy for the entire world market, 'global strategic partnerships'.

The growth of joint venture activity is due to a number of factors but particularly important has been the rapid rate of technological change and an increased emphasis on a strategy of globalization. In industries characterized by technological sophistication and rapid technological change, such as semiconductors and computers, only the very largest firms can independently carry the risks of accelerating R and D costs. At the same time shrinking product life cycles leave less time over which to recover these costs. Thus firms, especially those not the largest in their industry, may cooperate in order to reduce the risks involved. Another important new use that firms have made of joint ventures has been in developing global strategies, which recognize that competition can no longer be confined to a single nation's boundaries. Increasingly, joint ventures are being established as part of the network of business units that firms use to cope with world-scale competition (Harrigan, 1985).

The transaction cost approach to joint ventures, following Coase (1937) and Williamson (1975) as developed by Buckley and Casson (1988) identifies three primary motives for the establishment of joint ventures. These are (1) the existence of net benefits from internalizing a market in one or more intermediate goods or services between the joint venture and the parties' other operations, (2) an element of economic indivisibility which results in benefits from avoiding splitting up the joint venture in one or more separately owned facilities and (3) the existence of disadvantages to merger. Doz *et al.* (1990) examined international collaboration as the working out of 'key capabilities'. Three are identified: Strategic control, anticipation and redeployment. The challenge of maintaining integration, responsiveness and flexibility can be undermined by transnational partnerships. Their belief is that instability will cause many joint ventures to implode into unitary ownership. Resource dependency theory (Pfeffer and Salancik, 1978) also holds some fundamental propositions on organizational – environmental interdependencies. Its application to joint ventures (Pfeffer and Nowak, 1976) takes them as exemplary of interorganizational linkage. Interim links, such as joint ventures are, in this approach, undertaken in order to manage interfirm interdependence. Firms which control resources required by others but who do not depend on others for resources have a strong position in the network.

It is often suggested that the increasing frequency and strategic importance of joint ventures are likely to continue during the 1990s (Anderson, 1990). It is also a popular view that UK firms have been caught up in the accelerating trend to establish joint venture agreements. To date, however, no study has presented data which specifically considers the detailed activity of UK firms in joint venture formation over a significant period of time. This paper attempts to rectify the paucity of data reported on UK joint venture formation. The principal goal is to provide a factual picture of joint venture formation between UK firms and partner firms in Western Europe, USA and Japan over the decade of the 1980s. To this end the rest of the paper is set out as follows: Section 2 considers the nature of international cooperation and the way in which joint ventures have been defined for the purpose of this study. Section 3 indicates the nature of the data source. Section 4 reports the patterns of international joint venture formation by UK firms during the 1980s. A summary and conclusions are presented in Section 5. A summary of the hypotheses relating to the findings and the results of the relevant statistical tests are shown in Table 8.15.

## 2   DEFINING JOINT VENTURES

Cooperative arrangements between firms of different nationalities are of many kinds, serving many purposes and encompass joint ventures, licensing agreements, supply agreements, marketing agreements and a variety of other arrangements (Contractor and Lorange, 1988b: 5; Root, 1988: 69; Porter and Fuller. 1986: 315). Joint ventures are therefore a subset of cooperative activity. A joint venture is considered to be international if at least one partner has its headquarters outside the venture's country of operation or if the joint venture has a significant level of operation in more than one country (Geringer and Hebert, 1989).

It is usual to distinguish between equity joint ventures (EJVs) and non-equity joint ventures (NEJVs). Killing (1988: 56) views EJVs as 'traditional joint ventures', which are created when two or more partners join forces to create a newly incorporated company in which each has an equity position, thereby each expects a proportional share of dividend as compensation and representation on the board of directors. This conforms to Harrigan's (1985: 2) analytical concept of a joint venture where she studies joint ventures as 'separate entities with two or more active businesses as partners', where the emphasis is on the 'child' – i.e. 'the entity created by partners for a specific activity' (1985: 3). EJVs thus involve two or more legally distinct organizations (the parents), each of which invests in the venture and actively participates in the decision-making activities of the jointly owned entity (Geringer, 1991).

In contrast, NEJVs are agreements between partners to cooperate in some way, but they do not involve the creation of new firms. Contractor and Lorange (1988b: 7) point out that in these

:ases carefully defined rules and formulas govern the allocation
)f tasks, costs and revenues. They give three examples by way of
llustration, each of which involves different risk/return trade
)ffs for the partners.

(i) Exploration consortia, which often involves the sharing
of the venture's costs and revenue from a successful find
by formula.
(ii) Research partnerships, where, by comparison, costs may
be allocated by an agreed formula but the revenue of each
partner depends on what the company independently does
with the technology created.
(iii) Co-production agreements, where each partner's costs are
a function of its own efficiency in producing its part,
while revenue is a function of the successful sales of the
dominant partner.

Vith NEJVs, the compensation to each firm is dependent on the
evel of profits earned and there is at least a moderate degree of
nter-organizational dependence, as is the case with EJVs. All
)ther types of cooperative arrangements, such as franchising and
icensing, may be considered as contractual arrangements where
:ompensation is not determined by profits earned and inter-
)rganizational dependence is low to negligible. Such contractual
irrangements are not considered to be joint ventures and do not
'orm part of the data base reported here.

# 3  THE DATA SET

)espite their increased importance systematic data on the inci-
lence of joint ventures from official sources is not readily avail-
ible. There appears to be a number of reasons for the lack of
iard statistics on the existence of joint venture operations
OECD 1986: 12). Apart from the lack of a common definition
)f joint ventures the competition laws of the majority of OECD
:ountries do not provide the requirement of a legal notification or
)fficial reporting for the establishment of a joint venture. Where

data is collected it is often highly selective, some countries only record 50–50 EJVs, or only record those joint ventures above a certain (variable) size level, or only those in particular industries often the manufacturing sector.

The relative absence of official statistics has obliged researchers to amass their own data bases, the most common approach being to record announcements reported in the financial press, (Hergert and Morris, 1988; Ghemawat *et al.* 1986; Harrigan, 1985; Kogut, 1989; Osborn and Baughn, 1987) This study follows the established precedent and reports on EJV and NEJV formation by UK firms with Western European United States and Japanese partners announced in the *Financial Times* over the period 1980–1989. It should be noted that this data base differs from the one amassed by Hergert and Morris (1988) which includes aggregate data for the EEC and does no identify joint venture formation at the individual country level. In contrast the data reported on here is disaggregated to the level of the UK.

The focus of the study is on the flow of new joint venture rather than the total stock of existing ventures although Ghemawat *et al.* (1986: 346) argue that when tracked over a suitably long period, flows of new coalitions also capture most of the stock in existence at the end of it. It is important to note that the data does not include joint venture partnerships organized through national or international government agencies, particularly EC programmes such as ESPRIT. These fall outside the discussion, partly because they have been examined elsewhere (see for example Mytelka and Delapierre, 1987; Hare *et al.*, 1989) but largely because an attempt has been made to record the free association of firms where the venture was grounded in an independent strategic rationale rather than being provoked by the stimulus of an incentive from an external agent. Finally it should be noted that the data only records international ventures domestic joint ventures between UK firms are therefore no considered.

Although a number of studies have relied on press announcements of joint venture activity, there are some standard caveats that apply in the interpretation of any finding drawn from such data sources. It is likely that only major ventures – involving

elatively large and well known firms – will be reported in the
ress, with perhaps many small ventures going unreported.
Vhile recognizing this apparent weakness, Ghemawat *et al.*
1976: 348) note that the fixed costs of international, inter-firm
greements, would seem to deter small firms from participating
n joint ventures. The potential bias in the data towards larger
irms should, therefore, not be exaggerated.

Hergert and Morris (1988) point out that for many of the
ublished articles the source of information is likely to be press
eleases by the firms involved in the venture. These press
eleases may be biased accounts of the characteristics of the joint
enture. In particular, participating firms may seek to mislead
ompetitors over their motives and activities by deliberately mis-
resenting themselves to the financial press. While the reporting
f deliberate falsehoods is a possibility it is very difficult to
udge the extend of this kind of bias. Nor is it possible to esti-
nate the extent of joint venture activity that goes unreported
ecause the firms involved maintain such strict confidentiality
hat there is in effect nothing for journalists to report.

## PATTERNS OF ACTIVITY OF UK INTERNATIONAL OINT VENTURES

### Frends in UK International Joint Venture Activity Over Time

Jew joint venture formation over the 1980–1989 period is
hown in Figure 8.1. The total flow of new joint ventures fell
teadily at the beginning of the decade to a low in 1983. From
hat date joint venture formations rose in each year except for a
all in 1987. The final two years of the decade experienced
ignificant growth in joint venture formation.

The downturn in venture formation in 1987 is largely
ccounted for by the considerable fall in new joint ventures
stablished with United States firms which at that date fell to the
owest number recorded over the period. From the beginning of
he decade until 1987 the USA was the leading country for joint

*Figure 8.1*  UK joint venture formation region by year: 1980–89

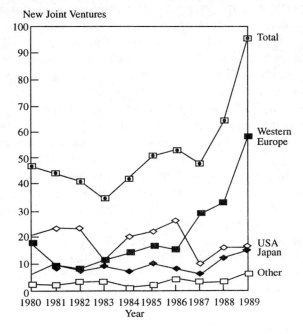

venture partnerships. From 1987 Western Europe became the leading partner. The rising trend in total new venture formation from the low point in 1983 has clearly been driven by the growth in joint venture activity with firms in Western Europe. Without the greater incidence of joint venture formations with Western Europe, there would be no appreciable growth in joint venture activity over the decade.

The total number of new joint ventures formed over the decade is shown in Table 8.1. From the total of 520 joint ventures recorded, the majority of just over 40 per cent were formed with firms in Western Europe, with the United States a close second responsible for about 36 per cent of the partnerships. While the actual number of ventures formed with Japanese firms is quite significant at 90, in proportional terms it is well below the other two geographical combinations.

Also shown in Table 8.1 are the number of EJVs and NEJVs formed. Over the decade there were marginally more EJVs (55.9

per cent) established than NEJVs (44.1 per cent). It should be recalled that these results are derived from data based on press releases, hence it is necessary to be prudent when generalizing about trends in EJVs and NEJVs. It is not clear, for instance, that companies will have the same policy in terms of announcing NEJVs in the press as they would for EJVs, with the latter probably attracting more publicity than the former. The actual incidence of NEJVs may in fact be greater than EJVs. Given this weakness in the methodology, the reader is cautioned to bear this in mind when considering the rest of the discussion.

Roughly the same proportions of EJVs and NEJVs were formed in each of the geographic regions. There appears, therefore, to be no concentration of a particular contractual form of joint ventures in any of the geographic regions. This may be stated more formally as follows:

H1: The contractual form of the joint venture and the region of the foreign partner are independent.

The chi-square test of independence clearly shows that H1 cannot be rejected (Table 8.15).

The formation of joint ventures in total over the decade has obviously been influenced by the somewhat contrasting experi-

*Table* 8.1   Joint venture formation: 1980–89

| Region | Total | | EJVs | | NEJVs | |
|---|---|---|---|---|---|---|
| | No. | % | No. | % | No. | % |
| Western Europe | 213 | 41.0 | 120 | 42.7 | 88 | 39.6 |
| USA | 188 | 36.2 | 100 | 35.6 | 78 | 35.1 |
| Japan | 90 | 17.3 | 48 | 17.1 | 41 | 18.5 |
| Other* | 29 | 5.6 | 13 | 4.6 | 15 | 6.8 |
| Total[†] | 520 | 100.0 | 281 | 100.0 | 222 | 100.0 |

* 'Other' refers to joint ventures formed between UK firms and partner firms from more than one of the regional groupings, for example, Western Europe and the USA. It also includes joint ventures formed between partners in Western Europe and a country other than the USA and Japan.
[†] For 17 of the joint ventures it was not possible to identify the contractual form.

ence of EJV and NEJV formation. In particular the general fall in incidence over the early part of the decade was driven by the decline in NEJV formation to the low point in 1983. The significant growth at the end of the decade was largely due to the acceleration in the formation of EJVs, particularly with Western European partners. There has been a smoother trend in the incidence of EJV formation compared with that of NEJV formation which has tended to be more erratic.

The popular view that joint ventures have become more common is supported by the data on the UK over the period of the 1980s. The trend is not universal, however, with most of the increase originating with partnerships in Western Europe. There has also been some increase in activity with Japan. The general trend with United States firms has been downwards for most of the second half of the 1980s, with marginally fewer joint ventures formed in the second half of the decade compared with the first half.

To test the view that the incidence of joint venture formation had changed over the period of the 1980s, the number of joint ventures established in the first half of the decade (1980–1984) was compared with the number formed in the second half of the decade (1985–1989) according to the region of the foreign partner. The hypothesis was:

> H2: The time period of the joint venture formation (first or second half of the decade) and the region of the foreign partner are independent.

The chi-square test of independence was conducted for all of the joint ventures and for the sub samples of EJVs and NEJVs with the results that the hypothesis can be rejected; the data does reveal a changed incidence of joint venture formation with partners in each geographic region over the 1980s (Table 8.15).

## Industry Characteristics of the Joint Ventures

The number of joint venture formations across industry groupings during the 1980s is shown in Table 8.2. The greatest number of joint ventures was formed in financial services (13.7 per cent),

147

Table 8.2  Joint venture formation by industry: 1980–89

| Industry | 1980 | 1981 | 1982 | 1983 | 1984 | 1985 | 1986 | 1987 | 1988 | 1989 | Total No. | % |
|---|---|---|---|---|---|---|---|---|---|---|---|---|
| Food and drink | 3 | 0 | 1 | 0 | 0 | 3 | 2 | 4 | 3 | 2 | 18 | 3.5 |
| Metals and minerals | 4 | 1 | 2 | 2 | 0 | 1 | 1 | 0 | 2 | 3 | 16 | 3.1 |
| Energy | 4 | 1 | 1 | 0 | 1 | 0 | 0 | 1 | 2 | 2 | 12 | 2.3 |
| Construction | 2 | 1 | 1 | 1 | 0 | 2 | 2 | 2 | 1 | 6 | 18 | 3.5 |
| Chemicals | 6 | 2 | 1 | 4 | 2 | 2 | 1 | 3 | 4 | 2 | 27 | 5.2 |
| Pharmaceuticals | 1 | 1 | 1 | 5 | 1 | 1 | 3 | 1 | 2 | 1 | 17 | 3.3 |
| Computers | 0 | 3 | 1 | 1 | 2 | 4 | 2 | 2 | 2 | 4 | 21 | 4.0 |
| Telecommunications | 2 | 4 | 7 | 5 | 3 | 4 | 10 | 7 | 7 | 10 | 59 | 11.3 |
| Other electrical | 1 | 3 | 4 | 3 | 5 | 0 | 1 | 4 | 1 | 6 | 28 | 5.4 |
| Automobiles | 2 | 3 | 3 | 2 | 3 | 6 | 5 | 5 | 6 | 3 | 38 | 7.3 |
| Aerospace | 6 | 4 | 4 | 2 | 4 | 7 | 7 | 3 | 7 | 12 | 56 | 10.8 |
| Other manufacturing | 2 | 8 | 2 | 5 | 5 | 7 | 9 | 6 | 10 | 13 | 67 | 12.9 |
| Transport | 1 | 2 | 0 | 0 | 0 | 1 | 1 | 2 | 2 | 2 | 11 | 2.1 |
| Distribution | 0 | 1 | 1 | 0 | 2 | 4 | 5 | 2 | 2 | 6 | 23 | 4.4 |
| Financial services | 7 | 7 | 8 | 4 | 13 | 5 | 3 | 6 | 6 | 12 | 71 | 13.7 |
| Other services | 6 | 3 | 4 | 1 | 1 | 4 | 1 | 0 | 7 | 11 | 38 | 7.3 |
| Total | 47 | 44 | 41 | 35 | 42 | 51 | 53 | 48 | 64 | 95 | 520 | 100.0 |

other manufacturing (12.9 per cent), telecommunications (11.3 per cent) and aerospace (10.8 per cent). The other industry groupings each recorded well under 10 per cent of the total number of joint ventures established over the period.

There is no clear pattern of growth or decline in venture formation in particular industries over the period. For 10 of the 16 industry groupings the incidence of joint venture formation was higher over the second half of the decade compared with the first, consistent with the general increase in new joint ventures. In four cases over 70 per cent of the ventures were established in the second half of the decade: Food and drink; construction; transport; and distribution. In six of the industry groupings, however, there were marginally fewer joint ventures formed in the second half of the decade: Metals and minerals; energy; chemicals; pharmaceuticals; other electrical and financial services.

To test the hypothesis:

H3: The industry of the joint venture and the time period (first or second half of the decade) of the joint venture formation are independent;

would involve several cell sizes with fewer than five observations. To avoid this the data was reclassified into the following *three broad industry groupings*: Group 1. Manufacturing: Food and drink; metals and minerals; energy; construction; chemicals. Group 2. Manufacturing: Pharmaceuticals; computers; telecommunications; other electrical; automobiles; aerospace; other manufacturing. Tertiary: Transport; distribution; financial services; other services.

The distinction between Group 1 and Group 2 manufacturing was made because of the generally more sophisticated technology assumed to be embodied in the products and processes of Group 2 manufacturing.

Joint venture formation by these broad industry groupings and time period are shown in Table 8.3. The chi-square test shows that the hypothesis that the broad industry groupings and the time period of joint venture formation are independent cannot be rejected. The hypothesis similarly cannot be rejected when the

*Table* 8.3   Joint venture formation – broad industry grouping by time period

| Broad industry grouping | Time period | | | | | |
| | 1980–1984 | | 1985–1989 | | Total | |
| | No. | Row % | No. | Row % | No. | Col % |
| --- | --- | --- | --- | --- | --- | --- |
| Group 1 manufacturing | 40 | 44.0 | 51 | 56.0 | 91 | 17.5 |
| Group 2 manufacturing | 108 | 37.8 | 178 | 62.2 | 286 | 55.0 |
| Tertiary | 61 | 42.7 | 82 | 57.3 | 143 | 27.5 |
| Total | 209 | 40.2 | 311 | 59.8 | 520 | 100.0 |

subsamples of EJVs and NEJVs are considered separately (Table 8.15). There appears to be no association, therefore, between particular industry groupings and the incidence of joint venture formation over the two halves of the decade.

The geographical distribution of the industry groupings is shown in Table 8.4. Discounting the other category, at least one joint venture was established in each of the industries in each of the three main geographical areas. The leading three industry groupings in Western Europe were other manufacturing (14.6 per cent), financial services (12.2 per cent) and aerospace (11.7 per cent). For joint ventures with firms from the USA, the leading three industries were telecommunications (16 per cent), followed by financial services and other manufacturing (each with 14.4 per cent of the US total). The leading Japanese industry partnerships were in financial services (16.7 per cent), other electrical (14.4 per cent) and automobiles (13.3 per cent). Clearly, the financial services industry has played a prominent role in joint venture formation across all three geographical regions. Moreover, the Tertiary sector comprises about one quarter of all new joint ventures in both Western Europe and Japan rising to almost one-third in the USA.

It is notable that Japan has a relatively weak presence in the Group 1 manufacturing industries as well as the Tertiary sector. In the Group 1 manufacturing industries, links with Western European firms are particularly strong in chemicals.

Within the Group 2 manufacturing industries, links with US firms dominate in telecommunications. Links with Japan are par-

*Table 8.4* Joint venture formation by industry and region: 1980–89

| Industry | Western Europe | | USA | | Japan | | Other* | |
|---|---|---|---|---|---|---|---|---|
| | No. | % | No. | % | No. | % | No. | % |
| Food and drink | 9 | 4.2 | 5 | 2.7 | 2 | 2.2 | 2 | 6.9 |
| Metals and minerals | 8 | 3.8 | 5 | 2.7 | 2 | 2.2 | 1 | 3.4 |
| Energy | 4 | 1.9 | 7 | 3.7 | 1 | 1.1 | 0 | 0.0 |
| Construction | 7 | 3.3 | 8 | 4.3 | 3 | 3.3 | 0 | 0.0 |
| Chemicals | 17 | 8.0 | 5 | 2.7 | 4 | 4.4 | 1 | 3.4 |
| Pharmaceuticals | 8 | 3.8 | 3 | 1.6 | 6 | 6.7 | 0 | 0.0 |
| Computers | 10 | 4.7 | 6 | 3.2 | 5 | 5.6 | 0 | 0.0 |
| Telecommunications | 16 | 7.5 | 30 | 16.0 | 8 | 8.9 | 5 | 17.2 |
| Other electrical | 8 | 3.8 | 5 | 2.7 | 13 | 14.4 | 2 | 6.9 |
| Automobiles | 15 | 7.0 | 11 | 5.9 | 12 | 13.3 | 0 | 0.0 |
| Aerospace | 25 | 11.7 | 20 | 10.6 | 2 | 2.2 | 9 | 31.0 |
| Other manufacturing | 31 | 14.6 | 27 | 14.4 | 8 | 8.9 | 1 | 3.4 |
| Transport | 6 | 2.8 | 2 | 1.1 | 1 | 1.1 | 2 | 6.9 |
| Distribution | 9 | 4.2 | 8 | 4.3 | 5 | 5.6 | 1 | 3.4 |
| Financial services | 26 | 12.2 | 27 | 14.4 | 15 | 16.7 | 3 | 10.3 |
| Other services | 14 | 6.6 | 19 | 10.1 | 3 | 3.3 | 2 | 6.9 |
| Total | 213 | 100.0 | 188 | 100.0 | 90 | 100.0 | 29 | 100.0 |

See footnote* to Table 8.1.

cularly weak in aerospace, telecommunications and other
manufacturing, compared with the other two geographical areas.
Japan has a strong presence, however, with partnerships in the
other electrical industry.

From this discussion it would appear that there are relatively
strong and weak links between partner nations in particular industries. This view was considered more formally in terms of the
broad industry groupings by means of the following hypothesis:

H4: The broad industry groupings and the region of the
foreign partners are independent. Eliminating the other category and conducting a chi-square test of independence
shows, however, that H4 cannot be rejected (Table 8.15). In
terms of broad industry groupings, therefore, there is no association between the industry of the joint venture and the region
of the partner firm.

## Joint Venture Purpose

The purpose underlying joint venture formation over the 1980s is
shown in Table 8.5. The purpose is the operating function of the
joint venture as recorded in the press releases and is not an indication of partner motives for establishing the venture. The greatest proportion of joint ventures (just over 27 per cent) were
classified as service provision. This means that the venture was
formed in order to carry out a service activity, for example, provision of insurance services or banking services. It should be
noted that the service provision applies to joint ventures formed
by firms in non-service industries as well as those in service industries, an example of the former being architectural design
consultancy offered by firms in the construction industry. Almost
one-quarter of the joint ventures were formed for the purpose of
production with the third largest category that of marketing (13.7
per cent).

Hergert and Morris (1988: 107) reported that the INSEAD
data indicated that cooperative behaviour begins to occur very
early in the product development cycle, partly explained by the
difficulties in managing the venture as the project gets closer to

Table 8.5  Joint venture formation by purpose: 1980–89

| Purpose | 1980 | 1981 | 1982 | 1983 | 1984 | 1985 | 1986 | 1987 | 1988 | 1989 | Total No. | Total % |
|---|---|---|---|---|---|---|---|---|---|---|---|---|
| R and D | 2 | 1 | 6 | 4 | 3 | 9 | 5 | 4 | 10 | 10 | 54 | 10.4 |
| Production | 10 | 6 | 10 | 10 | 7 | 9 | 16 | 16 | 18 | 23 | 125 | 24.0 |
| Marketing | 7 | 10 | 6 | 4 | 6 | 6 | 9 | 6 | 10 | 7 | 71 | 13.7 |
| Development and production | 7 | 6 | 4 | 1 | 3 | 8 | 10 | 5 | 4 | 8 | 56 | 10.8 |
| Development and marketing | 1 | 3 | 1 | 2 | 2 | 1 | 0 | 3 | 1 | 3 | 17 | 3.3 |
| Production and marketing | 4 | 8 | 1 | 4 | 6 | 4 | 1 | 2 | 3 | 5 | 38 | 7.3 |
| Development, production and Marketing | 2 | 0 | 0 | 1 | 0 | 0 | 2 | 0 | 1 | 7 | 13 | 2.5 |
| Service provision | 12 | 10 | 13 | 8 | 15 | 14 | 10 | 12 | 17 | 31 | 142 | 27.3 |
| Not known | 2 | 0 | 0 | 1 | 0 | 0 | 0 | 0 | 0 | 1 | 4 | 0.8 |
| Total | 47 | 44 | 41 | 35 | 42 | 51 | 53 | 48 | 64 | 95 | 520 | 100.0 |

its eventual market. The incentive to cheat or to otherwise benefit at a partner's expense tends to increase as the venture approaches the marketing phase. Hence it may be argued that non-marketing joint ventures are likely to be more common than those involving marketing. This hypothesis appears to be supported by the UK data. The joint ventures formed for the purpose of R and D production, and development and production, are 45.4 per cent of the total (where the purpose of the joint venture is known). This compares with 26.8 per cent of total ventures which involve marketing (excluding service provision).

Comparing the incidence of joint ventures by purpose over the second half of the decade with the first half, there was an increase in the number of ventures for each purpose, except for slight falls in the combined categories of development and marketing, and production and marketing. The greatest increase in purpose was in the combined development, production and marketing category with over three times more joint ventures recorded in the second half of the decade, however, this category has the smallest number of joint ventures in total. R and D had almost two and a half times more joint ventures recorded in the second half of the decade; production had almost twice the number recorded, with strong growth also in the combined category of the development and production. This would indicate that over the 1980s there was an increasing propensity to establish joint ventures at the early phase of the product-development cycle.

In order to test for an association between the purpose of the joint venture and the time period of the decade during which it was formed, the following three *broad purpose classifications* were derived, based on whether or not the purpose included marketing:

(1) Non-marketing related i.e. the purpose categories of R and D, production, and development and production.
(2) Marketing related i.e. the purpose categories of marketing, development and marketing, production and marketing, and development, production and marketing.
(3) Service provision, the original purpose category. Joint ventures here may or may not include marketing activities, but

it is not possible to determine from the press reports which joint ventures contain significant marketing activity and which do not. Given this uncertainty and the distinctly different nature of this purpose, it was left as a separate category.

Joint venture formation by these broad purposes and time period are shown in Table 8.6. The following hypothesis was subjected to a chi-square test of independence.

H5: The broad purpose of the joint venture and the time period of formation are independent.

H5 can be rejected for all joint ventures and EJVs but not for NEJVs (Table 8.15). There is an association between the broad purpose of the joint venture and the time period of formation (i.e. first or second half of the decade) for EJVs but not for NEJVs.

The distribution of joint ventures by purpose and geographical location of the foreign partner is shown in Table 8.7. In each region about two-thirds of joint venture formation is accounted for by only three purposes. Joint ventures formed with firms in Western Europe were principally for the purpose of production (30 per cent), service provision (26.3 per cent) and R and D (11.7 per cent). The purposes of joint venture formation in the USA were dominated by service provision (29.8 per cent), production

*Table* 8.6   Joint venture formation-boad purpose by time period

| Broad purpose* | 1980–1984 | | 1985–1989 | | Total | |
| --- | --- | --- | --- | --- | --- | --- |
| | No. | Row % | No. | Row % | No. | Col % |
| Non-marketing related | 80 | 34.0 | 155 | 66.0 | 235 | 45.5 |
| Marketing related | 68 | 48.9 | 71 | 51.1 | 139 | 26.9 |
| Service provision | 58 | 40.8 | 84 | 59.2 | 142 | 27.5 |
| Total | 206 | 39.9 | 310 | 60.1 | 516 | 100.0 |

* For four joint ventures purpose not known.

155

*Table* 8.7  Joint venture formation by purpose and region: 1980–89

| Purpose | Western Europe | | USA | | Japan | | Other* | | Total | |
|---|---|---|---|---|---|---|---|---|---|---|
| | No. | % | No. | % | No. | % | No. | % | No. | % |
| R and D | 25 | 11.7 | 18 | 9.5 | 6 | 6.7 | 5 | 16.9 | 54 | 10.4 |
| Production | 64 | 30.0 | 37 | 19.2 | 19 | 21.1 | 5 | 17.2 | 125 | 24.0 |
| Marketing | 19 | 8.9 | 29 | 15.4 | 18 | 20.0 | 5 | 17.2 | 71 | 13.7 |
| Development and production | 22 | 10.3 | 20 | 10.6 | 11 | 12.2 | 3 | 10.3 | 56 | 10.8 |
| Development and marketing | 8 | 3.8 | 4 | 2.1 | 3 | 3.3 | 2 | 6.9 | 17 | 3.3 |
| Production and marketing | 13 | 6.1 | 15 | 8.0 | 8 | 8.9 | 2 | 6.9 | 38 | 7.3 |
| Development, production and marketing | 4 | 1.9 | 7 | 3.7 | 2 | 2.2 | 0 | 0.0 | 13 | 2.5 |
| Service provision | 56 | 26.3 | 56 | 29.8 | 23 | 25.6 | 7 | 24.1 | 142 | 27.3 |
| Not known | 2 | 0.9 | 2 | 1.1 | 0 | 0.0 | 0 | 0.0 | 4 | 0.8 |
| Total | 213 | 100.0 | 188 | 100.0 | 90 | 17.3 | 29 | 5.6 | 520 | 100.0 |

* See footnote to Table 8.1.

(19.7 per cent) and marketing (15.4 per cent). The same rank order applies to Japan, with 25.6 per cent, 21.1 per cent and 20 per cent by each of these purposes respectively. As a single purpose relatively few R and D joint ventures were formed with the Japanese, while marketing features less prominently as a purpose for joint venture formation with Western European firms.

The broad purpose classifications by region are shown in Table 8.8. This table indicates that over 50 per cent of joint ventures with Western European firms were non-marketing related compared with about 40 per cent for the USA and Japan. While just over 20 per cent of joint ventures with firms in Western Europe include marketing, this rises to almost 30 per cent for the USA and about 35 per cent for Japan. There appears, therefore, to be a greater willingness for UK firms to engage in joint ventures which involve marketing with firms from Japan and the USA, than firms in Western Europe. The reason for this is not readily apparent, but it may be a function of proximity in that JVs with more geographically remote partners such as the US and Japan, maybe used as market entry mechanisms and thus these JVs have to involve marketing activities. This is not the case as often in Europe to the extent that UK firms are already in the market and consequently use JVs for other purposes. There may also be a presumption of greater understanding of each other's markets by UK and European firms than is the case for either the USA or Japan, thereby reducing the need for joint marketing initiatives. There is another plausible reason, however, based on the general argument that firms would be less willing to engage in marketing activities because of the greater inducement to cheat as the venture approaches the marketing phase. It could be concluded that UK firms tend to trust Japanese and US firms more than Western European firms, and *vice versa*.

To test the hypothesis:

H6: The purpose of the joint venture and the region of the foreign partner are independent,

the three broad purpose categories of non-marketing related, marketing related and service provision were again used.

Table 8.8  Joint venture formation – broad purpose by region

| Broad purpose* | Region | | | | | | | | | | |
|---|---|---|---|---|---|---|---|---|---|---|---|
| | Western Europe | | USA | | Japan | | Other† | | Total | |
| | No. | Row % | No. | Row % | No. | Row % | No. | Row % | No. | Col % |
| Non-marketing related | 111 | 47.2 | 75 | 31.9 | 36 | 15.3 | 13 | 5.5 | 235 | 45.5 |
| Marketing related | 44 | 31.7 | 55 | 39.6 | 31 | 22.3 | 9 | 6.5 | 139 | 26.9 |
| Service provision | 56 | 39.4 | 56 | 39.4 | 23 | 16.2 | 7 | 4.9 | 142 | 27.5 |
| Total | 211 | 40.9 | 186 | 36.0 | 90 | 17.4 | 29 | 5.6 | 516 | 100.0 |

* Purpose of four joint ventures not known.
† See footnote * to Table 8.1.

Eliminating the other regional group from the analysis, the ch
square test of independence showed that while H6 can
rejected for all the joint ventures, it cannot be rejected for each
the subsamples of EJVs and NEJVs (Table 8.15).

A further refinement of the data is to be consider the purpo
of the joint venture in terms of the industry groupings, as show
in Table 8.9. The R and D category includes a relatively sma
number of pure research ventures, which are concerned with t
increased understanding of products and processes, but is dom
inated by ventures formed to undertake joint product develo
ment. R and D is concentrated in the aerospace industry whic
accounts for about one-third of ventures for this purpos
Aerospace also dominates the development and production ca
egory with again about one-third of ventures for this purpos
Production joint ventures are more common than R and D in a
of the industries in which they occur apart from aerospace. T
production joint ventures are concentrated in the other man
facturing, chemicals and automobiles sectors, together accoun
ing for almost half of joint ventures for this purpose. Apart fro
energy and construction, marketing partnerships exists in a
industry groupings with the tertiary sector accounting for we
over one-third of the total. Service provision ventures, as wou
be expected, are concentrated in the Tertiary sector, particular
in the financial services industry, where almost half of t
ventures for this purpose occur. There is, however, also
significant proportion of service provision ventures in the tel
communications industry (16 per cent).

To test the following hypothesis:

H7: The industry of the joint venture and the purpose of t
joint venture are independent,

the three broad industry groupings were crosstabulated with t
three broad purpose categories previously defined. H7 was r
jected with the chisquare test of independence for all the joi
ventures, as well as for the subsamples of EJVs and NEJVs.
may be concluded from the data that there is an associati
between the industry of the joint venture and the purpose of t
joint venture (Table 8.15). It may be suggested that this resu
can be construed to support a resource dependency approach.

Table 8.9  Joint venture formation by industry and purpose: 1980–89

| Industry | R and D No. | R and D % | Production No. | Production % | Marketing No. | Marketing % | Development and production No. | Development and production % | Development and marketing No. | Development and marketing % | Production and marketing No. | Production and marketing % | Development production and marketing No. | Development production and marketing % | Service provision No. | Service provision % | Not known No. | Not known % | Total No. | Total % |
|---|---|---|---|---|---|---|---|---|---|---|---|---|---|---|---|---|---|---|---|---|
| Food and drink | 2 | 3.7 | 5 | 4.0 | 9 | 12.7 | | | 1 | 5.9 | 1 | 2.6 | | | | | | | 18 | 3.5 |
| Metals and minerals | 2 | 3.7 | 11 | 8.8 | 1 | 1.4 | | | 1 | 5.9 | | | | | | | 1 | 25.0 | 16 | 3.1 |
| Energy | 5 | 9.3 | 6 | 4.8 | | | | | | | | | | | 1 | 0.7 | | | 12 | 2.3 |
| Construction | | | 9 | 7.2 | | | 2 | 3.6 | | | 1 | 2.6 | | | 6 | 4.2 | | | 18 | 3.5 |
| Chemicals | 2 | 3.7 | 16 | 12.8 | 1 | 1.4 | 3 | 5.4 | 1 | 5.9 | 5 | 13.2 | 3 | 23.1 | | | | | 27 | 5.2 |
| Pharmaceuticals | 1 | 1.9 | 2 | 1.6 | 6 | 8.5 | 1 | 1.8 | 1 | 5.9 | 3 | 7.9 | | | 3 | 2.1 | | | 17 | 3.3 |
| Computers | 4 | 7.4 | 6 | 4.8 | 4 | 5.6 | 3 | 5.4 | 1 | 5.9 | 2 | 5.3 | | | 1 | 0.7 | | | 21 | 4.0 |
| Telecommunications | 6 | 11.1 | 7 | 5.6 | 9 | 12.7 | 6 | 10.7 | 3 | 17.6 | 3 | 7.9 | 2 | 15.4 | 23 | 16.2 | | | 59 | 11.3 |
| Other electrical | 6 | 11.1 | 8 | 6.4 | 4 | 5.6 | 2 | 3.6 | 3 | 17.6 | 3 | 7.9 | 2 | 15.4 | | | | | 28 | 5.4 |
| Automobiles | 2 | 3.7 | 16 | 12.8 | 2 | 2.8 | 9 | 16.1 | 1 | 5.9 | 4 | 10.5 | 2 | 15.4 | | | 2 | 50.0 | 38 | 7.3 |
| Aerospace | 18 | 33.3 | 11 | 8.8 | 2 | 2.8 | 20 | 35.7 | 3 | 17.6 | 2 | 5.3 | 1 | 7.7 | | | | | 56 | 10.8 |
| Other manufacturing | 6 | 11.1 | 28 | 22.4 | 6 | 8.5 | 10 | 17.9 | 1 | 5.9 | 12 | 31.6 | 1 | 7.7 | | | | | 67 | 12.9 |
| Transport | | | | | 3 | 4.2 | | | | | | | | | 1 | 0.7 | | | 11 | 2.1 |
| Distribution | | | | | 9 | 12.7 | | | | | | | 1 | 7.7 | 7 | 4.9 | | | 23 | 4.4 |
| Financial Services | | | | | 2 | 2.8 | | | | | 1 | 7.7 | | | 13 | 9.2 | | | 71 | 13.7 |
| Other services | | | | | 13 | 18.3 | | | 1 | 5.9 | 2 | 5.3 | 1 | 7.7 | 69 | 48.6 | | | 38 | 7.3 |
| Other services (cont.) | | | | | | | | | | | | | | | 21 | 14.8 | | | | |
| Total | 54 | 100.0 | 125 | 100.0 | 71 | 100.0 | 56 | 100.0 | 17 | 100.0 | 38 | 100.0 | 13 | 100.0 | 142 | 100.0 | 4 | 100.0 | 520 | 100.0 |

## Contractual Form of Joint Ventures

The contractual form of the joint ventures by industry groupings
is shown in Table 8.10. Apart from metals and minerals both
EJVs and NEJVs were established in all industry sectors. In 10
out of the 16 industry groupings, EJVs were established more
frequently than NEJVs. Taking the number of EJVs as a proportion of NEJVs there appears to be a greater preference for EJVs
in the Tertiary sector, particularly in distribution, financial services and other services, with chemicals also having a high proportion of EJVs. On the other hand, both aerospace and
telecommunications display relatively high proportion of NEJVs.

The chi-square test of independence was conducted on the following hypothesis:

*Table* 8.10    Joint venture formation – contractual form by industry: 1980–89

| Industry | Equity No. | Row % | Non-equity No. | Row % | Total* No. | Col % |
|---|---|---|---|---|---|---|
| Food and drink | 9 | 52.9 | 8 | 47.1 | 17 | 3.4 |
| Metals and minerals | 15 | 100.0 | 0 | 0.0 | 15 | 3.0 |
| Energy | 4 | 33.3 | 8 | 66.7 | 12 | 2.4 |
| Construction | 11 | 68.8 | 5 | 31.2 | 16 | 3.2 |
| Chemicals | 18 | 75.0 | 6 | 25.0 | 24 | 4.8 |
| Pharmaceuticals | 9 | 52.9 | 8 | 47.1 | 17 | 3.4 |
| Computers | 7 | 33.3 | 14 | 66.7 | 21 | 4.2 |
| Telecommunications | 22 | 38.6 | 35 | 61.4 | 57 | 11.3 |
| Other electrical | 16 | 59.3 | 11 | 40.7 | 27 | 5.4 |
| Automobiles | 16 | 42.1 | 22 | 57.9 | 38 | 7.6 |
| Aerospace | 15 | 27.8 | 39 | 72.2 | 54 | 10.7 |
| Other manufacturing | 43 | 66.2 | 22 | 33.8 | 65 | 12.9 |
| Transport | 5 | 50.0 | 5 | 50.0 | 10 | 2.0 |
| Distribution | 18 | 78.3 | 5 | 21.7 | 23 | 4.6 |
| Financial services | 49 | 70.0 | 21 | 30.0 | 70 | 13.9 |
| Other services | 24 | 64.9 | 13 | 35.1 | 37 | 7.4 |
| Total | 281 | 55.9 | 222 | 44.1 | 503 | 100.0 |

\* For 17 joint ventures the contractual form is now known.

H8: The industry of the joint venture and the contractual form are independent.

s the cross tabulation associated with Table 8.10 contains two lls with less than five observations, the hypothesis was tested sing the broad industry groupings of Group 1 manufacturing, roup 2 manufacturing and Tertiary. The test statistic shows that 8 can be rejected. It may be concluded, therefore, that there is a association between the industry of the joint venture and the ntractual form (Table 8.15). This result is in line with the ider predictions of transactions cost theory.

The contractual form of the joint venture by purpose is shown Table 8.11. Although EJVs and NEJVs were used in each of e purpose categories, there appears to be a preference for a par- cular contractual form by purpose. EJVs predominate in pro- uction and production-related ventures as well as in service

*able* 8.11   Joint venture formation – contractual form by purpose: 1980–89

| urpose | Equity | | Non-equity | | Total | |
|---|---|---|---|---|---|---|
| | No. | Row % | No. | Row % | No. | Col % |
| and D | 8 | 15.7 | 43 | 84.3 | 51 | 10.2 |
| oduction | 85 | 71.4 | 34 | 28.6 | 119 | 23.8 |
| arketing | 35 | 49.3 | 36 | 50.7 | 71 | 14.2 |
| evelopment and oduction | 19 | 34.5 | 36 | 65.5 | 55 | 11.0 |
| evelopment and arketing | 5 | 33.3 | 10 | 66.7 | 15 | 3.0 |
| roduction and arketing | 26 | 68.4 | 12 | 31.6 | 38 | 7.6 |
| evelopment, oduction and arketing | 9 | 69.2 | 4 | 30.8 | 13 | 2.6 |
| ervice provision | 93 | 67.4 | 45 | 32.6 | 138 | 27.6 |
| otal | 280 | 56.0 | 220 | 44.0 | 500 | 100.0 |

For one EJV the purpose is not known, for two NEJVs the purpose is not known, for a rther 17 joint ventures the contractual form is not known.

provision. NEJVs are the most frequent in R and D and develop-
ment-related ventures. There is an almost equal split in the contractual form in joint ventures established for the purpose of
marketing.

The chi-square test shows that the hypothesis:

H9: The purpose of the joint venture and the contractual form
of the ventures are independent,

can be rejected (Table 8.15). It would appear, therefore, that the
particular contractual form chosen for the joint venture is at least
in part associated with the purpose of the joint venture.

**Number of Partners**

The number of partners in each of the joint ventures formed over
the 1980s is shown in Table 8.12. A clear majority of ventures
(almost 85 per cent) involved only one foreign partner, with
roughly similar proportions of one partner ventures in both EJV
and NEJVs. This is perhaps not surprising as a joint venture will
become more difficult to coordinate and manage as the number
of partners grows. Despite this a small number of ventures are
created with a relatively large number of partners.

The chi-square test shows that the hypothesis:

*Table* 8.12   Number of partners by contractual form*

| Partners | Equity No. | Row % | Non-equity No. | Row % | Total No. | Col % |
|---|---|---|---|---|---|---|
| 1 | 244 | 57.1 | 183 | 42.9 | 427 | 84.9 |
| 2 | 22 | 51.2 | 21 | 48.8 | 43 | 8.5 |
| 3 | 5 | 45.5 | 6 | 54.5 | 11 | 2.2 |
| 4 | 2 | 33.3 | 4 | 66.7 | 6 | 1.2 |
| >4 | 8 | 50.0 | 8 | 50.0 | 16 | 3.2 |
| Total | 281 | 55.9 | 222 | 44.1 | 503 | 100.0 |

* For 17 joint ventures the contractual form is not known.

H10: The number of partners in joint venture and the contractual form are independent,

nnot be rejected (Table 8.15). The contractual form chosen for e joint venture appears, therefore, not to be associated with the umber of partners in the venture.

## quity Shareholding

he extent of UK partner firms' shareholding in EJVs is shown Table 8.13. In about one-third of the EJVs no information was available concerning the UK partner's shareholding, hence the ta in Table 8.13 and the discussion which follows relates only the 180 EJVs where this information is known. Table 8.13 ows that 50–50 shareholding is found in well over a third of e total ventures, ranging from about one-quarter with Japan to st over half with the USA. In about 65 per cent of cases UK ms have at least a half share in the venture, ranging from about per cent in Western Europe to almost 75 per cent in the USA. iven the relatively high proportion of 50–50 joint ventures, wever, UK firms have a majority shareholding in only 25.6 per nt of the ventures. For the regional groupings, UK firms have ajority shareholding in only about 21 per cent of the ventures Western Europe, 24 per cent in the USA, but almost 40 per nt in Japan.

It is clear that for the most part UK firms have either not been le to negotiate majority shareholdings in EJVs, or have been epared to accept at best a half shareholding. This is reflected in e mean equity shareholding of UK firms by region of the part-rs. With partners in Western Europe the mean equity share-olding is 44.97 per cent, the USA, 47.1 per cent and Japan .18 per cent. One-way analysis of variance (Scheffe pro-dure) shows that the mean equity shareholding is significantly fferent between partner firms in Western Europe and Japan $< 0.05$). The corollary of this is that the mean equity share-olding is not significantly different between partner firms in estern Europe and the USA, and partner firms in the USA and pan. Quite why UK firms are apparently more able to negotiate

*Table* 8.13  UK partners' shareholding in equity joint ventures

| Equity share (%) | Region | | | | | | | | | | |
|---|---|---|---|---|---|---|---|---|---|---|---|
| | Western Europe | | USA | | Japan | | Other* | | Total† | |
| | No. | % | No. | % | No. | % | No. | % | No. | % |
| >74 | 1 | 1.4 | 3 | 4.8 | 7 | 18.4 | 1 | 12.5 | 12 | 6.7 |
| 50–74 | 14 | 19.7 | 12 | 19.1 | 8 | 21.1 | 0 | 0.0 | 34 | 18.9 |
| 50–50 | 28 | 39.4 | 32 | 50.8 | 10 | 26.3 | 0 | 0.0 | 70 | 38.9 |
| 25–49 | 21 | 29.5 | 10 | 15.9 | 11 | 29.0 | 4 | 50.0 | 46 | 25.6 |
| <25 | 7 | 9.8 | 6 | 9.5 | 2 | 5.3 | 3 | 37.5 | 18 | 10.0 |
| Total | 71 | 100.0 | 63 | 100.0 | 38 | 100.0 | 8 | 100.0 | 180 | 100.0 |

* See footnote * to Table 8.1.
† Total of equity joint ventures where UK shareholding is known.

majority shareholdings with Japanese firms rather than firms in Western Europe is, however, not clear at this aggregate level of analysis.

The hypothesis:

H11: The proportion of UK equity shareholding in the JV and the regional location of the foreign partner are independent,

could not be tested using the cross tabulation in Table 13 because of the number of cells with fewer than five observations (the chi-square test of independence is generally considered not to be reliable when cell frequencies are less than five).

To overcome this problem the UK equity shareholding data was reclassified into the following categories (following Blodgett, 1991).

(i) UK partner majority: > 51 per cent.
(ii) Approximately equal: 49–51 per cent.
(iii) UK partner minority: < 49 per cent.

Eliminating the other regional grouping from the analysis the chi-square test of independence using the reclassified data produced the result that H11 cannot be rejected. There is no association between the amount of equity held by the UK partner and the geographical location of the foreign partner (Table 8.15).

A further three hypotheses were tested using the reclassified data:

H12: The proportion of the UK equity shareholding and the time period of the joint venture formation (first or second half of the decade) are independent.

H13: The proportion of the UK equity shareholding and the broad industry grouping of the joint venture are independent.

H14: The proportion of the UK equity shareholding and the broad purpose of the joint venture are independent.

The statistical results show that H12 can be rejected, H13 and H14 cannot be rejected (Table 8.15).

On the whole, the chi-square tests indicate no association between the UK partners' equity shareholding and other important variables such as industry, purpose or region of the foreign partner. To an extend, these results may have been partly generated by the way in which the shareholding data was reclassified into three tight groups. To avoid this problem and to throw further light on the determinants of the level of UK equity shareholding, a number of regression equations were constructed. This analysis is considered in the following sub-section.

**Empirical Findings from Regression Analysis**

A multiple regression analysis was undertaken in an attempt to identify the main predictors of the UK equity share of joint ventures. The dependent variable was, therefore, the percentage equity stake of the UK partner in the joint venture. The independent variables were treated as zero/one dummy variables. Table 8.14 shows the results of a multiple regression equation examining the percentage UK equity shareholding as a function of the time period, the region – or location – of the foreign partner, joint venture purpose and industry of the venture.

Regression equation 1 has a relatively poor explanatory value with low $R$ square and overall $F$ value. Apart from the intercept term the only significant coefficients are those of the three region variables and the metals and minerals industry variable. In an attempt to improve on this result a set of multiple regression equations was estimated where groups of variables were successively dropped from equation 1. The most successful form was regression equation 2, also shown in Table 8.14. Of those estimated this was the only regression equation which was statistically significant. In a further attempt to improve on equation 1 a second set of regression equations was estimated where the independent variables were combinations of the broad purpose and broad industry classifications and a number of interaction terms derived from the rejected hypotheses, H1 to H14 (i.e. where the chi-square tests indicated an association between variables). This

*Table* 8.14  Multiple regression on percentage UK equity shareholding

|  | 1 | 2 |
|---|---|---|
| Constant | 27.366* | 31.625* |
|  | (4.455) | (5.917) |
| Time period | 1.348 |  |
|  | (0.503) |  |
| W. Europe | 15.499* | 13.418[†] |
|  | (2.629) | (2.378) |
| USA | 17.728* | 15.470* |
|  | (2.943) | (2.727) |
| Japan | 23.719* | 21.560* |
|  | (3.880) | (3.666) |
| R and D | 3.075 |  |
|  | (0.354) |  |
| Production | −2.838 |  |
|  | (−0.551) |  |
| Marketing | −2.121 |  |
|  | (−0.447) |  |
| Development and production | 0.988 |  |
|  | (0.155) |  |
| Development and marketing | −1.568 |  |
|  | (−0.148) |  |
| Production and marketing | 4.299 |  |
|  | (0.739) |  |
| Development, production and marketing | −1.068 |  |
|  | (−0.153) |  |
| Food and drink | 5.990 |  |
|  | (0.485) |  |
| Metals and minerals | 21.883* |  |
|  | (2.667) |  |
| Energy | 5.452 |  |
|  | (0.596) |  |
| Construction | 7.330 |  |
|  | (0.920) |  |
| Chemicals | 2.267 |  |
|  | (0.319) |  |
| Pharmaceuticals | 4.433 |  |
|  | (0.523) |  |
| Computers | −6.944 |  |
|  | (−0.929) |  |
| Telecommunications | −1.199 |  |
|  | (−0.230) |  |
| Other electrical | 5.388 |  |
|  | (0.779) |  |
| Automobiles | 3.127 |  |
|  | (0.436) |  |

*Table* 8.14    Contd.

|  | 1 | 2 |
|---|---|---|
| Aerospace | 0.969 | |
|  | (0.122) | |
| Other manufacturing | 0.742 | |
|  | (0.122) | |
| Transport | −6.664 | |
|  | (−0.712) | |
| Distribution | 5.189 | |
|  | (0.930) | |
| Other services | 1.547 | |
|  | (0.271) | |
| N | 179 | 180 |
| R square | 0.191 | 0.083 |
| Adj. R square | 0.053 | 0.067 |
| F value | 1.38 | 5.27* |

*$p < 0.01$; †$p < 0.05$.
$t$ Ratios in brackets.
Second half of the decade is the Time period reference category; Other is the Region
reference category; Service Provision is the Purpose reference category; Financial
Service is the Industry reference category.

set of regression equations produced disappointing results and
are not reported in full here. Apart from the intercept terms the
only significant coefficients on this second set of regression
equations were those on the region variables and the variables
for Group 1 manufacturing.

From the data available from press announcements it would
appear that the simplest possible equation that best captures the
impact of the independent variables on UK equity share is
regression 2 in Table 8.14. The regression as a whole is
significant at the 1 per cent level; of the three independent variables two are significant at the 1 per cent level and one at the 5
per cent level. The $R$ square for this regression is quite low,
however, as were the $R$ square statistics on all of the other estimated regression equations. The available data therefore explain
very little of the variance of the percentage equity share of UK
firms. This would imply that other variables have an important
influence. These influences can only be found at the individual
company level for firms involved in the joint ventures.

*Table* 8.15   Summary of chi-square tests

---

**H1:** The contractual form of the joint venture and the region of the foreign partner are independent

All JVs: Cannot reject.
Chi-square statistic = 1.44; $d.f.$ = 3; $p$ = 0.7

**H2:** The time period of the joint venture formation (first or second half of the decade) and the region of the foreign partner are independent

All JVs: Reject*   EJVs: Reject†   NEJVs: Reject*
All JVs: Chi-square statistic = 23.4; $d.f.$ = 3; $p < 0.01$
EJVs:        Chi-square statistic = 9.57; $d.f.$ = 3; $p < 0.05$
NEJVs:     Chi-square statistic = 13.00; $d.f.$ = 3; $p < 0.01$

**H3:** The industry of the joint venture and the time period (first or second half of the decade) of the joint venture formation are independent

All JVs: Cannot reject   EJVs: Cannot reject
NEJVs: Cannot reject
All JVs:        Chi-square statistic = 1.6; $d.f.$ = 2; $p$ = 0.45
EJVs:          Chi-square statistic = 0.47; $d.f.$ = 2; $p$ = 0.79
NEJVs:       Chi-square statistic = 1.33; $d.f.$ = 2; $p$ = 0.52

**H4:** The broad industry groupings and the region of the foreign partners are independent

All JVs: Cannot reject   EJVs: Cannot reject
NEJVs: Cannot reject
All JVs:        Chi-square statistic = 3.87; $d.f.$ = 4; $p$ = 0.42
EJVs:          Chi-square statistic = 6.2; $d.f.$ = 4; $p$ = 0.19
NEJVs:       Chi-square statistic = 2.58; $d.f.$ = 4; $p$ = 0.63

**H5:** The broad purpose of the joint venture and the time period of formation are independent

All JVs: Reject†   EJVs: Reject†   NEJVs: Cannot reject
All JVs:        Chi-square statistic = 8.13; $d.f.$ = 2; $p < 0.05$
EJVs:          Chi-square statistic = 6.37; $d.f.$ = 2; $p < 0.05$
NEJVs:       Chi-square statistic = 1.86; $d.f.$ = 2; $p < 0.40$

**H6:** The purpose of the joint venture and the region of the foreign partner are independent

All JVs: Reject†   EJVs: Cannot reject   NEJVs: Cannot reject
All JVs:        Chi-square statistic = 9.97; $d.f.$ = 4; $p < 0.05$
EJVs:          Chi-square statistic = 6.35; $d.f.$ = 4; $p$ = 0.174
NEJVs:       Chi-square statistic = 4.31; $d.f.$ = 4; $p$ = 0.365

**H7:** The industry of the joint venture and the purpose of the joint venture are independent

All JVs: Reject *   EJVs: Reject*   NEJVs: Reject*
All JVs:        Chi-square statistic = 269.63; $d.f.$ = 4; $p < 0.01$
EJVs:          Chi-square statistic = 153.36; $d.f.$ = 4; $p < 0.01$
NEJVs:       Chi-square statistic = 101.77; $d.f.$ = 4; $p < 0.01$

*Table* 8.15    Contd.

---

H8:      The industry of the joint venture and the contractual form are
         independent
             All JVs: Reject *
             All JVs:    Chi square statistic = 25.25; *d.f.* = 2; *p* < 0.01

H9:      The purpose of the joint venture and the contractual form of the
         joint venture are independent
             All JVs: Reject *
             All JVs:    Chi-square statistic = 70.4; *d.f.* = 7; *p* < 0.01

H10:     The number of partners in the joint venture and the contractual
         form are independent
             All JVs: Cannot reject
             All JVs:    Chi-square statistic = 2.62; *d.f.* = 4; *p* = 0.63
             (Two cells have less than five observations)

H11:     The proportion of UK equity shareholding in the joint venture and
         the regional location of the foreign partner are independent
             EJVs: Cannot reject
             EJVs:       Chi-square statistic = 5.55; *d.f.* = 4; *p* = 0.24

H12:     The proportion of the UK equity shareholding and the time period
         of the joint venture formation (first or second half of the decade)
         are independent
             EJVs: Reject *
             EJVs:       Chi-square statistic = 5.91; *d.f.* = 2; *p* < 0.01

H13:     The proportion of the UK equity shareholding and the broad
         industry grouping of the joint venture are independent
             EJVs: Cannot reject
             EJVs:       Chi-square statistic = 5.85; *d.f.* = 4; *p* = 0.20

H14:     The proportion of the UK equity shareholding and the broad
         purpose of the joint venture are independent.
             EJVs: Cannot reject
             EJVs:       Chi-square statistic = 4.98; *d.f.* = 4; *p* = 0.29

---

*Significant as 1 per cent level; [†] significant at 5 per cent level.

## 5    SUMMARY AND CONCLUSIONS

This paper has analyzed a new data set on the formation of joint
ventures between UK firms and firms in Western Europe, USA
and Japan over the 1980s. The main characteristics of this
activity can be summarized as follows:

(i) There was an uneven pattern of joint venture formation
    over the period but a distinct increase in the final two

years of the decade largely caused by the growth in the number of joint ventures with firms in Western Europe.

(ii) The majority of joint ventures were formed with firms in Western Europe with partnerships with United States firms a close second.

(iii) Almost half the total of joint ventures formed were grouped in just four industries: financial services, other manufacturing, telecommunications and aerospace, with the financial services sector playing a prominent role in joint venture formation across all three geographical regions.

(iv) The greatest proportion of joint ventures were formed for the purpose of service provision.

(v) The clear majority of joint ventures involved only one foreign partner, however, there was some willingness on the part of UK firms to enter into joint ventures with multiple partners.

(vi) Equity joint ventures were formed rather more often than non-equity ventures but there was not an overwhelming preference on the part of UK firms to adopt equity ventures.

A regression analysis investigated the factors influencing the proportion of UK equity shareholding in EJVs. The results of this analysis indicates that the regional location of the foreign partner plays a significant effect in determining UK equity share. Very little of the variance in UK equity shareholding is explained by the data available from press releases however.

These findings shed new light on an increasingly important aspect of corporate activity over recent years. Given the caveats with respect to the data source it is clear that the details of the findings must be considered tentative. Despite this, it is fair to say that the broad trends in UK joint venture formation with the world's major trading blocks are adequately represented by the findings presented in this paper.

While data of this nature is useful in building up a picture of joint venture activity there are a considerable number of significant issues that are not addressed. The strategic motivation driving the ventures is an obvious lacuna. Information on stra-

tegic rationale is often not included in the press reports and tha
which is tends to be sketchy and difficult to classify, hence it i
not recorded here. While press reports on joint venture for
mations are generally comprehensive the incidence of join
venture termination is not. This means that it is not possible t
gauge from the number of joint ventures formed in the 1980
those which are still in existence or to know the reasons under
lying the termination decisions. Measures of how successful th
ventures are perceived to be by both the partners and the way i
which the ventures are managed are both important issues whicl
cannot be considered with data of the nature reported here
Another important consideration is the way in which firms selec
partners for joint ventures. It is hoped to develop these aspects o
UK joint venture activity by more closely investigating th
partner firms included in this data set.

# References

Anderson, E. (1990). 'Two Firms, One Frontier: On Assessing Joint Ventur
Performance', *Sloan Management Review*, **31**(2) pp. 19–30.
Blodgett, L. L. (1991). 'Partner Contributions as Predicators of Equity Share i
International Joint Ventures', *Journal of International Business Studies*
**22**(1), pp. 63–78.
Buckley, P. J. and M. Casson (1988), 'A Theory of Co-operation i
International Business', in: F. J. Contractor and P. Lorange (eds)
*Cooperative Strategies in International Business*. Lexington Books
Lexington MA.
Coase, R. H. (1937). 'The Nature of the Firm', *Economica*, (New Series), **4**
pp. 386–405.
Contractor, F. J. and P. Lorange (eds) (1988a). *Cooperative Strategies i*
*International Business*. Lexington Books, Lexington, Mass.
Contractor, F. J. and P. Lorange (1988b). 'Why Should Firms Cooperate? Th
Strategy and Economics Basis for Cooperative Ventures', in: F. J. Contracto
and P. Lorange (eds), *Cooperative Strategies in International Business*
Lexington Books, Lexington, MA.
Doz, Y., C. K. Prahalad, and G. Hamel (1990). 'Control, Change an
Flexibility: the Dilemma of Transnational Collaboration', in: C. A. Barlett
Y. Doz and G. Hedlund (eds), *Managing the Global Firm*, Routledge
London.
Geringer, J. M (1991). 'Strategic Determinants of Partner Selection Criteria i
International Joint Ventures', *Journal of International Business*, **22**(1)
pp. 41–62.
Geringer, J. M. and L. Hebert (1989). 'Control and Performance o
International Joint Ventures', *Journal of International Business*, **20**(2)
pp. 97–101.

Ghemawat, P., M. E. Porter and R. A. Rawlinson (1986). 'Patterns of International Coalition Activity', in: M. E. Porter (ed.), *Competition in Global Industries*, Harvard Business School, Boston.

Hare, P., J. Lauchlan and M. Thompson (1989). *An Assessment of ESPRIT In The UK*. HMSO, London.

Harrigan, K. R. (1985). *Strategies for Joint Ventures*. Lexington Books, Lexington, Mass.

Harrigan, K. R. (1988). 'Joint Ventures and Competitive Strategy', *Strategic Management Journal*, **19**, pp. 141–158.

Hergert, M. and D. Morris (1988). 'Trends in International Collaborative Agreements', in: F. J. Contractor and P. Lorange (eds), *Cooperative Strategies in International Business*, Lexington Books, Lexington MA.

Hladik, K. J. (1985). *International Joint Ventures: An Economic Analysis of US–Foreign Business Partnerships*. Lexington Books, Lexington, Mass.

Killing, J. P. (1988). 'Understanding Alliances: The Role of Task and Organisational Complexity', in: F. J. Contractor and P. Lorange (eds), *Cooperative Strategies in International Business*. Lexington Books, Lexington MA.

Kogut, B. (1989). 'The Stability of Joint Ventures: Reciprocity and Competitive Rivalry', *The Journal of Industrial Economics*, **XXXVIII**(2), pp. 183–198.

Lyons, P. L. (1991). 'Joint Ventures as Strategic Choice – A Literature Review', *Long Range Planning*, **24**(4), pp. 130–144.

Mytelka, L. and M. Delapierre (1987). 'The alliance strategies of European firms in the Information Technology industry and the role of ESPRIT', *Journal of Common Market Studies*, **26**(2), pp. 129–151.

OECD (1986). *Competition Policy and Joint Ventures*. OECD, Paris.

Osborn, R. N. and C. C. Baughn (1987). 'New Patterns in The Formation of US/Japanese Cooperative Ventures: The Role of Technology', *Columbia Journal of World Business*, Summer, pp. 57–65.

Pfeffer, J. and P. Nowak (1976). 'Joint Ventures and Interorganisational Interdependence', *Administrative Science Quarterly*, **21**, pp. 398–418.

Pfeffer, J. and G. Salancik (1978). *The External Control of Organisations*. Harper & Row, New York.

Porter, M. E. and M. B. Fuller (1986). 'Coalitions and Global Strategy', in: M. E. Porter (ed.), *Competition in Global Industries*. Harvard Business School, Boston.

Root, F. R. (1988). 'Some Taxonomies of International Cooperative Arrangements'. In: F. J. Contractor and P. Lorange (eds), *Cooperative Strategies in International Business*. Lexington Books, Lexington MA.

Viesti, G. (1988). 'International Cooperative Agreements: New Strategies for International Growth and Technological Learning?' Paper presented to the 14th Annual meeting of the European International Business Association, Berlin, 11–13 December.

Williamson, O. E. (1975). *Markets and Hierarchies: Analysis and Anti-Trust Implications*. Free Press, New York.

# Part III

# Asia-Pacific Issues

# Europe 1992 and its Impact on Pacific Futures*

(*with* Hafiz Mirza and Kate Prescott)

As the Single European Market (SEM) develops into an economic reality it is inevitable that this will have an impact on the world economic order. Although Europe has for many years been a loose affiliation of countries belonging to the European Community (EC), and the European Free Trade Association (EFTA), as well as the CMEA, nothing compares with the coherence which '1992' and the Single European Market Act has begun to initiate. The wider market which the EC has now become, although not fully exploited by all firms to date, offers new potential for European companies to expand and raise their stature on a global scale. Similarly, the SEM represents both a threat and an opportunity to non-European firms, including the disparate enterprises of Asia-Pacific. However, it is necessary to recognize at the outset that many of the Europe-related threats and opportunities exist irrespective of the SEM. Since there is sometimes confusion in this regard, this issue will be dealt with first.

## 'NON-1992' EUROPEAN–ASIAN-PACIFIC RELATIONS

During the course of the post-war era, political-economic power, wealth, and growth has been concentrated in the United States, Western Europe, and Japan, with a further diffusion into neighbouring economies; a configuration which is aptly captured in Ohmae's notion of 'triad power'.[1] Given that a major element in

*The Pacific Review*, Vol. 4, No. 4, 1991, pp. 368–74 (reprinted by permission).

this expansion has been international trade and investment, it is not surprising that European and Asian-Pacific (including Japanese) firms have played a major role in each other's domain.[2] Having said this a number of qualifications are essential. First, both European and Asian-Pacific firms have hitherto had closer relations with the United States than each other. Thus as their mutual trade and investment increased during the 1980s and into the 1990s, partly as a result of United States protectionism against Asian-Pacific firms (especially those of Japan and the NIEs), it is not surprising that a secular expansion of Asian-Pacific business relations with Europe has been confused with the specific expansion/reaction related to the SEM.[3] Secondly there are huge differences between the nature of economic relations between Western Europe and Asian-Pacific countries. The latter, in particular, range from the highly industrialized such a Japan; through newly industrializing economies (NIEs) such as South Korea, Taiwan, Hong Kong, and Singapore; to countries a varying levels of development. In the last category, the resource rich ASEAN countries (the Association of South East Asian Countries, including Malaysia, Indonesia, Thailand, the Philippines, Brunei as well as Singapore) and China are perhaps the most significant. The consequence of this diversity is that the nature of relations with Western Europe (and responses to the SEM) varies quite dramatically with the type of Asian-Pacific economy. Thus, whereas with Japan and the NIEs much of the discussion during the 1980s revolved around their trade and investment penetration of the EC, the ASEAN countries were perhaps more concerned with maintaining an adequate inflow of foreign direct investment (FDI) from Europe as well as from their other sources (excluding other countries, of the total inflow of FDI into ASEAN in 1989, 32 per cent was from the EC, 43 per cent from Japan, and 25 per cent from the United States). Thirdly, much of the expansion of Asian-Pacific foreign investment into the EC (and the rest of Western Europe) can be explained through non-SEM factors such as the normal search for business opportunities, the benefits of an 'insider presence' and – especially – the rapid appreciation (at various times) of Asian-Pacific currencies such as the yen and the won which made exporting less viable compared to other forms of foreign marketing servicing.[5] Finally, the rapid expansion of Asian-Pacific firms into the EC resulted in a series of protectionist moves, mirroring the earlier United States protectionism, against imports from Japan and the NIEs. Anti-dumping, local content, voluntary restraints and other measures[6] generated some 'barrier jumping' investment in the 1980s and, linked with the general fears against 'Fortress Europe', there is sometimes a conflation (not entirely unjustified) of the earlier – continuing – protectionism and the measures relating to the SEM.

## THE RATIONALE OF THE SINGLE EUROPEAN MARKET

For many years the fragmented nature of Europe – consisting of a number of relatively small, highly distinct national markets – was believed to be one of the major causes of the poor competitiveness of European firms. The barriers to operating on a pan-European scale, restricting firms to domestic market operations, hampered the development of large firms and the realization of economies of scale. With the anticipated removal of barriers the scope for expanding across Europe has heightened and with it comes the new hope that EC firms will develop their capabilities and secure their positions as leading Multinational Enterprises.

The potential for European firms to strengthen their standing in international markets poses a threat to multinationals around the world. The Japanese and Americans, two of the world's major trading blocs, originally saw the creation of a unified Europe as the throwing down of the gauntlet by the European Commission heralding the start of major competitive warfare. Policies for restricting competition from outside the EC in the early round of developing the internal market were also regarded as the foundations of a fortress Europe which threatened to engender anti-competitive reactions from the Japanese and Americans.

The realization by the Commission (encouraged by anti-protectionist Member State governments) that shielding Europe from the rest of the world would be damaging in terms of a new global order of business activity, resulted in a relaxation of external competition policy. Europe has, therefore, come to look less like a fortress and more like a rejuvenated trading area taking a more active role as the third leg in the world triad of economic power next to America and Asia-Pacific. Nevertheless, protectionism is not absent from EC policy and because of the need to reunify EC companies (a good example is provided by the electronics and IT industry)[7] may yet become integrated with the SEM strategy and so needs examining.

## THE SIREN CALLS OF PROTECTIONISM

In much the same way that global oligopolies involve a small number of large dominant companies, the new world economic order is dominated by a relatively small number of major trading blocs. The growing propensity of countries to affiliate themselves with large economic unions reflects increased awareness that large unrestricted markets give rise to internal efficiency and economic welfare which has a bearing on outward trade and investment flows. The United States of America, which has been identified as an example of economic and political union, has been in the forefront of world trade and investment for a long time. Although recent years have witnessed a sharp erosion of their dominance, particularly in those sectors which have been encroached upon by the Japanese, the long-standing success of American firms is thought to be partly attributable to the coherence of the integration between the individual states and the size and stature of the American market. This also provides a strong platform for future economic development.

Indeed, the success of the United States as a world power and the benefits accruing to American firms from their being free to operate in such a wide market is often believed to have contributed to the greater competitiveness of American firms over their European counterparts. The larger scale of the former permits them greater scope to attain economies of scale and more resources for future investment; and the scale of the American market provides a wider pool of personnel on which to draw. One of the important motivations, then, for developing the SEM has been to emulate the United States' high degree of integration in an attempt to give firms free access to a wider market, promote internal efficiency and strengthen the position of Europe *vis à vis* the other leading world trading blocs.[8]

Taking the analogy of the global oligopoly one stage further, aggressively competitive actions by one party are matched by equally aggressive counteractions by others. It was not surprising, therefore, that signals by the EC of increased economic integration and consolidation led to threats by the Japanese and Americans of renewed protection against European imports. Fearing greater internal efficiency would lead to more effective competition, as firms are able to attain greater scale economies and improve their dynamic efficiency and thus their innovatory expertise, there were rumblings among American and Japanese industrialists, keen for their governments to shield them from the potential new threat, of a new round of world protectionism. Aiding and abetting this belief were reports emanating from Brussels which seemed to suggest that, along with the new internal freedoms for competition across the EC, external trade policies, in the short-term at least, would be designed to protect the EC from external pressures in an effort to allow firms and industries alike to strengthen their position in the new Europe.

Notwithstanding any efforts being made by the Commission to shield EC firms from external trade, evidenced by a reassessment of rules on dumping, increased attention to 'rules of origin' and a renewed effort to ensure 'reciprocity', the support of a strict, anti-competitive, external trade policy was not unanimously supported by all EC member states. Some countries, traditionally open to external competition, found this new protectionism ran contrary to their own national policies and, indeed, internal EC competition policy which was keenly promoting free competition and restricting any form of protectionism as detrimental to the promotion of efficiency. No country was more against a protectionist external trade policy than Britain, and Margaret Thatcher in her critique of the Community presented in Bruges in 1988 is quoted as saying:

My fourth guiding principle is that Europe should not be protectionist. It would be a betrayal if, while breaking down constraints on trade to create the single market, the Community were to erect greater external protection. We must make sure our approach to world trade is consistent with the liberalisation we preach at home.

Mrs Thatcher's comments are in keeping with the principle that protectionism stifles economic growth as it allows industries to avoid adjusting to changes in international competition, consumer demand and new technologies, a principle keenly supported by the Conservative party during its tenure of office throughout the 1980s. Nevertheless, some would argue that this approach has not served to promote adjustment by United Kingdom industry which has, in many sectors, atrophied and died in the face of aggressive competition. Added to this, the Japanese success story and latterly that of other Asian-Pacific NIEs, which is one of rapid economic development and external trade expansion, partly rests on an element of protectionism. Import substitution policies allowed Japan, Korea, and other countries to reduce their dependence on developed countries and establish their own industries to produce goods which were previously imported.

Porter argues that protection only works under three conditions.[9] The first is domestic rivalry, which acts as a surrogate to international competition and stimulates efficiency. Second, is the development of competitive advantages in the domestic market which can be transferred and sustained internationally. Finally, success depends on protection being implemented for a limited period as, in all cases, it ultimately serves to retard competitiveness. Japanese protectionism may be explained in these terms: firms in protected sectors faced aggressive internal, often oligopolistic, competition between the *keiretsu* groups. The nature of competition also served to militate against firms competing on price and encouraged innovation and differentiation, competitive advantages which could be transferred to international markets. Over time, this allowed Japanese firms to climb the quality ladder in their products and services. Finally, although protectionism has historically been a feature of the

panese and other Asian-Pacific markets, they have begun to
nbrace a more liberalized stance to foreign trade and
vestment although some barriers do remain.

The case of Japan and Asia-Pacific, then, while not dis-
uraging protectionism outright, provides some potential
ound-rules for the EC concerning which sectors should be
forded a degree of protection and for how long. What is less
ear, however, is how common external trade policy will affect
ading links between the EC, trading blocs, and other world
gions. In 1987 the signing, finally, of the United States-Canada
e-trade agreement was shrouded in accusations that moves of
is kind were serving to create trading blocs in which internal
ade was facilitated, external trade made more sensitive (often
ing based on the notion of reciprocity and 'tit-for-tat' agree-
ents) and countries outside the blocs became more isolated.
e overall effect has been the concentration of trade in highly
veloped economic regions. Increased momentum for the
eation of the SEM, with its directives to be in place by 1992,
elled the argument that there is a dominance of economic
wer in the leading industrialized countries (Ohmae's market
ad), which is potentially damaging to the global balance of
de and investment as it excludes those outside the core – the
ss developed countries in particular, including, of course,
SEAN, China and many other Asian-Pacific countries. On the
her hand, many of the imports from these latter countries are
oduced by the overseas subsidiaries of European firms and so
ey are less likely to suffer from specific (as opposed to general)
otectionist measures than, say, the Japanese, South Korean,
d Taiwanese.

## HE IMPLICATIONS OF THE SEM FOR ASIAN-PACIFIC
## RMS

e SEM, once realized, through the elimination of physical,
chnical, and fiscal barriers to business access will both open up
e opportunity of a unified market of 340 million consumers to
y firm in Europe, and simultaneously, unleash the threat of

new competition from any other location within the Community
Allied with ancillary benefits, such as economies of scale, it is
clear that firms will be faced with a new environment where new
strategies regarding organizations' alliances, pricing, distribution, and communications, etc., need to emerge. Table 9.1
indicates the various alternative strategies towards the SEM
available to both EC and Non-EC companies, including Single
Country versus Pan-European strategies.

Asian-Pacific firms (mainly Japanese firms such as Nissan
Sony, and Toshiba) with an existing strong representation in the
EC are among the best placed to take advantage of the SEM
since, unlike many localized European firms, they already have a
wider European perspective. Lower internal barriers (especially in
industries such as pharmaceuticals and telecommunications) will
allow their earlier access into the future reaches of the community
market, although they may find themselves faced with stiffer competition from emerging 'Pan-European' firms. Firms expanding
their representation in the EC (mainly Japanese and the NIE firms
such as Fujitsu, Samsung, and Tatung) are also able to take advantage of the 'greenfield' nature of their entry, as well as benefit from
ancillary factors such as access to European design and R & D
facilities.[10] Kume's analysis of Japanese companies (the main
Asian-Pacific entrants) manufacturing in Europe illustrates the
complex basis of European/Asian-Pacific interaction.[11] He shows
that of 242 respondents, 90 per cent indicated that their reason
for entering the EC was the need to 'globalize' (including the
opening of new markets), 28 per cent referred to trade friction
requiring entry and only 10 per cent mentioned SEM and
European Integration (multiple responses were allowed). In addition, a range of other primary and secondary factors were mentioned, including servicing the other Japanese MNEs in Europe
and securing new materials and information gathering.[12] An additional reason for entering the EC would be to fend off the anticipated increased competitiveness of European firms, both in
Europe and on a global front. Entry would aid Asian-Pacific firms
in their competition against European firms by:

- allowing them to take advantage of the benefits of the SEM
- allowing them to learn and gather information on the
  competitors, and

| Headquarters location | Current position | Alternative strategies | Comments |
|---|---|---|---|
| EC Companies | Single country focus | • Consolidate domestic market position through mergers, acquisitions, alliances<br>• Identify local market niches and tailor products/services to local needs<br>• Sell out to an expanding pan-European company<br>• Become a pan-European company by identifying a specialized customer segment with common needs throughout Europe<br>• Become an OEM supplier in multiple markets to pan-European companies | • Vulnerable to larger European competitors<br>• Vulnerable to lower-priced standard Europroducts |
| | Pan-European | • Fill in gaps in European product market portfolios (via acquisitions, alliances) to create a more strategically balanced pan-European company<br>• Develop European plan in context of global strategy | • Sales of many so-called pan-European companies are today weighted heavily toward the headquarters country market<br>• Avoid European myopia as markets become more global |

186

*Table* 9.1  Contd.

| Headquarters location | Current position | Alternative strategies | Comments |
|---|---|---|---|
| Non-EC Companies | Weak EC representation | • Consolidate domestic market position | • Stronger European competitors will attempt further penetration of non-EC markets |
| | | • Establish alliances with EC firms (especially for mutual distribution of products) | • Easier to penetrate multiple EC countries with trade barriers removed |
| | | • Sell out to EC firm expanding overseas | |
| | | • Establish initial or additional offices and manufacturing plants within EC before 1992. Acquire or invest if large company; joint venture if small company | • EC protectionism, local content, and reciprocity requirements may impede exports into EC after 1992 |
| | Strong EC representation | • Fill in gaps in European product/market portfolios to become even more strategically balanced | • Already see EC as one market – need to consolidate further as EC companies develop same perception |

*Source*: John A. Quelch and Robert D. Buzzell, 'Marketing Moves through EC Crossroads', *Sloane Management Review*, Vol. 31, No. 1, 1989.

- in an oligopolistic situation, permitting an 'exchange of threats' in each others' home triad economies.

The alternative to entry into Europe for a firm is to continue to foster its underlying competitive edge in the home economy, something which Asian-Pacific firms continue to do.[13] It is possible for companies to attempt to do both!

Of course, not all Asian-Pacific firms wishing to take advantage of the SEM will be able to enter the market or enter easily, in which case alternatives need to be sought. These include: (a) alliances with European and non-European firms with established positions in the EC; (b) entry via nearby locations, such as East Europe[14] and North Africa, with treaty access to the EC where Asian-Pacific firms, especially those from the NIEs and ASEAN, can implement their expertise (e.g. in using cheap, skilled labour) and technology in 'unsecured' economies; (c) attention to other countries, including the United States (which is already an established market) and other developing countries (the recent Korean and Japanese attention to Mexico is similar to using East Europe as access to both the local and EC market);[15] (d) continue to restructure at home and use the enhanced competitiveness to service the European market by exports; and (e) expand economic relations with other Asian-Pacific economies.

This last possibility is, of course, already occurring in any case under the dynamic, intertwined and rapid economic growth throughout the region; although the ultimate solution would be the establishment of a Pacific Asian Economic Community, a concept hitherto resisted in its multitude of forms by many Asian-Pacific economies because of the central role of Japan, but now under serious consideration.[16] An SEM related spur to this might result from the relative 'retreat' of European firms from Asia-Pacific because of either the need to consolidate their position in Western Europe or the availability of cheap, skilled labour in Eastern Europe. Although there is no real evidence of this occurring, countries such as China and ASEAN members are clearly concerned because of their comparative dependence on offshore production. It is for this reason that many ASEAN countries have become more sympathetic towards the idea of a

Pacific-Asian Economic Community, which is certainly broadly feasible as a concept. If this was to occur, there would be three major trade blocs of comparable size: North America[17] with a total product of $5.9 billion in 1989 (the United States accounting for 90 per cent); Europe[18] with a total product of $6.2 billion (the EC accounting for 81 per cent); and Asia-Pacific[19] with a total product of $3.7 billion (Japan accounting for 76 per cent).[20] With Asia-Pacific growing most rapidly (around 6 per cent per annum in 1990 compared to 1 per cent for North America and 3 per cent for Western Europe) it would be ironic if a major consequence of the SEM, a strategy aimed at making European firms more competitive, ended up 'locking them out' of the most dynamic region in the world.

## Notes

1. Kenichi Ohmae, *Triad Power* (New York: The Free Press, 1985).
2. 'The Stateless Corporation', *Business Week*, 14 May 1990.
3. Gorota Kume, 'Japanese Manufacturing Investments in the European Community: Motivations and Locations', *EXIM Review*, Vol. 10, No. 1, 1991.
4. EC, *The European Community's Relations with ASEAN* (Brussels: European Information, Commission of the European Communities, 1991).
5. Hafiz Mirza, Peter J. Buckley, and John R. Sparkes, 'New Multinationals for Old? The Political Economy of Japanese Internationalisation', *Japan Forum*, Vol. 2, No. 2, 1990.
6. Soistu Watanabe, 'Trends of Japan's Direct Investment in Europe', *EXIM Review*, Vol. 9, No. 1, 1988.
7. EC, *The European Electronics and Information Technology Industry: State of Play, Issues at Stake and Proposals for Action* (Brussels: DG XIII, Commission of the European Communities, 1991).
8. For various aspects of the issues involved see, Paolo Cecchini, 1992: *The Benefits of a Single Market* (London: Wildwood House, 1988); Nicholas Colchester and David Buchan, *Europe Relaunches: Truths and Illusions on the Way to 1992* (London: Economist Books, 1990); John Dunning, 'European Integration and Transatlantic Foreign Direct Investments: The Record Assessed' (Paper presented at the UK Academy of International Business, 6–7 April 1990, Strathclyde University); 'A Survey of the European Community: an Expanding Universe', *The Economist*, 7 July 1990; John A. Quelch and Robert D. Buzzell, 'Marketing Moves through EC Crossroads', *Sloane Management Review*, Vol. 31, No. 1, 1989; John Burton, 'Single Market Changed Swedish Priorities', *Financial Times*, 21 February 1990; and 'The New Rush to Europe', *Business Week*, 26 March 1990.

9. Michael E. Porter, *The Competitive Advantage of Nations* (London: Macmillan Press, 1990).
0. *Japan in a Changing Europe* (London: Anglo-Japanese Economic Institute, 1991).
1. *ibid.*
2. See JETRO, *Current Situation of Business Operations of Japanese-Manufacturing Enterprises in Europe* (Tokyo, 1990) and Sung-Jo Park, 'Accessibility of Non-European Multinationals to the European Community in 1992', *The Pacific Review*, Vol. 3, No. 4, 1990.
3. BOT, 'Structural Changes in South Korean Economy', (Bank of) *Tokyo Financial Review*, June 1990.
4. Nina McPherson, 'Eastern Europe's Attractions', *Billion*, Vol. 2, No. 5, 1990.
5. See 'Building a Wider Path for Mutual Benefits', *Korean Chamber of Commerce and Industry, Quarterly Review*, July 1990; and Terutomo Ozawa, 'The Dynamics of Pacific Asian Industrialization: How Mexico Can Join the Asian Flock of "Flying Geese"', in: Riordan Roett (ed.), *Mexico's External Relations in the 1990s* (Boulder and London: Lynne Rienner, 1991).
6. Peter Drysdale, *International Economic Pluralism: Economic Policy in East Asia and the Pacific* (Sydney and London: Allen and Unwin, 1988); Kate Grosser and Brian Bridges, 'Economic Interdependence in East Asia: The Global Context', *The Pacific Review*, Vol. 3, No. 1, 1990; and Achim von Heynitz, *Some Guidelines for an European Policy Towards the Asian Newly Industrializing Economics* (Ebenhausen: Stiftung Wissenschaft und Politik (SWP), 1989).
7. The United States, Canada, and Mexico.
8. The EC, EFTA, and Eastern Europe (excluding the Soviet Union, Turkey, Malta and Cyprus).
9. Japan, China, the East Asian NIEs, and ASEAN.
0. These figures were calculated from BIS (1991) *Bank for International Settlements: 61st Annual Report*, Basle; Asian Development Bank (1990), *Key Indicators of Developing Asian and Pacific Countries*, Manila; UBS (1991) 'Eastern Europe: Waiting for a Market', *UBS International Finance*, Spring, 1991.

# 10 Forms of Enterpreneurial Cooperation between Chinese and Foreign Enterprises: Taxation Implications*

(*with* Eugen Jehle)

## INTRODUCTION

Hardly an economic development in the period since World War II has attracted the interest of the international business community in such an intensive manner as did the announcement in 1978/79 of the policy to open the Chinese economy to foreign enterprises. Quite a number of 'recession-hit' enterpreneurs and managers believed that they had finally discovered a country with almost unlimited cooperation possibilities, in a market of around one billion people. And indeed: 'in geographical size and internal diversity, in the age and richness of its civilization, and in its recent political history, China is unique' (World Bank, Vol. I, 1983).

The unlimited enthusiasm of the early days was quickly replaced by a more realistic view when China's economic, social and political constraints were properly evaluated. Two of those constraints serve as examples (World Bank, Vol. I, 1983):

1.   The structure of China's economic system, consisting almost exclusively of a largely urban state economy characterized by public ownership, centralization of economic decisions, strictly hierarchical control, and little reliance on markets or prices, and a rural commune economy in which large

* Nigel Campbell and John S. Henley (eds) *Advances in Chinese Industrial Studies, Part B*, JAI Press, Greenwich, Conn, 1990 (reprinted by permission).

d most capital are owned and used collectively and in
nich, although to a lesser extent, central directives must be
llowed.

2. The development policy that had been followed until then
ncentrated on two main objectives: industrialization, and in
rticular the development of a heavy industrial base; and
imination of the worst aspects of poverty. These two con-
aints played a central role: an extreme shortage of cultivatable
nd in relation to population, and a high degree of international
olation.

The almost exclusively domestic orientated enterprise struc-
re, strict central control, little flexibility for change, and
ina's international isolation resulted in a situation where there
as no legislative framework available in 1978/79 within which
w large scale cooperation between Chinese and foreign enter-
ises could be organized. The Chinese government chose a
licy of introducing legislation in the field of investment and
xation on an ad hoc basis. In the early phase of liberalization,
terested parties had considerable freedom to develop and
sign cooperation schemes on the basis of individual contracts,
itially without underlying legislation. The experience gained
as then incorporated in laws and regulations promulgated in the
st few years to form the legislative framework for subsequent
reign investment in China. This method of learning from
perience continues to feed into legislation still in preparation.

The legal and taxation implications of involvement with a
reign investor are not simply technical matters. Several factors
fecting business strategy are also involved.

First, legal and taxation factors affect whether or not foreign
operation takes place. From the host country's point of view,
ws and taxes may be designed to restrict foreign involvement
rhaps in a particular region or industry. From the foreign col-
borator's viewpoint, laws and taxes are important ingredients
the 'investment climate' of a host country and may make the
fference between a decision to invest or to seek opportunities
sewhere.

Second, laws and taxation requirements may affect the form of
reign involvement through the choice of cooperation mode. In

this paper we discuss tax regulations governing wholly foreign
owned ventures, equity and contractual joint ventures
technology transfer and compensation trade agreements.

Third, the choice of location for the foreign entrant may be
affected by differential types of legislation, particularly tax
legislation.

Fourth, the regulatory framework can influence the location of
decision-making power within joint ventures, determining in part
whether decisions are taken by the foreign parent company, the
local partner or jointly in a cooperative fashion (Buckley and
Casson, 1988).

Because the Chinese open door policy is less than ten years
old and despite the immense progress that has already been
made, the situation is still changing and, indeed has to change
very rapidly if the envisaged goals are to be achieved.


## A BRIEF OVERVIEW OF THE TAX SYSTEM OF CHINA AS IT AFFECTS FOREIGN INVESTMENT

After the revolution in 1949, China completely changed its fiscal
system (Jehle, 1982). Industrial and commercial cooperative
enterprises were subject to the industrial and commercial income
tax, based on the provisional regulations of December 10, 1950.
Agricultural undertakings (people's communes and/or sub
divisions thereof) were (and still are) subject to the agricultural
tax, based on regulations released on June 3, 1958, as amended.
Any transaction effected or services rendered by an industrial
commercial, trade or service business was and, to some exten
still is, subject to the industrial and commercial consolidated tax
based on regulations and detailed rules promulgated or
September 13, 1958, as amended. In addition to these major
taxes, there were a number of levies of minor significance such
as the urban real property tax, the motor vehicles tax, and the
salt tax.

With the announcement of the policy of the 'four modern
izations' in 1978, major changes were gradually introduced s
that today, some 9 years later, far-reaching reform of the entir

scal system is at an advanced stage. This affects almost all forms
f ownership of enterprises, public or collective, domestically-
wned or those in which foreigners have an interest. With respect
o purely domestic enterprises, state-owned enterprises are subject
o an income tax (based on the law of April 29, 1983), col-
ectively-owned enterprises engaged in industrial and commercial
ctivities are subject to the collective enterprise income tax (based
n the law of April 11, 1985), privately-owned enterprises are
ubject to the income tax concerning urban and rural individually
perated industrial and commercial businesses (based on the law
f January 7, 1986). Since this paper is confined to different
spects of cooperation between Chinese and foreign enterprises,
evelopments in the domestic sector of the Chinese economy and
scal system are not discussed.

As far as foreign enterprises and foreign individuals working
n China are concerned, there are currently three major pieces of
ax legislation:

- the Income Tax Law for Equity Joint Ventures of
  September 10, 1980, as supplemented and amended;
- the Individual Tax Law of September 10, 1980, as supplemented and amended; and
- the Foreign Enterprise Income Tax Law of December 18,
  1981, as supplemented and amended.

With respect to the taxation of transactions, it is still the indus-
rial and commercial consolidated tax to which the turnover of
nterprises with a foreign interest is subjected. Whether China is
oing to adopt the European system of Value Added Taxation
VAT) instead of the present system with its cascade taxation
ffect, remains to be seen. The implementation of VAT in the
Chinese economy would appear, at least at first glance and disre-
arding possible administrative constraints, to be mainly posi-
ive, for more diversification of industrial production would be
ncouraged through the introduction of VAT as turnover tax neu-
rality would be achieved by crediting previously paid VAT
gainst the firm's own VAT tax liability.

Mention must also be made of Chinese customs duties. Most
mports are subject to an import duty; the rates at which this duty

is levied depends on the type of commodity imported. Furthermore, a distinction is made between the 'general rates' and 'minimum rates' that apply to imports from those countries with which China has a trade agreement. On a small number of items, China charges an export duty.


## MAJOR TAXES AFFECTING FOREIGN ENTERPRISES AND INDIVIDUALS

These taxes are important to all foreign enterprises and individuals working in China (Jehle, 1985):

Equity joint ventures operating in China are, in principle, subject to a flat 30% national income tax and a 3% local income tax, bringing the total tax burden to 33%.

Foreign enterprises operating in China in a form other than an equity joint venture are taxed as follows:

Operating profits are, in principle, taxed at progressive rates ranging from 20% on an annual profit below 250,000 yuan to 40% on an annual profit exceeding 10 million yuan. In addition to this national tax, local authorities may levy an additional 10% surtax which brings the total tax burden to 30% on a profit up to 250,000 yuan, and to approximately 50% for profits exceeding 10 million yuan.

Nonoperating income ('passive income' received by enterprises not present in China) such as dividends, interest, rentals, royalties or other payments described as taxable income by the Ministry of Finance is, in principle, taxed at a flat rate of 20%.

Foreign individuals living in China for more than 5 years are, in principle, subject to Chinese personal income tax on their world-wide income.[1] Those living in China for less than 5 years are, in principle, liable to Chinese income tax on their Chinese-source income. Employment income is subject to tax at progressive rates which are divided into 7 brackets; the first 800 yuan per month are tax exempt, the next bracket (801–1500 yuan) is taxed at a rate of 5% and the last bracket (monthly income exceeding 12,000 yuan) is taxed at the (marginal) rate of 45%. Other categories of income, compensation for personal services, royalties and rentals are, in principle, taxed at a flat rate of 20% (for residents of China, an allowance is available so the effective rate is reduced 16%); the same rate of 20% applies to interest, dividends and bonuses for all taxpayers (but no allowance for residents). It must be remembered that the tax situations referred to above apply only 'in principle.' Under certain circumstances tax incentive measures or tax treaty provisions may bring about deviations from the tax treatment described here.

Another type of tax encountered by foreign enterprises operating in China is the industrial and commercial consolidated tax. The applicable rate of this tax depends, broadly speaking, on the degree of necessity which the goods or services have for an average citizen; it is nil or low (1.5%) for daily necessities, and as high as 69% for luxury products. Four broad distinctions are made (Jehle, 1986):

| Type of activity | Tax rate |
| --- | --- |
| Industrial and agricultural commodities | 1.5–69% |
| Retail Sales | 3.0% |
| Transportation and telecommunication services | 2.5% |
| Service commissions | 3.7% |

The tax rates referred to above represent national rates; on top of these a local surcharge of 1% is added. Thus, where the national tax rate is 30%, the total tax rate amounts to 30.3%. Since July 16, 1985, China charges an 'import regulatory tax' on a number of items, in addition to the import duty and the industrial and commercial consolidated tax that are levied on imports. The commodities that fall under this tax include:

- motor cycles which are taxed at 20%
- peripheral equipment for computers is taxed at 30%
- polyester yarn, tyre cord and similar fabrics of a synthetic nature are taxed at 40%

- electronic valves, motor vehicles for transport and motor lorries are taxed at 50%
- video recorders, color tv sets and spare parts are taxed at 70%, and
- calculators and photocopy equipment are taxed at 80%.

In addition to these taxes, foreign enterprises and individuals living in China are in most cases subject to:

- building tax (based on legislation promulgated on September 15, 1986) for the premises they rent, and to
- motor vehicles tax (based on legislation promulgated on September 15, 1986) for any vehicles or boats they make use of in China.

Certain forms of entrepreneurial cooperation between Chinese and foreign enterprises employing Chinese personnel may also be subjected to social security payments. Such payments may amount to as much as 30% of the payroll for all Chinese employees. The contract must be concluded with the People's Insurance Company of PRC.


## FEATURES OF THE TAX INCENTIVES GRANTED IN CHINA

Tax incentives available in China may be broadly categorized into two groups:

1. with respect to taxes on income (profits):
   - a low tax rate (commonly 15% national tax plus 10% local surcharge, thus a 16.5% total tax burden on operation profits, and a 10% withholding tax on nonoperation profits), available on a more or less permanent basis, as it is granted with respect to operations in Special Economic Zones, Economic Development Zones and 'Old City Areas';
   - an initial tax holiday and a tax rebate following the tax holiday period; this type of tax incentive is frequently made available by the underlying tax law and/or by specific legislation for specific activities;

- a refund of tax for (previously taxed) profits that are reinvested, for example, as provided for in the joint venture income tax law;
, with respect to the industrial and commercial consolidated tax and customs duties:
  - an exemption from or a reduction in levies on imported business assets, components and parts, and raw materials, used in the joint venture. Commodities produced by the enterprise may enjoy special tax treatment if they are exported or sold within a Special Economic Zones or Economic Development Zone.

The above represent only very broad categories. Provincial or )cal regulations may lead to deviations in general rules )ncerning taxation; also land use fees and similar charges.

While the formal tax 'environment' influences investment con-derations, the strategic decision is made when the form of cooper-ion is chosen. Much will, of course, depend on the specific rcumstances of a concrete case, including the kind of partner(s) d the size of a given undertaking. In this context, the advice of )ecialized consultants, lawyers and accountants, enterprises ready operating in China, specialized Chinese investment bodies d commercial banks is indispensable for 'newcomers.' Even ose enterprises which have extensive experience in one province ay face completely different problems in other parts of China. ew and unfamiliar cooperation schemes also may cause prob-ms. Nothing should be taken for granted in China (Stephanek, 982; Zhang Shangtang, 1984, Chiang, 1984; Lee and Ness, 1986).

AX ISSUES AFFECTING DIFFERENT FORMS OF OOPERATION WITH PARTICULAR REFERENCE TO RITISH COMPANIES

## Vholly Foreign Owned Ventures

### omestic Chinese Taxation

he income (profit) of a wholly foreign owned enterprise is bject to the Foreign Enterprise Income Tax. Where such an enterprise reinvests after-tax profits, it may apply for a refund of the taxes previously paid. Turnover is usually subject to the Industrial and Commercial Consolidated Tax, and other minor taxes may apply.

## *The Tax Treaty between China and UK*

At present, China does not levy a withholding tax on profit distributions of wholly owned foreign enterprises.

Article 23 of the tax treaty provides that a UK taxpayer could claim a credit for the Chinese withholding tax levied or, where tax incentive measures in China apply, a tax sparing credit would be available (i.e., a credit for fictitiously paid Chinese taxes). Where a British enterprise owns at least 10% of the equity in the wholly owned foreign venture in China, it may also claim an 'indirect' tax credit, that is, it may also – in addition to the possible withholding tax – set off the Chinese (Foreign Enterprise Income) tax paid by the wholly owned foreign venture against its (British) tax liability, on a proportional basis.

## Equity Joint Ventures

### *Domestic Chinese Taxation*

An equity joint venture is subject to the Joint Venture Income Tax which is, as a general rule, levied at a flat rate of 33%.

Where the foreign partner transmits his share in the profit abroad, a 10% remittance tax usually falls due which may, however, also be waived by tax incentive provisions.

Where the foreign partner reinvests his share of the profit for at least 5 years after the distribution has taken place, he may claim a refund of 40% of the tax previously paid on that share of the profit.

The turnover of an equity joint venture is generally subject to the industrial and commercial consolidated tax where the products produced are sold within China, unless specific tax incentive rules provide otherwise. The same applies to customs duties.

Equity joint ventures may be held responsible for the payment of the Building Tax and the Motor Vehicles Tax.

*The Tax Treaty between China and UK*

An equity joint venture is subject to the Equity Joint Venture Tax Law which regards the venture as a legal person, and profit distributions are, therefore, classified as dividends for purposes of the tax treaty. Such dividends may be subject to a 10% withholding tax which is creditable against British tax ('direct tax credit') or, where a tax incentive measure in China applies, a tax sparing credit is available (a credit for fictitiously paid Chinese taxes). Where a British enterprise owns at least 10% of the equity in the equity joint venture in China, it may also claim an 'indirect tax credit,' that is, it may also – in addition to the possible withholding tax – set off the Chinese (foreign enterprise income) tax paid by the equity joint venture against the (British) tax liability, on a proportional basis.

## Contractual Joint Ventures

*Domestic Chinese Taxation*

Since the legal status of contractual joint ventures is not always clear, there is some uncertainty as to the tax treatment. Where a contractual joint venture is beyond doubt not a legal entity, its income (profit) is subject to the Foreign Enterprise Income Tax whereby taxation takes place at the level of the partners. Where the status is doubtful, and where taxation according to the Joint Venture Income Tax is regarded to be more favorable, the partners should apply to the competent authorities to be treated like an equity joint venture.

The turnover of contractual joint ventures is usually subject to the industrial and commercial consolidated tax, and other minor taxes may apply.

*The Tax Treaty between China and UK*

In applying the tax treaty with respect to the profit distributions of contractual joint ventures, some complications can occur due to uncertainties concerning the legal status of a contractual joint venture.

Where a contractual joint venture is clearly modeled along th
lines of the equity joint venture law, and confirmation is obtaine
concerning tax treatment, there can be little doubt that any pro
distributions will qualify as dividends, with the consequenc
outlined under 'equity joint ventures.' Where contractual joi
ventures are, however, taxed according to the foreign enterpri
income tax law, the situation could be different. It may b
assumed that the income of a contractual joint venture represen
'business income' in the sense of Article 7 of the tax treat
Then, China would have the right to tax any such busine
income, and the UK would allow a tax credit for the Chine
taxes paid or, where tax incentives are granted by China, a ta
sparing credit subject to a maximum of 10 years. The credit pr
cedure is outlined in Article 23 (2) and (3) of the tax treaty.

## Transfer of Technology Agreements

*Whether or Not a Tax Liability Arises in Connection wi
Transfer of Technology Depends on the Precise Contents of th
Agreement*

The sale of hardware is usually not subject to income tax.
there is building, construction, installation or assembly wo
involved, a tax liability may occur if a permanent establishme
exists. This would give rise to liabilities to the Forei
Enterprise Income Tax, either on the basis of an account syste
or on a deemed profit calculation. With respect to payments su
as interest, royalties and technical fees (including training fee
the ordinary withholding tax of 20% would apply. It mu
however, be borne in mind that with respect to the transfer
technology, a wide range of specific tax incentives is availab
provided certain conditions are met.

### The Tax Treaty between China and UK

As regards the question of whether a permanent establishme
exist in connection with building, construction, installation
assembly work, Article 5 states that this is only the case if it la
for more than 6 months. As regards payments such as intere

oyalties and technical fees, the rate is lowered to 10% in the
ase of interest (Article 11), 10% in case of royalties for patent
ights (Article 12 (2) (a)), and effectively 7% in the case of
oyalties for use of industrial, commercial or scientific equip-
nent (Article 12 (2) (b)) or technical fees (Article 13).

In all these cases, the UK will grant its taxpayers a tax credit
or the Chinese taxes paid, or where tax incentives are granted by
China, a tax sparing credit (Article 23).

## Compensation Trade Agreements

### Domestic Chinese Taxation

As a general rule, straight-forward compensation trade agree-
nents do not evoke a tax liability to the foreign enterprise
nvolved (Maaren, 1986).

If there are, however, elements included such as the instal-
ation of equipment, transfer of technology, provision of know-
ow and/or training, extension of loans, and so forth, a liability
o the Foreign Enterprise Income Tax may occur. A liability to
he Industrial and Commercial Consolidated Tax (and import
uties) may be given where imported equipment or finished
roducts are sold within China (Jack, 1986; Gelatt and Pomp,
984).

### The Tax Treaty between China and UK

Where no tax liability and tax payment occurred in China, no
elief measure need be provided for in the UK. The tax treaty
oes not specifically refer to income from a source mentioned
nder the heading 'compensation trade.' Where, however, any
ayment made by a Chinese person to a UK person is classified
s loan interest, royalty or a technical fee, China has the right
o levy a withholding tax which is fixed at a maximum of 10%
n case of interest (Article 11) and 10% in case of royalties
or patent rights (Article 12 (2) (a)), and effectively 7% in
ase of royalties for the use of industrial, commercial or
cientific equipment (Article 12 (2) (b)) or technical fees
Article 13).

## CONCLUSION

Whether China's 'open door policy' can be described as a success depends, of course, on what expectations the Chinese government had when it introduced that policy. Some commentators feel that China is disappointed (Becker, 1986). However, given the absorption and adaptation problems which any economy isolated from other economies for a long time faces, and given the progress that has been made in establishing, within a relatively short period of time, an almost comprehensive domestic legal system in economic matters and a network of bilateral treaties (particularly investment protection agreements and treaties for the avoidance of double taxation) in support of efforts to attract foreign investment, progress has been substantial.

As far as taxation is concerned, the detailed rules of January 30, 1987 for the implementation of the Provisions of October 11, 1986 brought the clarity necessary to improve the 'fiscal climate' for foreign investment. The measures include:

- an exemption from the 10% tax on the repatriation of profits to partners in Sino-foreign export enterprises and technologically advanced enterprises (starting with fiscal year 1986);
- enterprises that export more than 70% of their production in terms of value (hereinafter export enterprises) enjoy a tax rebate of 50% after the expiration of the time period during which they have been fully exempt; where the application of the tax rebate would lead to an applicable tax rate of less than 10%, a 10% minimum tax rate shall nevertheless be applied for export enterprises;
- technologically advanced enterprises may enjoy a 3-year extension of the 50% tax rebate period;
- foreign investors who reinvest the profits distributed to them by their enterprises in order to establish or expand export enterprises or technologically advanced enterprises for an operational period of not less than 5 years can apply for a full refund of the enterprise income tax previously

paid on the reinvested portion of the profit; this rule applies to profits reinvested in years starting from 1986.

● the Provisions of October 11, 1986 do not apply to Sino-foreign enterprises undertaking joint exploration and exploitation of oil and previous metal resources.

Within an extremely short period of time, China has established a legislative framework, particularly for its internationally oriented economy which quickly approaches comprehensiveness and, as such, forms a good basis for many different forms of interpreneurial cooperation between Chinese and foreign enterprises. Moreover, China has become a party to many bilateral treaties that encourage the expansion of international cooperation, including investment protection agreements and treaties for the avoidance of double taxation.

However, the period during which foreign enterprises have been able to operate in China has been too short to build up sufficient experience of the operation of the tax system. The actual establishment of many ventures is of such a recent date that many of them are still in the tax holiday period and, as such, have not paid tax.

A big problem that remains is the bewildering variety of different pieces of legislation by provincial/local authorities which causes uncertainty among foreign investors, and extra costs. It is certainly reasonable, for instance, to charge different land use fees in urban and rural areas. But any such provision should easily be accessible, without extensive study of legislation. Matters would be much improved if legislation released by central government provided a model for provincial and local legislators to follow so that any deviations could be confined to rates of taxation.

Foreign business activity in China that is to have a long-term future will require an increasingly sophisticated approach. This paper can only offer a very brief introduction to the rapidly evolving Chinese system of taxation of foreign investment. Clearly, established forms of cooperation, as much as new ones, need to be evaluated in the light of charges in the tax regime.

## Note

1.  In order to avoid any confusion, it must be borne in mind that the personal income tax described applies to foreigners, that is, persons other than Chinese citizens who have a domicile in the People's Republic of China. For Chinese citizens who have a domicile in China, a specific individual Income Regulatory Tax was introduced on September 25, 198 (Li Jinyan, 1987).

## References

Becker, J. (1986). 'China Disappointed with Open Door Policy Results.' The *Guardian*, February 3.

Buckley, P. J. and M. Casson. (1988). 'A Theory of Cooperation i International Business,' in: F. J. Contractor and P. Lorange (eds *Cooperative Strategies in International Business*. Lexington, MA: Lexingto Books.

Chiang, J. (1984). 'Factors to Consider as China's Door Opens Wider: Checklist for Investors.' *The China Business Review*, November/December pp. 18–19.

Ernst & Whinney (1986). *Taxation – The People's Republic of China*. Hon Kong: Ernst & Whinney.

Gelatt, T. A. and R. D. Pomp. (1984) 'Tax Aspects of Doing Business with th People's Republic of China.' *Columbia Journal of Transnational Law* pp. 421–504.

Guangzhou Municipal Taxation Bureau. (1985). *Guide to Taxation in th People's Republic of China for Investors*. Hong Kong: Coopers & Lybrand

Jack, M. (1986). 'Update on the Most Tax Effective Structure for Your Chin Business.' Conference Paper, Zurich.

Jehle, E. (1982). 'The Tax System of the People's Republic of China – A Shor Survey.' Text of talk delivered on June 11, 1982 at the Workshop on Chines Law in Paris. (Reproduced in: *Bulletin for International Fisca Documentation*, 1982, pp. 447–451.)

Jehle, E. (1985). 'Taxation in the People's Republic of China – Tax Laws Tax Incentives – Tax Treaties.' *Bulletin for International Fisca Documentation*, pp. 405–427.

Jehle, E. (1986). 'The Tax System of the People's Republic of China, See from a European Viewpoint.' *APTIRC-Bulletin Singapore*, May: 212–219.

Lee, S.-J. and A. Ness. (1986). 'Investment Approval.' *The China Busines Review*, May/June, pp. 14–18.

Li, Jinyan. (1987). 'The New Regulatory Tax on Individual Income.' *Bulleti for International Fiscal Documentation*, April, pp. 167–171.

Li, S. (1987) *Bilateral Investment Promotion and Protection Agreements Practice of the People's Republic of China*. The Hague: Institute of Socia Studies.

Maaren, Th. van (1986). 'Legal and Tax Aspects of Doing Business in China. Caron & Stevens in cooperation with Baker & McKenzie, Amsterdam, Hon Kong, Beijing and Shanghai.

Ness, A. and S. J. Mitchell (1986). 'Taxing US Offices in China.' *The China Business Review*, September/October, pp. 36–39.

Stepanek, J. B. (1982) 'Direct Investment in China.' *The China Business Review*, September/October, pp. 20–22.

World Bank. (1983) *A World Bank Country Study: China – Socialist Economic Development*; Volume I: *The Economy, Statistical System, and Basic Data*, Volume II: *The Economic Sectors, Agriculture, Industry, Energy, Transport, and External Trade and Finance*; Volume III: *The Social Sectors, Population, Health, Nutrition and Education*, Washington, DC: World Bank.

Zhang, S. (1984). 'Investment in China Practice and Theory,' *International Business Lawyer*, September, pp. 361–365.

# 11 Government–Industry Relations: Japan versus UK*

(*with* Hafiz Mirza, C. L. Pass and John R. Sparkes)

## INTRODUCTION

Government–industry relations are a crucial element in fosterin industrial and international competitiveness. The rapid rate which new technologies are simultaneously promoting ar undermining existing industries, allied to the internation restructuring process, has led to the recognition that goc government–industry relations are essential for a smooth proces of transition.

We set out to examine these relations in Japan and the Unite Kingdom, the latter in a European context. Our objective was enhance the understanding of the mechanisms by which Japa and the UK/Europe manage the restructuring process. From th outset it was determined that emphasis would be placed c examining the Japanese context because it is generally reco nised that Japan has been proficient in promoting industri restructuring, particularly in the key area of internationall traded goods.

To provide a framework for the study, we investigated the pr motion of an expanding industry, pharmaceuticals, and sought compare government–industry relations in this particular cas with the management of an industry which had experienced period of decline as a result of the 'oil shocks' in 1973 and 197 viz petrochemicals. This paper is designed to test a model fc examining the specific mechanisms facilitating the process c

* *International Business Review*, Vol. 2, No. 1, 1993, pp. 15–37 (with kind permissic from Elsevier Science Ltd, The Boulevard, Langford Lane, Kidlington OX51GI England).

•vernment–industry relations. The model is developed in the
ction entitled 'Industrial Policy and Government–Industry
:lations in Japan' and, following a background section on
ιarmaceuticals and petrochemicals, applied primarily to Japan
n which the model was based) in the section entitled 'The
npirical Study'. Comparative material comparing our findings
ι government–industry relations in Japan with the European
uation is presented as appropriate in the sections entitled 'The
lobal Pharmaceuticals and Petrochemicals Industries:
ιckground and The Restructuring Process' and 'The Empirical
udy'. 'The Empirical Study' section also refers to the method-
ogy. The last section concludes with a discussion of future
search directions.

## IDUSTRIAL POLICY AND GOVERNMENT–INDUSTRY ELATIONS IN JAPAN

ιe question of the effectiveness of Japanese industrial policy is
:nerally agreed to hinge around government–industry or,
:rhaps more appropriately, bureaucracy–industry relations
Japan, but beyond this views diverge considerably. Three
oad categories of opinion can be discerned in the literature: the
ationality' view, the 'adversary' view, and the 'interest–
presentation' view (Aoki, 1988, p. 265). The *rationality view**
ιlds that the bureaucracy plays a complementary role to the
arket and that good and close relations with business ensure
·herent macroecomonic and industrial policies: the efficiency
 the market is enhanced. The 'Japanese mercantilism' model is
ι extreme expression of this position: market efficiency is re-
aced by alterative objectives which are pursued by the state in
ndem with business. The *adversary view*[†] argues that govern-
ent intervention is, at best, irrelevant to the success of Japanese
ιsiness and, at worst, positively harmful to it. This is a common

---

ιuthors taking this view include Johnson (1982), Vogel (1979), Zysmon and Tyson
•83), Fallows (1989) and (to some extent) Wolferen (1989).
ee, for example, Patrick and Rosovsky (1976), Saxonhouse (1979) and Adams and
imura (1983).

'neoclassical' position which is difficult to sustain in its pristin
form given the historically significant role of the Japanese stat
in ensuring economic development (Lockwood, 1954; Halliday
1975; Johnson, 1982; White, 1988). A more sophisticate
version of the adversary view argues that the role of the state wa
previously valuable, but new market and business relations nov
obviate further involvement. The *interest representation* viev
holds that the specific value and institutional structure in whic'
the Japanese bureaucracy is embedded places it 'in two in
separable roles: that of a semiautonomous rational regulatc
(policymaker) and that of a quasi agent of specific interests in th
economy' (Aoki, 1988, p. 267). Of course interest-representatio
is *not*, in principle, different from the situation i
other economies, but the specifics of their political economi
articulation in Japan may be significant. It would be a mistake
however, to assume that these three views are mutuall
exclusive.

Government–industry relations are thus a complex proces
and it is necessary to be wary of straitjacketing them along line
suggested by a particular 'view'. A reading of Ouchi's (1984
article on the development of the microelectronics industry i
Japan shows the importance of a nexus of interlinked organ
isations, institutions, advisory bodies, research groups, industr
associations, etc. He argues:

> It is these institutions which are the loci of the social memory
> Each actor participates in many such institutions and thu
> knows that the future memory of his or her current behaviou
> will be stored, remembered and justly rewarded or punishec
> Thus, five competitors can enter into joint research on
> critical subject without even the protection of clear pater
> agreement . . . [yet] self interest has not been diminished in th
> least (pp. 20–30).

The model developed later in this section will attempt to in
corporate this aspect of government–industry, industry–industr
relations, but the next section will first introduce the main sta
institutions involved in industrial policy in the context o
Japanese economic planning.

## Economic Planning in Japan and State Agencies Fostering Government–Industry Relations

The Japanese state has been involved in a process of formal economic planning since the country's abrupt entry into the world capitalist system after the Meiji restoration of 1868; indeed it could be argued that the 'embedded' nature of industrial policy can be largely ascribed to the country's status as a 'late developer' compared to other industrialised countries (Murakami, 1987; White, 1988). Since the Second World War there have been 11 five-year economic plans which are described in Table 11.1. These plans are formulated by the Economic Council through a process of consultation with other state organs and agencies and a co-ordination of their respective policies. The Economic Council consists of representatives from business, academia, labour, journalists, ex-bureaucrats, etc. and therefore is able to include the views of many interested groups.

In theory the 'economic plan' (essentially an exercise in indicative planning) is implemented during its tenure by the various ministries and other agencies (Fig. 11.1); in practice the process is two-way and, in addition, there is a great deal of industrial policy at the level of each ministry or agency. It is also questionable whether such a plan can affect more than a general guideline for action on the part of government agencies or business. In practice economic planning/industrial policy has to be formulated at a specific level and on an on-going basis. This is likely to be a complex process and we have attempted to capture some of this complexity.

## A Model of Japanese Government–Industry Relations

Figure 11.2 presents details of the research model utilised in our study of Japanese government–industry relations. It would be hubris to claim that the figure encompasses all the major issues relating to government–industry interaction, but it does attempt to model the complexity of these relationships and thereby facilitates a focus on key issues:

Table 11.1  Japan: the implementation of the plan – the role of some state organizations and agencies

| Name of plan | Date published Cabinet at the time of plan approval | Planning period (FY) | Aim | Average annual growth rate of real GNP (%) | Unemployment rate at the final year (%) | Average annual rise in consumer prices (%) | External balance (current accounts) at the final year (US$ 100 million) |
|---|---|---|---|---|---|---|---|
| | | | | \multicolumn{4}{Projection in the plan and actual performance} | | | |
| Five-Year Plan for Economic Self-Support | Dec. 1955 Hatoyama | 1955–60 | Self support of the economy, Full employment | 5.0 / 9.1 | – / 1.5 | – / 2.0 | 0 / –0.1 |
| New Long-Range Economic Plan | Dec. 1957 Kishi | 1958–62 | Maximization of growth, Improvement of national living, Full employment | 6.5 / 10.0 | – / 1.3 | – / 3.5 | 1.8 / –0.2 |
| Double National Income Plan | Dec. 1960 Ikeda | 1961–70 | do. | 7.8 / 10.3 | – / 1.2 | – / 5.7 | 1.8 / 23.5 |
| Medium-Term Economic Plan | Jan. 1965 Sato | 1964–68 | Rectifying imbalances | 8.1 / 10.4 | – / 1.1 | approx. 2.5 / 5.0 | 0 / 14.7 |
| Economic and Social Development Plan | Mar. 1967 Sato | 1967–71 | Balanced and steady economic development | 8.2 / 10.0 | – / 1.3 | approx. 3 / 5.7 | 14.5 / 63.2 |
| New Economic and Social Development Plan | Apr. 1970 Sato | 1970–75 | Construction of admirable society through balanced economic growth | 10.6 / 5.1 | – / 1.9 | 4.4 / 10.9 | 35 / 1.3 |
| Basic Economic and Social Plan | Fev. 1973 Tanaka | 1973–77 | Promotion of national welfare, Promotion of international cooperation | 9.4 / 3.5 | – / 2.1 | 4% level / 12.8 | 59 / 140.0 |
| Economic Plan for the Second Half of 1970s | May 1976 Miki | 1976–80 | Realization of a richer national life and stable development of our country's economy | a little over 6 / 4.9 | 1.3% level / 2.1 | 6% level / 6.4 | approx. 40 / –70.1 |

Table 11.1 Contd.

| Name of plan | Date published Cabinet at the time of plan approval | Planning period (FY) | Aim | Projection in the plan and actual performance | | | |
|---|---|---|---|---|---|---|---|
| | | | | Average annual growth rate of real GNP (%) | Unemployment rate at the final year (%) | Average annual rise in consumer prices (%) | External balance (current accounts) at the final year (US$ 100 million) |
| New Economic and Social Seven-Year Plan | Aug. 1979 Ohira | 1979–85 | Shift to a stable growth path. Enrichment of quality of national life, Contribution of the development of the international economic community | approx. 5.7 / 4.1 | approx. 1.7 / 2.6 | approx. 5 / 3.6 | Roughly balanced basic accounts / 550 |
| Outlook and Guidelines of Economy and Society in the 1980s | Aug. 1983 Nakasone | 1983–90 | Formation of peaceful and stable international relations, Forming an economy and society full of vitality, Ensuring a secure and affluent people's life | approx. 4 / 4.0(FY.1983–86) | approx. 2 / 2.7 | approx. 3 / 1.5(FY. 1983–86) | Internationally harmonious balance |
| Economic Management within a Global Context | May 1988 Takeshita | 1988–92 | Reducing the massive external imbalance, Creating diverse lifestyles and better quality of life, Promoting balanced economic and social development nationwide. | approx. 3¾ | approx. 2½ | approx. 1½ | - |

(Note) Average annual growth rates of real GNP are based on the SNA at CY 1980 prices. Top figures, Projected; Bottom figures, Actual.

*Figure 11.1* The implementation of the plan: the role of some state organizations and agencies

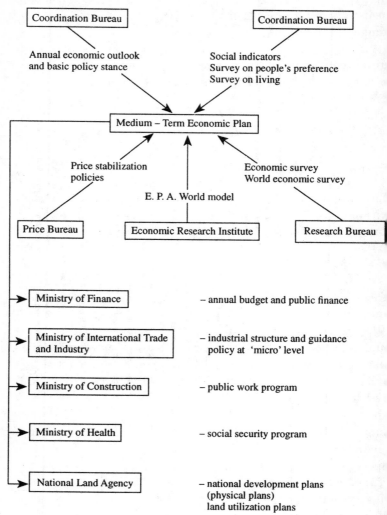

(1) Which are the primary entities in government–industry relations, from government departments and agencies, through joint working parties, and industry groups to individual firms? The relevant actors will, of course, differ from case to case.

(2) What is the nature and relative importance of the relationship between actors? For example, as Figure 11.2 depicts, consensus between ministries need not be assumed and there may be
a range of relationships, varying from co-ordination of activities
($C_4$) to competition ($C_2$). Neary (1989) refers to a case of competition between ministries in the promotion of biotechnology.
We hypothesise, however, that at the level of government departments and agencies, co-ordination and consultation is more important than competition.

However, this need not prevail in each specific case. The
structure of relationships will also help in determining which of
the 'views' of Japanese (and UK) government–industry relations
is closest to being correct. For example, if control/influence ($C_1$)
relationships are prevalent in a top-down hierarchical manner
then one of the *rationalist views* would be confirmed as being
most valid. Similarly the strength and direction of consultation
($C_6$) could help in confirming the validity of an *interest-
presentation* model, be this a simple 'triad' version (big business rules the Liberal Democratic Party which rules the
bureaucracy, which in turn rules big business!) or the more
complex forms suggested by Aoki (1988). Even Wolferen's
(1989) recent reworking of the multiple power centres theme
could be verified. Figure 11.2 also illustrates something which
Aoki calls isomorphism – i.e. relationships are repeated at a
number of stratified levels, e.g. consultation procedures at intra-
government, government–industry, intra-industry and even sub-
industry levels. Aoki (1988) suggests this is due to certain
features of Japanese culture, but the argument can be developed
in more specific historical terms. Either way, this feature may be
important.

(3) What are the mechanisms through which these relationships are articulated? Not all of these are depicted in Figure 11.2,
but include: (i) institutions and organisations such as industry
councils, government laboratories, symposia, industry associations, 'special legal entitles', keiretsu councils, etc.; (ii) human
resource flows, including practices such as shukko ('loan of personnel', such as the movement of government and company sci-
entists to research laboratories) and amakudari ('descent from
heaven' whereby former bureaucrats move to industry and may

214 *Asia-Pacific Issues*

*Figure 11.2* A model of Japanese government–bureaucracy–indu relations

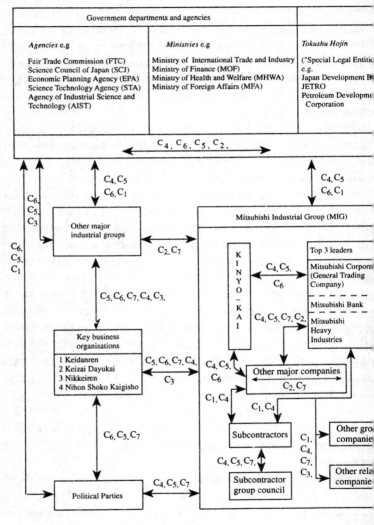

Notes:

◀━━▶Denotes relationships

C plus subscript denotes type of relationship

(i)     The relationships vary between actors. The hypothesised relationships include:
Control/Strong influence; $C_2$ = Competition (even within groups); $C_3$ = Concili
of differences; $C_4$ = Coordination of activities or approach; $C_5$ = Conse
seeking; $C_6$ = Consultation; $C_7$ = Cooperation.

(ii)    The order of the seven 'C's' implies the relative importance of each hypothe
relationship.

tes: Contd.

) Many agencies are directly linked to specific ministries, as are research laboratories etc. For example, the AIST is a part of MITI and controls a large number of research institutes and laboratories. The Patents Office and the Industrial Technology Council are linked to AIST within MITI.

) Mitsubishi Industrial Group is taken as an example. There are about 140 'group' companies, *excluding* subcontractors, smaller subsidiaries and other related companies. The activities of the Mitsubishi Group are coordinated (to some extent) by the three top leaders, the Sewanin-kai (top nine firms) and the Kinyo-kai which is the policy making body of the group. The Kinyo-kai consists of 28 firms *including* the top three. There is active competition, cooperation etc within MIG, as in all groups.

There are thousands of subcontractors tied to the group and these have their own council. This increases their bargaining power.

) The four key business organizations are very powerful. They are:
KEIDANREN – The Federation of Economic Organizations. Trade associations and leading companies are represented
KEIZAI DOYUKAI – Japan Committee for Economic Development
NIKKEIREN – Japan Federation of Employers' Organizations
NIHON SHOKO KAIGISHO – Japan Chamber of Commerce.

---

ay a role in the interest representation process); (iii) reports, hite papers, etc. (including the Maekawa report which in our search seemed to have had less coverage in Japan than in the est!); and (iv) legislation and 'administrative guidance' issued the authorities. Mechanisms (i) to (iii) taken together may be garded as 'networking' and, taking a cue from Ouchi, one uld argue that this network is the 'repository of social, political d business past and *anticipatory* memory'. Perhaps the key fference between industrial policy between Japan and other untries is the quality of this network.

## HE GLOBAL PHARMACEUTICALS AND ETROCHEMICALS INDUSTRIES: BACKGROUND AND HE RESTRUCTURING PROCESS

he petrochemicals and pharmaceuticals industries were chosen r investigation because of the potential benefits of comparing industry in (relative) decline, with one in the ascendent. In the ent, the dynamism of petrochemicals during much of the 980s confounded our expectations, but, arguably, this was rtly a result of the restructuring process. A comparison tween the two industries was of interest for another reason.

The industries are under the auspices of different ministries (Tl
Ministry of International Trade and Industry and the Ministry
Health and Welfare in Japan) and, therefore, one might find th
government–industry relations differ between state agencie
This is particularly the case since in pharmaceuticals, unlil
petrochemicals, the ministry concerned (MHW in Japan, tl
Department of Health in the UK) is not only a regulator, but al:
a direct participant as purchaser. This section gives the bacl
ground to both industries in order to facilitate the comparativ
analysis in the sections entitled 'The Empirical Study' ar
'Concluding Remarks'.

## The Global Pharmaceutical Industry

The term 'pharmaceuticals' covers a wide spectrum of heal
care products ranging from drugs used in the clinical treatme
of heart, respiratory, nervous system, etc., disorders (so-call(
ethical pharmaceuticals) to items used to treat more minor ai
ments such as headaches, coughs and colds. The global ethic
pharmaceutical market is dominated by multinational companie
reflecting the significance of economies of scale and the va
sums of money required to undertake risky research and deve
opment. However, niche markets exist, supporting a substanti
number of small and medium-sized companies. National go
ernments' drug approval and procurement practices have had
pervasive influence on the industry, tending to produce fra;
mented national markets and differential pricing levels. The cu
tomary policy of government, the main purchasers of ethic
pharmaceuticals, to place the bulk of their orders wi
indigenous producers has encouraged international companies
invest in local manufacturing plant or licence local supplier
rather than service these markets through exports. In cor
sequence, international trade in drug products overall is on tl
low side (around 20 per cent of total world sales) but for son
countries, the UK in particular, exports make an importai
contribution to foreign exchange earnings.

Competition in the industry is focused primarily on the searc
for new drugs. New products, protected by patent rights for 2

ears, can bring a substantial profit return if accepted on to governments 'approved' drug lists and then purchased in large quanties by public and private hospitals and clinics. For the leading ompanies Research and Development intensity is high (R&D xpenditures typically average 10 to 15 per cent of company urnover), with companies operating under a constant imperative o bring out a succession of new products to augment/replace ose whose patent protection has expired or which have been ade obsolete by technical advance.

Global sales of pharmaceutical products are dominated by rge multinational companies, mainly American and West uropean. However, although multinational companies occupy n important position in the industry at large, the degree of seller oncentration in the pharmaceutical industry is much lower than many other industries where the advantages of scale are simirly important. The pharmaceutical industry is characterised in ost countries by an active fringe of smaller and medium-sized ompanies operating in niche segments as well as the 'off-patent' eneric sectors.

A particular feature of the research-based sector of the industy is the fact that even major companies tend to be dependent on only a few products for a high percentage of their sales. In ese circumstances a company's market ranking is liable to be olatile unless an effective new product development can be ustained over the longer term.

In most countries there is a concentration of buying power in e hands of the State through its provision of publicly-financed ealth care facilities. In the UK, for example, the National Health ervice purchased some two billion pounds worth of drugs in 987, accounting for around 90 per cent of total UK ethical drug les. Such state controlled bureaucracies have in the past been riticised for being too price insensitive in their desire to obtain the ost effective drugs or too acquiescent in their dealings with the ug companies. More recently, governments' desire to moderate eir spending on drugs has been reflected in the application of ore stringent price controls and their support for generics.

Monopsonistic buying power has also affected the structure of e industry in one other important way. In most countries government procurement policies favour sourcing from indigenous suppliers and this has led foreign companies to establish local manufacturing subsidiaries and, to a lesser extent, the licensing of local producers. Historically, licensing arrangements have played an important part in the worldwide development of the industry. From a global perspective, buy-local policies have tended to result in plant proliferation and over-capacity in the industry world-wide. The European Community's 1992 harmonisation initiative will undoubtedly produce some rationalisation and restructuring of the European market, although the European Commission (surprisingly) estimates a saving of less than 1 per cent in production costs.

After growing rapidly in the 1960s and 1970s the demand for pharmaceuticals slowed down in the 1980s, following moves by many governments to limit expenditure on health care budgets and this has attenuated a number of competitive pressures facing the major drug companies, and influencing market structure. These include the high cost and risk involved in developing new products and getting them on to governments' 'approved' drug lists, tighter government regulation of drug prices and procurement policies, the erosion of patent protection, together with heightened competition from 'parallel imports' and the 'off patent-generics'.

## The Japanese Pharmaceutical Industry

In contrast to other Japanese industries such as motor vehicle and electronics which have capitalised on their 'home' market strengths to develop, initially, a thriving export trade, followed more recently by foreign direct investment, the Japanese pharmaceutical industry is characterised by its parochialism. Domestically, the industry is highly fragmented with around 1,300 producers, mostly small-scale, and even the largest firms have only relatively minor shares of the local market. The top ten Japanese companies have a combined market share of around 3. per cent, the remainder of the market being supplied by smaller local firms, foreign-owned subsidiaries of American and West European companies and imports. On the international scene the Japanese companies are dwarfed by the major American and West European concerns and export revenues as a percentage of companies' total revenues from pharmaceuticals are modest for all of the leading companies.

A combination of factors has contributed to the under-representation of Japanese companies in the world market. In the past profits on home sales have been very lucrative. Until the 1980s Japanese drug prices were some of the highest in the world propelled by a rapidly rising demand for pharmaceuticals and a high state funding programme (drugs account for around 40 per cent of Japan's state health bill compared to around 10 per cent in the UK). Thus, the Japanese market itself presented a 'sellers' market and reduced the imperative to seek overseas sales. A number of more technical factors have played their part. Japanese expertise in drugs research has lagged behind that of the Americans and Europeans. As a result many Japanese drug products have limited transferability to international markets. A lack of marketing know-how and experience in selling drugs in world markets together with a reluctance on the part of foreign governments to accept Japanese drug test data have also worked against the interest of the industry.

The situation is changing, however. The Japanese government has cut drug prices and has cultivated an 'open economy' policy, encouraging imports as well as inward investment by foreign companies to provide stiffer competition to 'complacent' indigenous producers. Import penetration in drugs is already much higher than in most other sectors of the economy, with Japan sustaining a large deficit on its drug trade. Foreign companies have found it easier to establish manufacturing subsidiaries in Japan and acquire local firms. The government has also attempted to upgrade and modernise the industry's research capabilities, targeting what many observers consider to be the key drug technology of the future, biotechnology, for special attention.

Japanese companies have stepped up their overseas involvement with various licensing arrangements with American and European-based concerns. They have also sought greater international penetration and the acquisition of local marketing know-how through joint-ventures, most notably in the US: Fujisawa-Smith Kline, Takeda-Abbott, Yamanouchi-Eli Lilly and Tanabe-Marion, while prominent joint-ventures in Europe

include Chugai and Takeda with Roussel and Eisai with Sandoz
As yet, however, investment in overseas subsidiaries is minimal

## The Global Petrochemical Industry

Between 1950 and 1973 the petroleum industry in the USA
Europe and Japan expanded rapidly as a result of boomin
demand conditions, low oil prices and the development of
widening range of end uses for basic and secondary petroleum
products. The quadrupling of the price of oil in 1973 and furthe
oil price increases in 1979, however, brought with it a world
wide recession and heightened the problems of excess capacity
and low profitability becoming evident in the industry in th
early 1970s. In the 1980s the European and Japanese petroleum
industries embarked upon a series of structural adjustments t
accommodate the changed conditions, centred primarily on th
'mothballing' and closure of existing capacity and a sever
curtailment of new investment.

Even before the first oil price increase of 1973 there wer
various signs that the extremely favourable conditions note
above were in the process of changing. End-user markets fo
basic and secondary chemicals were becoming more mature; th
scope for the further exploitation of economies of scale wa
limited; capital costs of construction were increasing and mor
stringent environmental requirements were additional factor
pushing up production costs. Nevertheless, the prevailing view i
the industry at this time was that high growth rates would con
tinue and in consequence many more new petrochemical plant
were commissioned.

Petrochemical plants take between three to five years to buil
and bring into operational use, and it was the case that extr
petrochemical manufacturing capacity was coming on stream a
the time of the 1973 oil price increase. The effect of the oil pric
increase was to plunge the world into recession and with it th
demand for petrochemical products. As demand fell, howeve
capacity continued to increase. From 1973 to 1978, for example
Western European ethylene capacity was increased by aroun
three million tonnes. *The Economist* commented on thi
investment behaviour thus:

Petrochemical investment has for years resembled a pursuit cycle race, with companies crawling along until one makes a break and the others follow because they do not want to be caught short of capacity when demand piles up. The plants are so expensive and their output so massive that one or two can change the whole balance between supply and demand. Each country anxious to improve its chemical balance of trade is then eager to offload products cheaply on to its neighbour (*The Economist*, 3 June 1978).

Little in fact had changed by the early 1980s, EEC ommissioner Davignon concluding that capacity had been eadily increased, because the petrochemical companies were aore preoccupied with what competitors were doing than what aarkets were telling them (Davignon, 1982). The overcapacity :verely constrained manufacturers' willingness and ability to aise their prices to cover cost increases and in consequence the rofitability of the industry collapsed, with most companies aaking losses in the early 1980s. The problem of the European adustry was further exacerbated by import competition from the 'SA.

By the beginning of the 1980s a consensus emerged in the uropean petrochemicals industry that the problem of over- apacity would only be tackled, in the medium term at least, by lant closures. The rationalisation of the sector involved both adividual initiatives and various collaborative deals between etrochemical companies to reduce capacity. Additionally, com- anies sought to internationalise their business through joint ven- tres and mergers (making a particular foray into the USA aarket) and the reorientation of their product portfolios acreasingly towards the supply of high value-added 'speciality' aemicals to boost growth prospects and profitability. Between 980 and 1986 plant closures involving both scrapping and nothballing' were effected by many companies unilaterally, articularly by those concerns which operated several plants 'here the removal of the least efficient units could be expected ○ make a significant improvement to the throughput of the maining plants. A major factor inhibiting collaborative :structuring initiatives in Europe, however, is the fact that they are generally viewed as being anti-competitive under Article 8 to the Treaty of Rome which declares illegal cartel agreemen between producers. On occasions, however, the Europea Commission has sanctioned the formation of 'crisis cartels' facilitate 'orderly' market conditions and restructuring. But, th diverse interests of producers, the complex vertical chain activities involved in petrochemical operations and the she number of companies involved all mitigated against securing common consensus on how best to tackle the industry's ove capacity problems. However, while ostensibly failing to come with a concerted approach to the control of production, this h not stopped a number of companies participating in 'illega price-fixing cartels. For example, in 1986, 15 companies we fined by the European Commission of colluding to fix the pri of polypropylene.

## The Petrochemical Industry in Japan

The petrochemical industry in Japan was established in the la 1950s as part of a wider national plan for expanding Japane industrial capabilities. The government had initially target basic chemicals and oil refining for expansion, but support f petrochemicals came to the fore also when the importance petrochemical applications such as plastics and synthetic fibr was perceived. Measures taken by the Ministry of Internation Trade and Industry (MITI) to assist the development of t industry included an allocation of crude oil supplies, a forei exchange allocation to enable the industry to import petr chemical plant and technology and the provision of loans by t Japan Development Bank to cover initial capital and operati costs. The initial entrants to the industry were four establish chemical companies (Sumitomo, Mitsui, Mitsubishi and Shov Denko), who established ethylene plants between 1957 a 1959, linking-up with an oil company in each case to secure su plies of crude oil. Oil refining companies began to enter t industry after 1960 together with other chemical companies. I 1982 the Japanese industry consisted of 18 producers, 12 which operated ethylene plants.

MITI continued to support the industry through its Basic
dustry Bureau and in 1965 established the Council for
trochemical Industry Co-operation through which it vetted
oposals for establishing new capacity. The general policy at
is time was to insist upon a minimum scale of cracker plant of
0,000 tons per year which encouraged the development of
mplexes in which the output of a single cracker plant serviced
e input requirements of several companies producing petro-
emical derivatives and products. By the late 1960s with
mand for petrochemicals booming the Council had increased
e minimum scale of cracker plant to 300,000 tons per year.
ith both existing companies and new entrants building plants
this size the industry's capacity at this time was generally
eater than current demand, but this was seen as being of
ategic importance (i.e. the avoidance of bottlenecks).
The slowdown of demand for the industry's products after the
l price increase of 1973, coupled with new large-scale plant
ming on stream, led to a substantial reduction in capacity
ilisation rates. This was exacerbated after a further increase in
e oil price in 1979 which left the industry with chronic over-
pacity problems.
Analysis of the industry's woes at this time was somewhat
nbivalent. For their part the companies blamed uneconomic
oduction partly on the fact that they were 'forced' to buy
phtha feedstock from domestic oil refineries at 'unrealistically'
gh prices. After 1973 MITI's Agency for National Resources
d Energy (ANRE) rationed oil supplies between users and
ould not allow petrochemical companies to import naphtha
rectly, a source of some friction *within* MITI between ANRE,
the one hand, and the Basic Industry Bureau which looked
ter the interests of the petrochemical companies, on the other.
ITI's view, however, was that a major restructuring programme
as required to adjust to the changed conditions facing the
dustry.
In 1981 MITI asked the Chemical Industry Committee and the
troleum Council, both coming under the auspices of the
dustrial Structure Council (a central, 'neutral' body used by
ITI to establish a broad political consensus behind major
licy decisions) to review the oil price situation. In April 1982

MITI endorsed their joint view that the industry be permitte
to import naphtha directly at world prices. Meanwhile
the Industrial Structure Council turned the matter of restruc
turing over to a specially convened Petrochemical Industria
Capacity Subcommittee. This subcommittee made two ke
recommendations:

> (i) That an improvement in the cost effectiveness of the indus
> try required the removal of unused capacity, the introductio
> of energy-saving technologies and the development of non-oi
> based raw materials; and (ii) the elimination of 'excessive
> competition.

Concurrent with the subcommittee's deliberations, th
Industrial Structure Division of MITI's Industrial Policy Burea
was working on proposals to sanction restructuring initiatives i
a number of industries (petrochemicals, pulp and paper, syntheti
fibres, chemical fertilisers, aluminium, etc.) considered to b
'fundamentally weak' because of high energy costs, overcapacit
and excessive competition. As a result of their work th
*Temporary Measures Law for The Structural Adjustment o
Specific Industries* became effective in May 1983. (It wa
repealed in June 1988.)

In the event, while the cut-backs in capacity and cartelisatio
helped the supply-demand balance, the revival of demand fror
1985 onwards led to higher prices and improved profitabilit
Indeed, some companies have been tempted to reopen capacit
In the longer term MITI and the industry are concerned with th
consequences of the steady build-up of the petrochemical indus
try in Korea and Taiwan and the eventual emergence of thes
countries as significant net exporters of petrochemical product
to Japan and the world market.

## THE EMPIRICAL STUDY

This section discusses the findings of our empirical research o
government–industry relations in Japan and, as appropriat

makes comparisons with the situation in the UK and Europe. Given the exploratory nature of the investigation, the methodology utilised a flexible, interview-based questionnaire which was categorised in five sections.

Section one asked the interviewees to give their views on the economic and commercial circumstances prevailing in the relevant industry in the early 1980s and to compare that with the contemporary situation. In the course of the interview, details were sought of changes in production, sales and profits; of measures of competitiveness and industry structure; of employment trends and industrial structure. In eliciting this background information we attempted to identify the main factors explaining change and the key players in the process of structural adjustment.

The second section of the questionnaire dealt with key institutions in the restructuring process, identifying here appropriate the role of various government bodies, private concerns, banks and labour organisations in the process of adjustment during the 1980s. Sections three and four dealt respectively with the organisational methods and the communicative mechanisms in the restructuring process, particularly in the context of the chronology of events in order to assess causality and significance. The final section invited predictions from interviewees for the future of government–industry relations in Japan and of industrial restructuring.

The questionnaire was applied to a wide range of individuals, firms and institutions who might either be associated with the process of government–industry relations (in either pharmaceuticals or petrochemicals), or be in a position to shed light on the process. Each interview took between one and a half and three hours to complete and the interviewees included senior executives from ten private companies, five Japanese and five European companies operating in Japan; Industry Associations; government bodies, including the Fair Trade Commission, the Ministry of Health and Welfare, three divisions of MITI, and the Economic Planning Agency; Keidanren; the Japan Institute of Labour; and three financial institutions.

The following discussion gives a broad sketch of the overall impression gained, as well as focusing on situations where, for example, there were significant differences of interpretation between the various actors in the process.

## Government–Industry Relations in the Pharmaceutical Industry

A crucial factor affecting business–government relationships in the pharmaceutical industry in Japan is the policy of the Ministry of Health and Welfare (MHW). The MHW attempts to fulfil two roles: to keep down the cost of health care provision and to ensure the continued development of the pharmaceutical industry. These aims are not always congruent. The situation is complicated by the fact that MITI plays a role in promoting new technology in areas like biotechnology.

A primary concern of MHW is with patient safety. The MHW has the right to permit new drugs to come on the market through its licensing approvals system and its supervision of patent applications. The ministry also controls drug prices. Securing safety and drug costs as a major (and controllable) part of social security costs are its 'bottom line' concerns. Worries about the management of the pharmaceutical industry are secondary. In a sense the MHW is sandwiched between pressure applied by the Ministry of Finance (MoF) on social security costs and pressures upward from the industry. 'Keeping the lid' on health care spending whilst giving the Japanese people access to the best 'state of the art' medicines and maintaining an indigenous pharmaceuticals industry is a difficult balancing act. The pressures arising from the ageing of the Japanese population make this an endemic and increasingly acute dilemma.

The downward pressure on drug prices has been strong. In 1971 drug spending was 45.8 per cent of total health care spending, in 1980 this was down to 28.5 per cent. The system of selling in Japan also places heavy burdens on drug companies. Approximately 85 per cent of all drug sales are direct to doctors through the Health Insurance Fund System. Any new drug which is an 'improvement' enters the market at a higher list price. This price is then eroded through successive price cuts by MHW. The programme of holding pharmaceutical expenditure below 30 per ent of total health spending therefore cannot be maintained xcept by continuing cuts.

The domestic industry is also under threat from foreign entry. apan's trading partners have put pressure on Japan to facilitate rug approval from foreign sources to allow more frequent entry nto the National Health Insurance (NHI) listings. This will ncrease competition. The OTC (over-the-counter) market owever is expanding. OTC drugs carry no NHI reimbursement. he rate of NHI coverage is likely to decline, which will make onsumers more cost conscious and increase leakage to OTC emedies.

The Japanese ethical drugs market remains huge in terms of bsolute size, per capita and as a proportion of GDP. This is artly as a result of doctors' willingness to prescribe drugs as ney profit from every prescription they write, for they dispense s well as prescribe drugs. They procure the drugs from the nakers or sales agents at a discount and sell at the full NHI list rice. Thus the margin of profit is added to the normal technical ee paid by NHI for a patient visit. It is likely that this fee struc-ure will be reformed before long. However, relations of the drug ompanies, through their agents, are very close to doctors and ales expenditures, not least on large numbers of 'detailmen' vho sell to doctors, are very high. Consumer resistance to multi-le prescriptions is rising as costs to the patient rise. Many pseudo-new' drugs have entered NHI listings and these 'me-oo' domestic drugs are likely to come under pressure. NHI list-ngs are now opened four times annually to new products (rather an twice) to allow new foreign drugs to enter. The price cutting ormula was revised in 1988. This entails across the board cuts very two years with no cuts in between. The price cut formula as also been revised so that price reductions on a drug whose ctual market price is close to the official list price will be pplied at a lower rate.

The MHW is also responsible for drug development and atent procedures in Japan. The theoretical 15 year patent life an become as little as four to six years, given the testing eriod. An extension of two to five years is granted if certain pecified conditions are met. (Revision of law effective January 988).

The industry response includes (i) increasing R&D expen
diture, (ii) internationalisation, (iii) hesitant moves toward con
solidation through mergers and acquisition, and joint venture
with foreign entrants and licences.

## R&D Expenditure

The actions of the Japanese government agencies in promotin
R&D in pharmaceuticals are diverse but not always effectivel
targeted. Government support for basic science and technolog
in this area began in fiscal year 1986 through 'The Japan Healt
Sciences Foundation' which organises the basic study fo
longevity, studies of biotechnology, development of medica
materials and the study of biophylaxis. This body is a joint gov
ernment, industry and university organisation. The promotion o
industrial technology development by private companies occur
through the tax system and through low cost financing. Specia
tax regimes have been introduced for research. They include: th
system for deduction of tax on increased research expenses, th
tax system for promotion of fundamental technology (establishe
1985), the tax system for the improvement of biotechnolog
research environment (1986) and the tax system for technica
bases reinforcement in minor enterprises (1985), Examples of in
vestment and financing systems are The Adverse Drug Reaction
Sufferings Relief and Research Promotion Fund (establishe
1987). Low interest, long term financing for facilities for drug
on biotechnology was established in 1987 through the Japa
Development Bank.

## Internationalisation

Japan has, as yet, no drug makers to compete with US an
European multinationals. One of the most internationalise
Takeda, has 7 per cent of sales from overseas, compared with 4
per cent for Merck, 45 per cent for Pfizer and 87 per cent fo
Glaxo – the norm is about 50 per cent. Government stimulatio
to internationalize the drug companies comes via MHW's use o
NHI pricing which awards higher prices to new products wit
international promise and lower prices to products with purel
domestic potential. However, it is also clear that unless Japanes

rug makers meet international product and R&D standards, they
'ill lose the domestic market too as the major multinationals es-
blish Japanese marketing networks. These firms are now less
'illing to license their products to Japanese firms. There is some
vidence that Japanese drug firms are splitting into two: one
roup internationalizing, the other attempting to defend the do-
estic market. The larger Japanese drug firms are cash rich and
an afford to internationalize, but they need to do this on the
ack of internationally competitive products. This issue is thus
timately related to the research issue.

## *Mergers, Acquisitions and Joint Ventures*

o an outsider, it is remarkable that the pressures on the Japanese
harmaceutical industry have not produced a wave of mergers
nd acquisitions (M&A). The need to consolidate, to achieve
conomies of scale in R&D, to maintain large sales forces and to
ternationalise all seem to point in this direction. In fact, a long
ar of attrition is being fought. It is likely that some firms will
ll victim to price wars and lack of R&D ability. There may then
e 'friendly' takeovers. The Japanese aversion to takeovers is
ne factor preventing rapid consolidation. So too, is the 'human
entred' nature of the industry as MHW fears a disappearance of
currently prescribed drug with its maker. Some small scale
I&A activity has taken place involving foreign companies and
is may be a harbinger of future moves but foreign M&A
ctivity is unpopular.

In contrast to M&A entry, joint ventures with foreign compa-
ies are a feature of the industry. The synergy between foreign
ultinationals' R&D, new products and know how and Japanese
istribution systems with their masses of detailmen and contacts,
ot least in MHW, is irresistible. New entry into the Japanese
arket is largely via joint ventures with existing Japanese com-
anies, followed only by a brave few with wholly owned
entures.

## *The Future*

key element in the future for the pharmaceutical industry is
he ageing of the population. This is already having an impact. In

1980 senior citizens composed 17.8 per cent of total nationa
health expenditure, by 1985 it was 25.4 per cent and it is pre
dicted to exceed 40 per cent in 20 years. The number of senic
citizens was 12 million in 1985 (10 per cent of the population
and is expected to double by 2010. It is likely that MHW wi
attempt to impose heavy price cuts on certain 'overpriced' cat
egories of age related drugs. To exploit this, and other key seg
ments, the Japanese industry must become internationall
competitive. So far it has succeeded where the mechanism fc
drugs is well known and a search for the theory behind th
disease is not essential, i.e. in searching for effective substance:
It has not succeeded in basic research. This remains the bi
unanswered question – can radically new treatments emerg
from Japanese companies? Here the respective roles of MITI an
MHW require clarification. For this question, it may be too muc
to ask MHW to be both regulator and innovation stimulator.

## Discussion of Findings on the Pharmaceuticals Industry

The main instrument chosen by the MHW to reform the industr
was a formula for price reductions on all drugs, applied on a
annual basis, although new drugs were allowed higher prices an
the amendments in the patents law ensured a higher appro
priation of returns to research. Overall the result of this polic
(i) increased the rate of innovation in Japanese pharmaceutical
companies; (ii) promoted the industry's internationalization; an
(iii) created a spurt of mergers and acquisitions which may we
result in larger, more diversified and fitter Japanese phama
ceuticals companies. Neary (1989) argues that this is not a
industrial policy since the restructuring is the result of measure
taken for other reasons (e.g. the reduction of state drug expen
ditures) rather than a deliberate approach. He may well be righ
in that the MHW position on whether it has an industrial polic
is ambiguous. If there is a lack of policy then this certainl
points to a clear difference in approach between MHW an
MITI, with the latter being more proactive and involved wit
industry (see the section entitled 'Government–Industr
Relations in the Petrochemical Industry'). However, there is th
need for a more careful scrutiny regarding MHW–Industry rela

ons because either the form of government–industry relations
ay be structured differently (e.g. we came across a number of
nts regarding the importance of amakudari in the industry) or
ere may simply be a reluctance to talk about such matters, par-
cularly given the ministry's dual role as regulator and procurer.
ven if the MHW does not have a policy for the pharmaceuticals
dustry, other ministries and agencies clearly have. For
ample, the Ministry of Agriculture, the MHW itself and
pecially MITI's Agency for Industry, Science and Technology
IST) are all promoting research in biotechnology in which the
armaceuticals industry participates. It is also worth mentioning
at MITI has a longer history of involvement in industry
ohnson, 1982).

Both the MHW (and similar bodies in Europe) are in the
ique position in government–industry relations of being both a
gulator of the pharmaceutical industry and a procurer of its
oducts, striving for 'value-for-money'. In consequence the pos-
bilities for 'consensus based' government–industry relations
e difficult and this may explain the haphazard, perhaps coinci-
ntal, nature of industrial policy in this industry. Further work
eds to be done for both Europe and Japan to see how proactive
dustrial policy actually is in pharmaceuticals – and the role of
overnment–industry networks in its conduct.

## overnment–Industry Relations in the Petrochemical
dustry

comparison with its counterparts in Europe and the United
ates, the Japanese petrochemical industry displays the follow-
g structural characteristics: (i) many petrochemical manu-
cturing companies are small; (ii) raw material producing
mpanies on a relatively large scale co-exist with processor-
pe companies on a small scale; (iii) a petrochemical manu-
cturing facility complex on a single site consists of several
mpanies instead of just one company; (iv) profits are generally
w; and (v) the Japanese petrochemical industry has a much
gher dependence on imported raw materials than its US or
uropean counterparts.

Nevertheless, in principle, the petrochemical industry in Japa has various advantages compared with Europe in affecting restructuring initiative. A single country rather than a mult country plan of action was required; there were fewer produce in the industry; and from the outset the government was deepl involved in the affairs of the industry. In practice, however, th restructuring of the industry proved to be far from smooth.

### The Restructuring Process

The fact that there was a capacity problem in the Japanese petr chemical industry was apparent to all the parties concerned lor before 1983 when measures were taken to alleviate the situatio Tracing the evolution of the problem is perhaps the best way t understand the process of restructuring that followed.

The Japanese petrochemical industry, like its counterpart Europe, was seriously affected by the downturn in busine activity in the 1970s. Diminishing domestic demand coupl with the scheduled construction of petrochemical plants Singapore, Canada and Saudi Arabia, some capable of producii petrochemical products at a very low cost and all expected concentrate on exports, foreshadowed radical changes worl wide in the demand-supply situation of petrochemical producer

By the early 1980s the situation forced the domestic petr chemical industry jointly with the Japanese government to fac up to the need for industrial restructuring. The process leading *The Temporary Measures Law for the Structural Adjustment Specific Industries* which came into effect in May 1983, difficult to focus. David Watts, reviewing Karel van Wolferen 'The Enigma of Japanese Power' (Macmillan 1989) in *The Tim* newspaper (3.8.89) likens Japanese power centres to a 'a mass soap bubbles, coalescing, separating and re-coalescing with r apparent focus and no identifiable centre of ultimate powei This is an apt description of the process of industrial restructu ing in the Japanese petrochemical industry. It did not, howeve prevent the various parties to the process claiming responsibili for what happened and for the way in which it happened. On th one hand the initiative for action was claimed to have come fro weaker firms who sought government action. MITI had to pe

uade hesitant (and presumably stronger) companies of the need
or a restructuring effort. The problems confronting the petro-
hemicals industry were shared by other industries. But it was
MITI's decision to establish *The Law*. Wolferen's enigma of
apanese power would suggest no ultimate responsibility. MITI
ees its own role with regard to *The Law* rather differently.
Consultation with business was very much part of the process,
ut 'responsibility lies with us', we were told.

MITI's persuasive powers centred on the need for companies
o co-operate in the face of a crisis and 'eventually all agreed' – a
iumph in MITI's eyes for practical needs over 'the peculiar
lea' of free market philosophy which would have seen
iefficient companies go to the wall. MITI's approach was to
iake forecasts of demand which were used as a basis for reduc-
ig production capacity. There was some disagreement among
roducers as to how much capacity should be cut so MITI 'infor-
ially' devised a formula to achieve the desired reduction, using
ie MITI forecast but with consultation. While MITI suggested
)ptimum' figures of capacity reduction, each producer judged
ieir own particular need for cuts. It was not uniform. The Japan
etrochemical Industry Association 'checked' capacity reduc-
ons, which were effected in several stages over a period
f time. The reductions were achieved through a consensus
ecision-making process with MITI, the producer association
nd individual companies recognising a common objective in
romoting adjustment to the benefit of all concerned.

*The Law* promulgated the following programmes:

(1) Abandonment of production capacity.
(2) Establishing joint sales companies.
(3) Providing investment assistance to new business that any
f the companies undertook.

The abandonment of production facilities was applied to 11
iemical products. A total of 2.02 million tons of ethylene
icilities amounting to 32 per cent of total production capacity
ere abandoned; and 0.45 million tons of PVC production
icilities amounting to 22 per cent of total capacity were also
andoned. To eliminate excessive competition and help
nprove prices and profitability, joint sales companies were
tablished for the sale of PVC and polyolefine. The sales

divisions of 18 companies were consolidated into four joint marketing companies.

MITI's communicative mechanisms depend on persuasion (backed by small subsidies) and consensus. If most producers agreed with MITI's proposals then MITI had the power to 'instruct' (euphemistically referred to as the issuing of guidelines) those who remained in disagreement to behave in harmony with the others. MITI sees its own role in the process as one of ensuring that the restructuring happens smoothly, a major policy objective. The companies by and large seemed to accept that they had to make sacrifices and trusted MITI to make the process as equitable as possible and compensate them if they suffered.

The Temporary Measures Law required temporary exemption from the anti-trust legislation in the setting up of a cartel arrangement between producers. The Antimonopoly Act (as amended 1977), while generally prohibiting cartel activities (a 1977 amendment introduced a surcharge system against illegal cartels), allows depression cartels (a cartel for combating a depression) under Section 24–3; and rationalisation cartels (a cartel to rationalise enterprises) under Section 24–4, as exceptions under limited special conditions, with prior authorisation from the Fair Trade Commission (FTC). In this instance the FTC was willing to sanction the setting up of a crisis cartel after consultations with MITI. The FTC did, however, force MITI to amend its original plan to set up only three joint sales companies as this was regarded as overly restrictive.

The crisis measures discussed above were seen as necessary to prevent industries seeking trade restrictive measures (which were applied to some petrochemical products) and exemplifies the delicate balance of power to be retained within MITI. Different divisions of MITI have different responsibilities which require internal discussion on what measures should be applied in particular circumstances. One division will have a wider perspective than another, for example in relation to the international repercussions of specific measures, or other industries' views on policy measures. The process of consensus building is therefore a matter for internal as well as external co-ordination with elaborate mechanisms of advisory councils, industry structure councils, steering committees, etc., all involved in the consultations

The process requires what one MITI official described as 'the endurance to wait for consensus'.

The end-purpose of the closure of plant capacity was 'to leave the broad competitive structure of the industry unchanged' after capacity adjustment. Consultations with firms by MITI about the adjustments were mainly through producers' associations with whom MITI has close involvement in a 'continuing dialogue' as it was described. In this way MITI is able to force the pace of adjustment, although there are well documented instances of MITI failing to get its proposal accepted – for example, in its abortive attempt to reduce the number of motor car manufacturers. Nevertheless, organisations like the Japanese Petrochemical Industry Association, a 'meeting place' for producers' interests, has an ongoing relationship with government, co-operates with MITI in supplying trade information, and seeks MITI's advice and support when necessary. It 'corroborated' the cartel set up under The Temporary Measures Law. If the industry has a problem which needs political judgement or policy, it is natural to put that problem to MITI. However, 'managing the problem is ultimately the industry's affair', and as in all Japanese business dealings, 'the group interests are paramount'.

## Discussion of Findings in the Petrochemical Industry

Within the context of the overcapacity issue and its resolution we detected only some sign of 'administrative guidance' on the part of MITI (though both sides claimed the initiative, with MITI stressing the role of its officials and The Industrial Council; and Industry stressing its own initiative and the significance of the Petrochemicals Association) since the crisis was recognised by both the government and industry. If anything, MITI played the role of a referee in ensuring a smoother restructuring than might otherwise have been the case. This could be regarded as a form of interest-representation (as described in the 'Industrial Policy and Government–Industry Relations in Japan' section).

A better example of MITI (or AIST) leading the industry is in fundamental research. We came across numerous projects (e.g. a 1981–1990 project developing high performance plastics) where firms expressed the belief that it was 'politic' to be involved even if no direct benefits were likely to be gained: MITI carries a lot of clout should it care to use it. On the other hand, arguably, firms get involved because of the benefits of networking. In contradistinction to the above mentioned projects, an example of industry taking the initiative is the '$C_1$' project which aimed to develop an alternative feedstock for the petrochemicals industry (because of the price of oil). This was a typical example of a research association with a government scientist leading the project, but using loaned personnel (who do not necessarily physically move) from the participating firms. In this case most financial resources came from industry and though the project was technically successful the results have been 'shelved' because of the fall in the price of oil.

Three points are particularly clear from our research. First, though a smooth restructuring was deemed useful by all actors in Japan and Europe, only in Japan was it possible to come to a quick resolution (see discussion for Europe in the section entitled 'The Global Pharmaceutical Industry'). This was despite the misgivings of a number of Japanese firms. This implies both a well-developed network and also a different corporate attitude (compared to Europe) in that co-operation is sought (and achieved) even at some cost to individual firms – in the belief of longer term reciprocity. Secondly, the network of relationships, as suggested by our model, is complex and probably fluctuates over time. It seems that there are multiple channels of communication (Industry Councils, trade associations, etc. for example) and these could be valuable, both for the reinforcement of views and as a 'double check'. Finally, neither business nor the government (or even a single ministry) should be seen as monolithic, our research showing a considerable diversity of views and hence the need to arrive at an 'internal' consensus.

## CONCLUDING REMARKS AND POINTERS TO FUTURE RESEARCH

In general our findings *tentatively* support the notion that Japanese Government–Industry relations are more in line with

e 'rationality' or 'interest-representation' models described in
e 'Industrial Policy and Government–Industry Relations in
pan' section; while the 'adversarial' model *may* be a better
flection of the situation in Europe. Of course this is a gross
versimplification and future research may determine alternative
uropean structures and mechanisms which are functionally
quivalent (in bringing about similar ultimate results) to those in
pan. In addition, the differences in relations found between
dustries, projects and ministries suggests that it is not possible
argue for a single structure of relations whether in Japan or the
K/Europe. The reason for these differences and their
nsequences need further study.

The network of relationships, even on cursory examination,
as been shown to be of crucial importance in ensuring smoother
dustrial restructuring in Japan (at least with regard to the role
f MITI's network and the reduction of capacity in the petro-
emicals industry). A glance at Fig. 11.2 shows that only a
nall part of our model has actually been investigated and a
ore extensive examination of the Japanese network is war-
nted. In particular the relationships *between* firms needs
ploring. It is worth asking why, under certain circumstances,
ese relationships (even those at a cross-keiretsu level) are less
versarial in Japan than in Europe.

Finally, though the preliminary empirical focus has been on
pan, it is by no means self-evident that Europe is bereft of a
twork similar to Japan's though this assumption is often made,
least with regard to the European Community and some
ember countries. It is therefore also necessary to build a model
r Government–Industry relations in Europe (perhaps by
apting Fig. 11.2) and apply this rigorously in future research.
he choice of research topic would ideally permit a valid
mparison of Government–Industry relations in Europe and
pan.

## eferences

dams, F. G. and Ichimura, S. (1983) Industrial Policy in Japan, in: Adams,
F. G. and Klein, L. R., *Industrial Policies for Growth and Competitiveness:
An Economic Perspective*. Lexington Books, Lexington.

Adams, F. G. and Klein, L. R. (eds) (1983) *Industrial Policies for Growth ar Competitiveness: An Economic Perspective.* Lexington Books, Lexington.

Aoki, Masahiko (1988) The Japanese Bureaucracy in Econom Administration: a Rational Regulator or Pluralist Agent?, in: Shoven, J. I *Government Policy Towards Industry in the United States and Japc* Cambridge University Press, New York.

British Chamber of Commerce in Japan (1988) *Seihin-Ka: How Japan Brin R&D to the Market.* Tokyo.

Buckley, P. J. and Mirza, H. (1985) The Wit and Wisdom of Japanes Management: An Iconoclastic Analysis. *Management International Revie* Vol. 25, No. 3.

Calder, K. E. (1988) *Crisis and Compensation: Public Policy and Politic Stability in Japan, 1949–86.* Princeton University Press, Princeton.

Caves, R. E. (1986) Industrial Policy and Trade Policy: a Framework, i Mutoh, H., Sekiguchi, S., Suzumura, I. K. and Yamazana, I., *Industri Policies for Pacific Economic Growth.* Aen and Unwin, Sydney.

Davignon, E. (1982) European Producers Must Now Shoulder the Responsibilities. *European Chemical News*, 1 November.

Eads, G. C. and Yamamura, Kozo (1987) The Future of Industrial Policy, i Yamamura, Kozo and Yasuba, Yasukichi (eds). *The Political Economy Japan, Vol. 1: The Domestic Transformation.* Stanford University Pre: Stanford.

Fallows, J. (1989) Containing Japan. *The Atlantic*, May.

Hallilay, J. (1975) *A Political History of Japanese Capitalism*, Pantheon Boo! New York.

Johnson, C. (1978) *Japan's Public Policy Companies.* AEI-Hoov Washington.

Johnson, C. (1982) *MITI and the Japanese Miracle: The Growth of Industr Policy*, 1925–1975. Stanford University Press, Stanford.

Lockwood, W. (1954) *The Economic Development of Japan: Growth a Structural Change.* Princeton University Press, Princeton.

Murakami, Yasasuki (1987) The Japanese Model of Political Economy, Yamamura, Kozo and Yasuba, Yasukichi, *The Political Economy of Japc Vol. 1: The Domestic Transformation.* Stanford University Press, Stanford

Mutoh, H., Sekiguchi, S., Suzumura, I. K. and Yamazawa, I. (1986) *Industr Policies for Pacific Economic Growth.* Allen and Unwin, Sydney.

Neary, I. J. (1989) An Industrial Policy for the Pharmaceutical Industry. *Jap Forum*, Vol. 1, No. 1.

Okimoto, D. I. (1989) *Between MITI and the Market.* Stanford Universi Press, Stanford.

Ouchi, W. G. (1984) Political and Economic Teamwork: The Development the Microelectronics Industry of Japan. *California Management Revie* Vol. XXVI, No. 4.

Patrick, H. T. and Rosovsky, H. (eds) (1976) *Asia's New Giant.* The Brookir Institute, Washington.

Peck, M. J., Levin, R. C. and Goto, A. (1988) Picking Losers: Public Poli towards Declining Industries in Japan, in: Shoven, J. B., *Government Pol Towards Industry in The United States and Japan.* Cambridge Univers: Press, New York.

Phillips, G. O. (1989) *Innovation and Technology Transfer in Japan a Europe: Industry–Academic Interactions.* Routledge, London.

axonhouse, G. (1979) Industrial Restructuring in Japan. *Journal of Japanese Studies*, Vol. 5, No. 2

hibauchi, Tetsuo (1988) *Impact of Asia NICs on Japan's Petrochemical Industry.* Nomura Research International Research Note Series, 88–1, Kamakura.

hoven, J. B. (ed) (1988) *Government Policy Towards Industry in the United States and Japan.* Cambridge University Press, New York.

BS Phillips & Drew (1989) *Pan-European Pharmaceutical Review*, March.

ergara, W. and Brown, D. (1989) *The New Face of the World Petrochemical Sector: Implications for Developing Countries.* World Bank Technical Paper No. 84, Washington.

ogel, E. (1979) *Japan as Number One.* Harper & Row, New York.

hite, G. (ed.) (1988) *Developmental States in East Asia.* Macmillan, London.

ilks, S. and Wright, M. (eds) (1987) *Comparative Government–Industry Relations: Western Europe, The United States and Japan.* Clarendon Press, Oxford.

olferen, K. van (1989) *The Enigma of Japanese Power.* Macmillan, London.

amamura, Kozo and Yasuba, Yasukichi (eds) (1987) *The Political Economy of Japan, Vol. 1: The Domestic Transformation.* Stanford University Press, Stanford.

oshikawa, Aki (1989) The Other Drug War: US–Japan Trade in Pharmaceuticals. *California Management Review.* Vol. 31, No. 2.

ysman, J. and Tyson, L. (1983) *American Industry in International Competition .* Cornell University Press, Ithaca.

# Index

241